D1067486

ASSAULT FROM THE SKY

ASSAULT FROM THE SKY

U.S. MARINE CORPS HELICOPTER OPERATIONS IN VIETNAM

DICK CAMP

CASEMATE
Philadelphia & Oxford

Published in the United States of America and Great Britain in 2013 by
CASEMATE PUBLISHERS
908 Darby Road, Havertown, PA 19083
and
10 Hythe Bridge Street, Oxford, OX1 2EW

Copyright 2013 © Dick Camp

ISBN 978-1-61200-128-9
Digital Edition: ISBN 978-1-61200-140-1

Cataloging-in-publication data is available from the Library of Congress and
the British Library.

All rights reserved. No part of this book may be reproduced or transmitted in
any form or by any means, electronic or mechanical including photocopying,
recording or by any information storage and retrieval system, without permission
from the Publisher in writing.

10 9 8 7 6 5 4 3 2 1

Printed and bound in the United States of America.

For a complete list of Casemate titles please contact:

CASEMATE PUBLISHERS (US)
Telephone (610) 853-9131, Fax (610) 853-9146
E-mail: casemate@casematepublishing.com

CASEMATE PUBLISHERS (UK)
Telephone (01865) 241249, Fax (01865) 794449
E-mail: casemate-uk@casematepublishing.co.uk

MIX
Paper from
responsible sources
FSC® C011935

CONTENTS

Prologue   7

PART I: THE BUILDUP, 1962–1966
ONE: Archie's Angels   13
TWO: HMM-364 Strike Mission   27
THREE: Death on the Flight Line   37
FOUR: One Very Bad Afternoon   56
FIVE: Ashau Valley Rescue   64
SIX: Helicopter Valley   80

PART II: HEAVY COMBAT, 1967–1969
SEVEN: Special Landing Force   95
EIGHT: A Month in the Tour of HMM-165   106
NINE: The Beach Rescue   115
TEN: Super Gaggle   125
ELEVEN: Lang Vei Rescue Attempt   147
TWELVE: Team Box Score   157

PART III: THE BITTER END, 1975
THIRTEEN: Operation Frequent Wind   185
FOURTEEN: Saigon Rooftops   196
FIFTEEN: Defense Attaché Compound   206
SIXTEEN: The Embassy   227

APPENDIX A: Marine Corps Helicopter Development 1948–1969   242
APPENDIX B: Pless Recommendation for Medal of Honor   248
APPENDIX C: Navy Unit Commendation Task Force 76   252

Bibliography   253
Index   257

HELICOPTERS ARE DIFFERENT

The thing is, helicopters are different from planes. An airplane by its nature wants to fly and if not interfered with too strongly by unusual events or by a deliberately incompetent pilot, it will fly. A helicopter does not want to fly. It is maintained in the air by a variety of forces and controls, working in opposition to each other; and if there is any disturbance in the delicate balance, the helicopter stops flying immediately and disastrously. There is no such thing as a gliding helicopter. This is why being a helicopter pilot is so different from being an airplane pilot; and why, in generality, airplane pilots are open, clear-eyed, buoyant extroverts and helicopter pilots are brooders, introspective anticipators of trouble. They know if anything bad has not happened it is about to.—*Harry Reasoner, ABC Evening News, 16 February 1971*

PROLOGUE

Adrenaline surged through my blood stream as black puffballs of antiaircraft fire erupted in the distance. It was a wake-up call, the North Vietnamese were alive and well in the Ashau!

I was sitting on the outboard jump seat of a U.S. Army Huey; it's side door was wide open. My heart was in my mouth as I stared down at the jungle several thousand feet below. It was not a pleasant experience! Several minutes earlier I had seen a CH-54 "Flying Crane" carrying a small bulldozer take a hit and crash in a great ball of fire. Neither was my confidence bolstered by the fact that our pilot, the fifty-plus-year-old Army Maj. Gen. John J. Tolson III, had only gone through the short, senior officer flight course at Fort Rucker. Helicopters are unforgiving—experience counts! I glanced to my right and observed my boss, Marine Maj. Gen. Raymond G. Davis, totally absorbed in the action. Operation Delaware, the air assault into the North Vietnamese Army's (NVA) backyard was being conducted by the 1st Cavalry Division (Airmobile), the Army's elite helicopter-borne assault division, and we had been invited to observe it. The assault was a classic helicopter strike. The landing zone had been prepped by B-52 and Marine and Air Force fighter-bombers followed by the main assault force, UH-1H troop-carrying helicopters, escorted by rotary-wing gunships, while command and control helicopters circled overhead monitoring the tactical situation on the ground. The operation was the "Cav's" typical way of fighting. Major General Davis intended to introduce this concept of "high mobility" into the 3rd Marine Division's scheme of maneuver when he assumed command.

General Davis used the time before taking command of the division to study the Army's use of helicopters. He took every opportunity to discuss operational matters with the Cav's senior leadership and visit their units in the field. As his aide de camp, I was along for the ride, and the assault into the Ashau Valley was one of those occasions I would have gladly passed up.

Regardless of my trepidation, the view at ten thousand feet over the valley was extraordinary. The sky was literally black with helicopters: aerial rocket artillery (ARA) from the 2nd Battalion, 20th Field Artillery Regiment's gunships was pounding enemy antiaircraft emplacements; the 1st Squadron, 9th Cavalry's aero-weapons, aero-scout, and aero-rifles choppers (known as "Reds," "Whites," and "Blues," respectively) flitted through the sky stalking enemy personnel as the troop-carrying birds arrived in waves. Sensational! That day in 1968 confirmed in my mind that Vietnam was truly a helicopter war.

In June, two months later, I accompanied General Davis to the '1st Cav's headquarters at Camp Evans. On that particular day our regular bird, a Huey, was unavailable so we were being flown by a Marine Corps UH-34D helicopter, a model which was being phased out by the newer turbine-driven CH-46A. After shutting down the engine, the pilots climbed down from the cockpit and joined the crew chief and gunner waiting for the return of the general. Before long a large crowd of young Army warrant officer pilots gathered to see "the relic that their fathers had flown many years before." They were amazed that the ancient bird was still in service; the Army had replaced them at least a decade before. The UH-34D, known affectionately as the "Dog," had first entered service in the late 1950s and had served as the mainstay of the Corps' medium helicopter lift for over a decade and a half. In March 1966 the Vertol CH-46 "Sea Knight," known colloquially as the "Phrog," started arriving in Vietnam, relegating the Dogs to an increasingly minor role.

The Phrogs were a Godsend to the "grunts" (infantrymen) because they could carry a full squad, compared to the Dog's five or six combat-loaded Marines. Regrettably, the '46 was not quite ready for prime time. In September 1967, the entire fleet was grounded because of a series of unexplained crashes. An observer saw one of the crashes and described seeing the tail fly off in flight; the crew died in the crash. An investigation found that structural failures were occurring in the after pylon. As a result of the grounding, approximately half the Marine Corps' tactical/logistic airlift in Vietnam was lost until the problem was fixed and the CH-46s were placed back in service. To take up the gap, the tried and true UH-34Ds were given a new lease on life.

Most Marines, particularly my infantry contemporaries, were beneficiaries of helicopter support. The birds carried the grunt into combat, provided him with rations, ammunition, close air support, and carried him out of battle, dead or alive. I, for one, can never forget the stench of JP-4 (jet fuel), the hot blast of engine exhaust, the drip of hydraulic fluid, the orange-colored nylon seats, and the leap of faith jumping off the ramp off a hovering '46 into the ten-foot high elephant grass . . . and the medevac helicopter's promise of life. The memory of holding a critically wounded Marine's head in my hands, and praying for the life flight, is still an open wound.

———

The first U.S. Marine Corps helicopter deployment began in 1962 and ended with the evacuation of Saigon in 1975. During that decade of America's involvement in South Vietnam over four hundred Marine Corps helicopters were lost in combat and operational accidents taking some eight hundred passengers and crewmen with them. *Assault from the Sky: U.S. Marine Helicopters in Vietnam Combat* is an account of the bravery and sacrifice of the helicopter flight crews during that involvement.

This book is organized into three parts that correspond to the American buildup (1962–1966), increasingly heavy combat (1967–1969), and the final evacuation (1975) of South Vietnam. Each part is comprised of several chapters that provide the reader with examples of the bravery, dedication and sacrifice of Marine Corps aircrews in support of their infantry brethren.

PART I:

THE BUILDUP, 1962–1966

CHAPTER ONE

ARCHIE'S ANGELS

Shufly was the confirmation of the whole concept of vertical envelopment in a jungle setting against an elusive guerrilla enemy.—Historian Beth Crumley, Marine Corps History Division

There was a hushed expectancy in the air as the pilots and aircrew gathered on the aircraft carrier USS *Princeton's* (LPH-5) hanger deck. "The Marines of Marine Medium Helicopter Squadron 362 [HMM-362] could sense something was about to happen," LCpl. Tyler Bush recalled. "The squadron commanding officer, Lt. Col. Archie J. Clapp had just called the men together for a briefing. It was announced that before daybreak the following morning, April 15, 1962, the darkened ship would steam to within twenty miles of Vietnam . . . [and] we would make a landing via helicopter and establish a base camp near the tiny village of Soc Trang." Lieutenant Colonel Clapp's squadron, nicknamed "Archie's Angels," after the skipper, was to be the first large Marine operational unit committed to South Vietnam. "It was an exciting time," 1st Lt. Bob Whaley explained. "We were Marines who were doing what we were trained to do. Our squadron had been together a long time, and we had a good number of pilots who had served during World War II or Korea. It was comforting to know that those leading us into Vietnam had prior combat experience, and we learned a lot from them." The squadron would join three companies of U.S. Army Piaseki H-21 Shawnee helicopters in support of South Vietnamese forces. Dubbed "Operation Shufly," HMM-362's mission was to provide increased tactical mobility for the South Vietnamese units attempting to hold the critical rice producing Mekong Delta. Operational control of the squadron was vested with Military Assistance Command, Vietnam (MACV), whose Joint Operations Center provided final approval of all missions.

ARCHIE J. CLAPP

Lieutenant Colonel Archie J. Clapp, squadron commander of HMM-362 (Archie's Angels), the first Marine Corps operational unit assigned to the Republic of South Vietnam.

Archie J. Clapp enlisted in the Marine Corps in 1940, rising to the rank of master sergeant before being commissioned. He received his naval aviator wings in 1943. In the closing months of World War II, Clapp was assigned to Marine Fighting Squadron 123 (VMF-123) aboard the USS *Bennington* (CV-20) in support of the invasions of Iwo Jima and Okinawa and in the first carrier strikes against the Japanese home-islands. Clapp is credited with shooting down three and a half enemy planes during the war. As quoted in James Bradley's book, "Flyboys," "Somebody would go down you knew like a brother, but you couldn't dwell on it" . . . . "You'd get briefed on the next mission and you knew it

might be your turn next." After the war, Clapp was one of the first pilots to transition from propeller driven planes to jets and then to rotary-wing aircraft. He served in Korea as a pilot with Marine Helicopter Transport Squadron 161 (HMR-161). In his April 2010 *Leatherneck Magazine* article "Shufly: The Marine Corps' Beachhead in Vietnam" David Hugel noted, "Following his return from Korea, Clapp served in various positions at Marine Corps Air Station, Miami; the Marine Corps Development Center, Quantico; and Headquarters, U.S. Marine Corps." After being promoted to lieutenant colonel, Clapp assumed command of HMM-362. While on an exercise in the Philippines, he was informed of a secret mission his squadron was going to be assigned in South Vietnam codenamed Operation Shufly.

Corporal Larry D. Shirley recalled, "Reveille aboard the *Princeton* sounded early on the morning of 15 April. Well before daybreak the ship's piper came blaring over the PA system with his morning wake-up call." Lance Corporal

Bush said, "We left the stifling heat below deck, clutching our rifles with sweaty palms. As soon as we stepped out topside we knew we were in a different world. Even at this early hour, the heat was intense and muggy. It felt like trying to breathe through a pillow." The men quickly boarded their assigned helicopters. "This was it," 1st Lt. Jim Shelton said, "we were it . . . the first Marine unit to be committed in South Vietnam. We were going to do the job we had trained so long and hard for." Lieutenant Colonel Clapp received clearance from *Princeton's* air boss and lifted off the amphibious assault carrier's flight deck. Captain Weldon Munter recalled, "It was still dark when we lifted off, all twenty-four aircraft in the squadron. One by one the flight of twenty-four HUS-1 "Sea Horse" (later known as the UH-34D) helicopters and three Cessna OE-1 "Bird Dog" aircraft followed their commanding officer toward the old Japanese-built landing strip near Soc Trang, located about eighty-five miles southwest of Saigon.

The USS *Princeton* (LPH-5), steaming toward Chu Lai, Vietnam with UH-34s of Marine Air Group-36 on her flight deck in August 1965.—*U.S. Navy*

SIKORSKY UH-34D "SEA HORSE"

The Sikorsky UH-34D "Sea Horse" (HUS-1 until September 1962) helicopter was the backbone of the Marine Corps' vertical lift capability from 1957 to the mid 1960s. The first one was delivered to tactical units in mid February 1957 and the last in 1964 for a total of 540 aircraft. Called the "Dog" by the flight crews, one pilot described it as "a fat, ugly, green insect. They were slow, vulnerable, noisy, and vibrated like a crazed washing machine. Crew members had to scream at one another to be heard. But, the men respected the craft because it was resilient; it could take punishment."

The UH-34D had a single main lifting rotor, fifty-six feet in diameter, with a smaller nine-and-a-half-foot anti-torque rotor on the tail pylon. The all-metal blades had a leading edge formed of a hollow steel "spar," which provided the bulk of its structural strength and lighter "pockets" bonded to the rear of the spar to provide aerodynamic lifting surfaces. The main blades could be folded and the rear anti-torque rotor could be unlocked and rotated 180 degrees until it was folded back parallel to the left side of the fuselage, allowing it to fit better aboard aircraft carriers. The UH-34D had a full set of controls for both the pilot and copilot, who sat above and behind the front-mounted engine and just forward of the main trans-mission. The troop compart-ment was placed directly un-der the main transmission and rotor, with the pilots and engines in front being coun-terbalanced by a long tail structure. The cabin meas-ured over thirteen feet long, almost five feet wide and six feet high with a large sliding door on the right side. Can-vas bucket seats for twelve passengers could be installed. In addition, a hook under-neath the aircraft, stressed to 5,000-pound capacity to carry loads externally, and a hoist mounted outside just above the cargo door could be used to lift loads of up to

Two Sikorsky UH-34 D Sea Horse transport helicopters are seen lifting off after bringing Marine riflemen into a landing zone. The UH-34s continued to be a mainstay of helicopter troop lift well into 1967.

400 pounds. The UH-34D had a cruising speed of 98 mph, with a top speed of 123 mph. A normal load in Vietnam included the crew (pilot, copilot, crew chief, and gunner), eight com-bat-equipped Marines, armor, weapons (two M60 7.62mm machine guns), and enough fuel for an hour-and-a-half mission.

Lance Corporal Bush recalled the flight to Soc Trang, "Archie's Angels boarded the choppers and shuddered off toward the Mekong Delta, won-dering if we were going to get shot in the next hour or two. Soon they were hop scotching over lush green foliage and skipping over water-filled rice pad-dies." First Lieutenant Shelton said, "The region lay before us. A level of peaceful looking land cut irrationally with canals and streamlets. The river lay below in a sleeping band of shaded browns and greens. It was difficult to realize a war could be in such a tranquil setting." A short time later, the squadron landed at an old Japanese airstrip three miles from the tiny village of Soc Trang. By mid-afternoon Lieutenant Colonel Clapp's squadron was ashore. The only problem the squadron experienced during the movement ashore was one of its OE-1s had to make an unscheduled landing back aboard the *Princeton* because of an engine malfunction. The pilot, Lt. Francis M. Walters, made an emergency landing without benefit of a tail hook or arresting wires. After repairs, he was able to fly ashore.

The commanders responsible for Shufly confer after arriving at Soc Trang in April 1962. Major General John Condon, Commanding General, 1st Marine Air Wing (fourth from left) confers with Col. John Carey (extreme right), the task group commander, and Lt. Col. Archie Clapp, HMM-362 squadron commander (third from left holding coat and briefcase).

CESSNA OE-1 BIRD DOG

The Cessna OE-1 Bird Dog—"O" signified an observation aircraft, while the "E" was a manufacturer-assigned letter—was a four-seat, single-engine liaison and observation aircraft. It had a maximum speed of 130 mph, a range of 530 miles and a service ceiling of 20,300 feet.

Cessna 0-1 Bird Dog, a light single-engine observation and air control aircraft. The Bird Dog was in the Marine Corps inventory from World War II through Vietnam.

During the Korean and Vietnam Wars OE-1s were used by Marine observation squadrons (VMO) for artillery spotting and forward air control. The Bird Dog was unarmed, except for its target-marking rockets. A Total of seven OE-1s were lost in action during the Vietnam War.

An advance party, Sub Unit 2 of Marine Air Base Squadron-16 (MABS-16) was already on the ground and hard at work preparing the field. They quickly erected sleeping quarters, hardback tents with wooden decks to keep the men out of the mud during the rainy season, office spaces in one of the few remaining hangers, a wooden mess hall and last but not least, wooden heads. Capt. James Perryman noted that, "the base was operational when we arrived. It was ready for us to set up shop and begin operations without much delay." Lance Corporal Bush recalled that the "airstrip had an old hanger into which we could pull our aircraft to work on. There were a few rooms that became offices for operations, administration, etc. Tents were erected for the troops in what was to become known as 'tent city' . . . at night we slept, rifles at the ready, under mosquito nets that barely slowed down the swarm of bugs that left our skin sore and itching with red welts. Rats that seemed as big as cats had a fondness for crawling into the sack with us. Fresh water and fuel had to be trucked in from Soc Trang. In less than twenty-four hours we were operational."

The airfield was protected by the South Vietnamese Army (ARVN, Army of the Republic of Vietnam, as opposed to PAVN, Peoples Army of Vietnam, aka NVA, North Vietnamese Army). "A Vietnamese mortar battalion and infantry battalion provided perimeter security," Bush remembered. "Inner defense and internal security was provided by our men. Language was a major problem—both sides had to make decisions more than once on whether a man would not obey a 'halt' command because he could not understand, or if he was really an enemy. There was also a language barrier between our helo pilots and Vietnamese support pilots—very dangerous when you need 'moment's notice' help."

LIVING CONDITIONS

Soc Trang was located in the Mekong Delta. Corporal Shirley observed, "Rice paddies were everywhere, trees lined the riverbanks, and villages were scattered throughout the region. There was water everywhere. However, when we arrived and for several weeks thereafter it was hot and dusty." Lance Corporal Bush recalled, "Dust blew so thickly around the base area that at times it was hard to see twenty feet. One minute it would be dry; then thick sheets of rain would come down, and in a few minutes we would be up to our ankles in water and mud. Tents often were blown down, soaking everything and everyone." Shirley said, "Twice the tent I slept in was blown down by strong winds, once even breaking the heavy timber center posts. Another time the top of a building blew off and the debris hit a Marine knocking him out cold for a while."

Living conditions were primitive. "Generators provided our only electricity supply," Shirley recalled. "When the lights were on large swarms of bugs would collect around them. Everyone had mosquito nets on their cots for protection. One night while sleeping in the office something woke me up running against my mosquito net. It took only a second or two to realize something was in bed with me. I came straight up off the cot and of course the mosquito net was over my head and it took a while to get all untangled. Somehow a large rat had gotten in the sack with me and could not get out." ""Despite the weather and primitive living conditions, "the squadron could have started accepting missions the next day," according to Lieutenant Colonel Clapp. However, it was a week before III Corps requested the first combat troop lift. "The intervening time was crowded with briefings conducted by MACV and ARVN personnel, area familiarization flights, indoctrination of Vietnamese troops in embark-and-debark procedures, and establishment of operating procedures with III Corps and 21st ARVN Division personnel," he recalled.

Soc Trang Airfield, Shufly's first operating base in the Mekong Delta. Flying from Soc Trang, the Marines learned many vital lessons in helicopter operations and tactics.

INNOVATION

On Easter Sunday, six days after arriving in Vietnam, HMM-362 received its first mission. "Operation Lockjaw," Clapp explained, "consisted of landing approximately 340 troops of the Vietnamese 7th Division on one side of a stream-divided village while a U.S. Army helicopter company landed a like number [of ARVN soldiers] on the other side. Opposition was light and no aircraft were hit, so the Corps gained some 'combat veterans' for a very reasonable price." It was well that there was no opposition. HMM-362's helicopters were not armed unlike their Army counterparts, which mounted machine guns and rockets. "We decided not to install machine guns on the helicopters," Clapp explained. "We figured that our best defense was to hold our time on the ground in the landing zone to a bare minimum. The best way to accomplish this is to have the cabin exit door clear and to have the crew chief help the troops debark rather than handle a machine gun. We did, however, carry two 'Grease gun' (.45 caliber) submachine guns in each helicopter. The copilot covered the left side of the helicopter while the crew chief covered the right when we were close to, or on the ground." (Early on the UH-34D had a three-man crew with a left-side door gunner being added later on.) After several opposed landings, it did not take long for the policy to change. M60 machine guns were soon installed on swivels in the cabin doorway. For personal protection, the aircrews carried side arms and M1 rifles. They wore standard infantry body armor over their tan flight suits. "This protective gear

Vietnamese infantrymen disembark from HMM-362 helicopters and move toward a tree line in one of the first operations attempted by a Marine squadron in the Mekong Delta.

was not ideal but it was all we had," Clapp said. "In the high heat and humidity, many of the crewmen developed fairly serious cases of rash from wearing the armor for extended periods of time."

On 24 April, during Operation Nightingale, the squadron suffered its first combat damage when a helicopter was forced down after its oil line was punctured by enemy small arms fire while landing troops of the ARVN 21st Division near Can Tho. "The pilot was able to take off and fly about a mile . . . before landing in a rice paddy near a Self-Defense Corps outpost," Lieutenant Colonel Clapp said. "A wingman landed and retrieved the crew, while a division of four helicopters proceeded to the forward loading site where it picked up the repair crew, who fixed the helicopter . . . all within two hours of the time it was hit." Squadron Commander Clapp insisted that his helicopters not fly by themselves. "I wanted two helos flying together, and they said, 'That's not being economical,' and I'd say, 'I don't care.' We were the only kind of [aircraft] with its own rescue means. I was a former fighter pilot, and I had enough of that feeling of flying over enemy territory where you might be shot down and captured right away. I wouldn't have that happen with my people. So they went in pairs, and nobody had done that before."

The squadron's most significant operation occurred on 9 May when it supported an assault on Cai Ngai, a Viet Cong fortified village. The six landing zones were prepped by Vietnamese fighter bombers five minutes before the landing. "According to the plan," Lieutenant Colonel Clapp recalled, "the

Lieutenant Colonel Clapp decreed that at least two helicopters fly on every mission so that if one was downed, the other could rescue the crew.

Vietnamese pilot broke off his attack as we came in sight. He had been work-ing the village over for about twenty minutes and several columns of rising smoke indicated that he had down his job well." However, as the helicopters swept in for landing, the enemy opened fire, hitting eight of twenty-two air-craft and forcing one to land a few miles from the objective at an ARVN outpost. Three others required field maintenance before returning to Soc Trang. The squadron's after-action message stated, "The lead HUS received two small arms hits at touchdown. An ARVN trooper in the third aircraft was hit in the stomach as he stepped out the door. Another trooper was wounded in the foot while a helo was in final approach. Flying glass from a bullet-pierced windshield caused the pilot to receive minor scratches."

The resistance caused Lieutenant Colonel Clapp to " . . . have serious reservations about preparatory air strikes in this type of operation. Besides the possibility of inflicting casualties on potential friends, forfeiture of the element of surprise is a certainty. There did not seem to be enough favorable results to offset these drawbacks." However, Clapp did not rule out air sup-port entirely. "Some on-call support would have been most welcome that day, and would probably have caused some VC casualties. But the language barrier between the attack pilots and helicopter flight leader precluded calling in the strike. After this mission we insisted on being covered by support fighter air-craft flown by English-speaking pilots."

The Marine Corps took immediate steps to armor the helicopter's most vulnerable areas. A team of systems analysts was sent to Vietnam to observe

UH-34 troop lift into a dry rice paddy landing zone. The bird on the right is discharging troops while the one in the middle is taking off and the one on the left on coming in for a landing. Smoke from a prelanding bombardment caused fires, which can be seen in the background.

and make recommendations. As part of the study, they prescribed the criteria for describing the intensity of enemy fire:

- 1–15 rounds per minute—light fire,
- 16–30 rounds per minute—moderate fire,
- 31 and over rounds per minute—intense fire.

The pilots were required to use these terms to describe the type of enemy fire. After a particularly "hairy" flight one of the pilots, wrote the word "withering" under the description of enemy fire. The next day he received a phone call from an indignant systems analyst asking just what constituted withering fire, to which the stalwart aviator replied, "One round through the cockpit!" Lieutenant Colonel Clapp remarked, "Fortunately, we were not meeting some of the heavy caliber stuff that came along later when the North Vietnamese Army entered the battle. We were pretty much contending with just guerrillas. While the Viet Cong created considerable work for the metalsmiths and mechanics, they fortunately did not manage to do any damage that came under the cognizance of the doctor."

During several operations, Marine aircrews noticed that the Viet Cong often were able to elude the ARVN troops by fleeing the area in small groups and blend in with the local population. "As the flight approached the village, armed men could be seen scurrying into the fields where they dove into tall weeds and literally disappeared," Clapp recalled. "A few of them, who happened to land in a sparse spot, could be seen lying on their backs firing upward at the helicopters as they passed only a few feet above them . . . one helicopter was hit, but was able to make it back to the forward loading site before repairs were made." Lieutenant Colonel Clapp devised an airborne reaction plan by using four helicopters loaded with ARVN soldiers on standby. "We could respond to what the enemy did on the ground by having other troops airborne in the vicinity. Then we could swoop in and take care of them," he said. Named "Eagle Flight," the concept was first tested on 18 June. *U.S. Marines in Vietnam, The Advisory & Combat Assistance Era 1954-1964* stated, "Heavy monsoon rains made the enemy particularly difficult to pin down, but the Marine pilots managed to sight 10 Viet Cong near the main landing zone. After landing near the enemy, the ARVN troops captured 10 Communist soldiers and wounded one other. Shortly after this incident another Eagle Flight made two eventful contacts with the enemy. The Marine helicopters landed their small force and the ARVN promptly killed four

Viet Cong and captured another. Twenty minutes later, after reboarding the helicopters, the South Vietnamese swept down upon a new prey, this time capturing four prisoners."

On 4 June the squadron lifted soldiers of the ARVN 7th Division into landing zones in the Plain of Reeds, west of Saigon. "When the troops landed on their first objective—a village situated at a stream junction—many armed and uniformed Viet Cong soldiers were flushed from the village," Clapp explained. "They headed north in the direction of the Cambodian border. This signaled the beginning of a huge checker game all over the sector." The ARVN commander sent in more troops as an "anvil," while landing others in various locations around the enemy to drive them like a "hammer" into the stationary forces. "Five more landings were made," Clapp noted. "On the last landing . . . the flight leader's copilot was leaning out the window using a submachine gun to spray a group of VC, who were firing at the flight as it lifted off." The flight leader heard a bullet hit the aircraft and looked around the cockpit to see if everything was still functioning. "He saw a large hole in the back of the copilot's helmet . . . and a small clean hole in the front . . . the bullet had gone through and through, passing through the half-inch-thick padding between the helmet and his head!" The copilot was none the worse for wear.

The squadron participated in its first jungle mission on 14 June, "supporting the ARVN 5th Division in a landing in the Viet Cong's D-Zone [a major "liberated" area north and northeast of Saigon]," Clapp said. "The landing site was a pear-shaped clearing about thirty-five miles north of Saigon, in which the VC had emplaced sharpened bamboo poles as an anti-helicopter device." The Viet Cong were trying to counter the Marine heliborne assault tactics. "By restricting us to a landing in a narrow perimeter, the VC had an ideal set-up for a mine or machine-gun defense," he surmised. Clapp said, "The squadron quickly learned that it was more difficult to remain oriented over a 'sea of trees' than over a patchwork of streams and canals. Dead reckoning can be employed over the jungle, and when it leads to a clearing that undoubtedly is the right spot. In the delta, however, most villages are similar enough in appearance that the objective could be any one of several in the immediate vicinity unless pinpoint navigation and accurate map reading is used to single out the proper one."

During the three and a half months of their deployment, April through August 1962, HMM-362 "came away with a keen awareness of the unique characteristics of this type of combat [guerrilla warfare]," Lieutenant Colonel Clapp noted. "My squadron had made some 50 combat troop-lift

UH-34 being directed into a hilltop landing zone by a Marine carrying a .30 caliber carbine and wearing an in-country manufactured camouflage uniform, while two heavily loaded Vietnamese wait to embark.

missions which entailed about 130 landings by flights of helicopters against Viet Cong opposition." Lance Corporal Bush wrote, "The operations provided us with additional on-the-job training and helped polish our expertise in helicopter support." The squadron did not lose a single helicopter nor suffer any casualties, even though seventeen of its twenty-four helicopters and two of the three OE-1 aircraft suffered battle damage. On 1 August, HMM-163 relieved Archie's Angels in what became a regular four-month rotation of Marine Corps helicopter squadrons supporting Operation Shufly. "All aircraft and gear changed hands at this point," Lieutenant Colonel Clapp reported, "although the actual work involved in the transfer had been going on for over a week. The incoming pilots had been flying on missions in increasing numbers over the same period, while my pilots were slowly phased back to Okinawa for return to the States. This created a minimum break in continuity. . . ."

SHUFLY ROTATION 1962-1964

USMC Squadron Time of Rotation

MABS-16, SubUnit	29 Apr 1962–30 Nov 1964
HMM-362	9 Apr 1962–31 Jul 1962
HMM-163	1 Aug 1962–11 Jan 1963
HMM-162	12 Jan–6 Jun 1963, 1 Jul–7 Oct 1964
HMM-261	7 Jun 1963–30 Sep 1963
HMM-361	1 Oct 1963–31 Jan 1964
HMM-364	1 Feb 1964–30 Jun 1964
HMM-365	8 Oct 1964–30 Nov 1964

CHAPTER TWO

HMM-364 STRIKE MISSION

*Sure Wind 202 would be the costliest and most viciously opposed heli-
borne assault attempted in South Vietnam during the 1962–1965 period.*
—U.S. Marine Corps History Division

HMM-364's "Purple Foxes" ready room buzzed with excitement.
The entire squadron had been assigned to lift a battalion of
ARVN soldiers into the rugged Annamite Mountains near the village of
Do Xa, located thirty miles due west of Quang Ngai in central Vietnam. The
area was reported to be a Viet Cong sanctuary and infiltration route from
Laos into the densely populated coastal lowlands of Quang Tin and Quang
Ngai provinces. Intelligence reports indicated that it was the headquarters
of the Communist military headquarters for Military Region 5 (MR-5).
The operation, code named Sure Wind 202 or Quyet Thang 202 in Vietnamese, was the first time South Vietnamese forces had penetrated the
rugged area in more than a year. It was expected that the enemy under General Nguyen Don would put up a fight to protect their ammunition and food
storage areas. The operation was scheduled to kick off on 27 April 1964, with
the first assault waves scheduled to touch down in the landing zone at 0930.

The assembled officers rose to their feet as their commander, Lt. Col.
John "Big John" La Voy entered the ready room. He strode purposefully to
the front of the assembly and, without ceremony, delivered a detailed mission
brief. The day before, he and Col Robert A. Merchant, the overall Marine
commander, had participated in the final planning session at Pleiku and
Quang Ngai with the ARVN II Corps commander, General Do Cao Tri.
The two Marines learned that HMM-364, supported by five U.S. Army UH-
1B Huey gunships (Dragon Flight), and two UH-34Ds from the South Vietnamese Air Force (VNAF, also Republic of Vietnam Air Force, RVNAF)
would helilift a 420-man battalion into Landing Zone (LZ) Bravo. At the

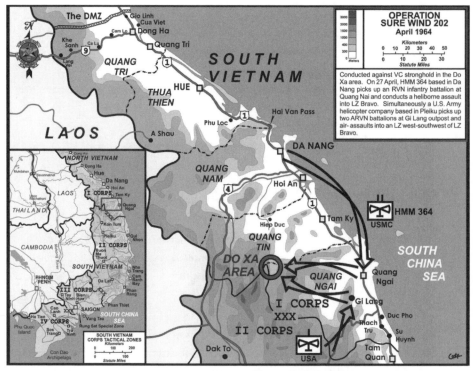

HMM-364 (Purple Foxes) was assigned to lift ARVN forces into an area close to the border of Laos in central South Vietnam. Called Operation Sure Wind 202 or Quyet Thang 202 in Vietnamese, it was one of the most costly helo operations in 1964.

same time, two other ARVN battalions were to be helilifted by the 52nd Aviation Battalion, which included both the 117th Aviation Company, based at Qui Nhon, and the 119th Aviation Company, at Pleiku, into a second landing zone approximately eight miles west-southwest of LZ Bravo. A U.S. Air Force U-10 aircraft was tasked to fly Colonel Merchant and several staff officer overhead to assist in coordinating the helilift into LZ Bravo. Twenty South Vietnamese A-1H Skyraiders were assigned to provide tactical air support for the operation. Twelve of these attack aircraft were scheduled to conduct preparatory strikes on and around the LZ; four were to orbit above the area after the landing, while the remaining four were to be positioned on strip alert at Da Nang.

Lieutenant Colonel La Voy covered the salient points of the mission in detail—conduct of the flight, radio frequencies, flight procedures, troop pick-up and insertion locations, and emergency procedures—answered questions, wished his men good luck, and dismissed them. The pilots hurried to the flight line to preflight the aircraft and brief their crewmen. On schedule the eighteen aircraft of HMM-364 lifted off and formed four divisions of four aircraft each, with a section of two aircraft in trail, for the flight to Quang Ngai. The two trail aircraft, designated rescue birds, were flown by CWO Dennis T. Mckee and Maj. John Braddon, the squadron maintenance officer. After reaching Quang Ngai, the helicopters refueled and boarded the first assault waves, heliteams (the number of combat soldiers that can be lifted in one helicopter at one time) comprising ten ARVN soldiers.

As the heliteams boarded HMM-364's UH-34Ds, Dragon Flight, under Capt. Jack Woodmansee, headed for the objective. "Tactically we flew in two sections of two UH-1B gunships each," Woodmansee explained. "As the leader, I was unattached and could fly with either section that had the most enemy to engage. I formed the two sections of guns ahead of and to my right and left." The Huey's flew in an inverted V formation with Woodmansee in the lead aircraft. He intended to make a low level pass and recon it by fire to see if it was defended or not. "I had one section of guns covering the 6 o'clock and the left (north) flank of the LZ and the right section covering the right flank and the 12 o'clock section of the LZ," he recalled. "I was in trail to see which one might draw fire. In the event either did draw fire, the tactical procedure was for the gunner to instantly throw out a smoke grenade. This would be the first signal that one was taking fire and would mark the ground in the vicinity of same. The wingman would then fire behind his lead aircraft as he saw the smoke go out. From the mark on the ground we could generally figure out where the fire was coming from."

There was only one LZ in the objective area that could accommodate a simultaneous landing of HMM-364's eighteen aircraft. Unfortunately it was dominated by high ground on three sides, with the open end facing west. Scores of natural caves scored the cliff face, which was later determined to contain numerous Viet Cong gun emplacements. As Woodmansee's Dragon Flight neared the objective, the Vietnamese Skyraiders attacked the area around the LZ with cannon, rockets and 500-pound bombs. Following the air strikes, the Army Huey's swept in. "On our

HMM-364 squadron commander Lieutenant Colonel John LaVoy had flown fixed-wing combat missions during World War II and Korea before transitioning to helicopters. He was admired and respected by the Purple Foxes.

first pass, low level at about 100 feet, all of my first four Dragon guns were throwing smoke out both sides of the aircraft," Woodmansee recalled. "I could see tracers crisscrossing the valley from both sides." The Viet Cong were firing .30 and .50-caliber machine guns from camouflaged positions in the cliff face. Lieutenant Colonel La Voy aborted the landing and ordered the squadron to orbit out of small arms range while the gunships attempted to suppress the enemy fire. "On one of my passes west to east, I was engaged by a .50 caliber [machine gun] from the south side," Woodmansee said. "There was [a] stream of tracers passing about 10 feet under my helicopter for at least 10 seconds." A wingman blasted the enemy position and knocked it out. "On [another] pass close to the hill on the south side, a VC machine gun surprised us and opened up at point blank range. My door gunner put a magazine of his M14 right into the VC position causing the fire to stop."

The gunships continued to pound the Viet Cong positions but were unable to silence them. Despite being low on ammunition, Woodmansee volunteered to mark a .50-caliber machine gun position for a Skyraider. "I got a running start south to north, popped over the southern ridge, got very low, below the machine gun . . . popped up just over it and my right door gunner threw a smoke grenade right into the position." He was so low that, "I saw that it was a .50 cal. with two shoulder braces and a big ring sight like those

UH-34 helicopter crews from HMM-261 (EM painted on the nose) standing by for the start of a mission.

on World War II ships. The VC soldiers were wearing camouflage uniforms and pith helmets." As he flew by the position, "The VC were getting up out of the ditch and one was swinging the machine gun around to shoot us. My first section leader was covering me from 1,000 feet when I called for him to suppress [it] so that we could get out of there safely." The section leader "slowed to a 1,000 foot hover . . . and placed a stream of fire around the smoke grenade. We never heard from that gun the rest of the day." As he pulled out, a Skyraider made a firing run. "He missed badly," Woodmansee recalled, " . . . and got stitched from a weapon on the south side of the valley. Smoke billowed from his engine."

Second Lieutenant Pham Van Hoa felt the impact of the thumb sized .50-caliber rounds tearing into his Skyraider. The aircraft shuddered, smoke started billowing from the engine, and the instrument panel warning lights flashed red. He knew it was only a matter of time before the engine seized up and he would be flying a rock. Fortunately the rescue helicopter was overhead. "The A-1 was hit and left the zone trailing smoke," Major Braddon recalled. "Since I was the pilot of a helicopter designated to rescue downed crews, I chased the A-1 and caught up with it when it crash landed in a field about 10 miles west of Quang Ngai." Lieutenant Hoa was unable to lower the landing gear and was forced to put the Skyraider down with the wheels up. The aircraft landed hard, throwing Hoa forward and smashing his face against the instrument panel. The impact broke his sunglasses and cut his face. Despite the injury, Hoa scrambled out of the wreckage and took cover in the brush near the aircraft wreckage. Braddon immediately landed. "My crew and I picked up the pilot and delivered him safely to Quang Ngai." Asked later about the rescue, Braddon said, "Lieutenant Hoa was supporting Marines. In that capacity he came under the umbrella that 'Marines take care of their own.' However briefly, he supported us and became one of us and we made sure he was cared for."

U.S. Army Capt. Jack Woodmansee, leader of Dragon Flight, which provided gunship support for HMM-364 during Operation Sure Wind 202.

By this time the Army gunships had expended their ordnance and were low on fuel. "I requested that we go back to Quang Ngai, rearm and decide what we wanted to do," Woodmansee explained. "I suggested they should pound the place with VNAF fixed wing aircraft before we returned. I wasn't at all convinced that we had made a dent in the enemy after our first hour's flight. My personal view was that we should look for another LZ because we had flown into an ambush." Colonel Merchant considered Woodmansee's recommendation and then ordered the transport helicopters and gunships back to Quang Ngai, while the Skyraiders pounded the objective area. The airstrikes continued until 1225 when the gunships returned from rearming. Shortly after the strikes ceased, Colonel Merchant ordered the first wave of transport helicopters to land the ARVN assault force.

Woodmansee escorted Lieutenant Colonel La Voy and the first division of three UH-34Ds. "As we approached the zone . . . my Dragon Flight moved forward and commenced suppressing the LZ," the Army officer recalled. "We raked the LZ with the division [UH-34Ds] right on our tail and then all hell broke loose." The Viet Cong opened up a devastating fire, which was returned by the gunships and the transports' door gunners. Crisscrossing streams of red [U.S.] and green [Viet Cong] tracers filled the air. Several helicopters in the first wave were shot up. Capt. William Cunningham's aircraft took a hit in the engine. "It appeared to me that Captain Cunningham and I got

UH-34s heading for a landing zone in the Mekong Delta. Note the boat in the river containing two Vietnamese.

stitched at about the same time," Maj. Albert N. Allen said. "He was lifting in a very steep climb, trying to clear some tall dead trees and I was on final. It was evident that Bill was coming down." Cunningham's aircraft crashed in the LZ.

Major Braddon rushed to the rescue. "It was only seconds after the bird went down that John [Braddon] called that he was coming down" Woodmansee said. "There was not a tinge of hesitation as to what he was going to do." The rescue aircraft spiraled in toward the downed UH-34 and its crew. "I positioned my helo between John and the horseshoe machine gun position," he continued. "We shot

Major John R. Braddon received the Silver Star for unhesitantly landing his aircraft under heavy enemy fire to rescue a downed flight crew.

some rockets into the trees above the position to get some air bursts, and hosed down the area while John was patiently waiting to get the crew on board." Braddon recalled that, "We took a lot of fire and our bird had many holes. As I lifted from the zone . . . I noticed that some of the electrical components were not working and there were some new terrible sounds coming from the engine compartment." Woodmansee heard Braddon say over the radio, "Dragon Six, Yankee Kilo coming out." The Army gunships covered him as he pulled out of the zone with Cunningham and his crew safely aboard.

Braddon's aircraft was so heavily loaded that he had could not clear a ridge. "I elected to go around a knob protruding into the LZ and up a creek bed. The knob had a bunch of VC on it and we were treated to a spectacular view of muzzle flashes all the way out!" As Braddon was trying to clear the zone, Major Allen's bird was having problems. "My crew chief reported that we had taken multiple hits on the left side of the aircraft which had entered low and exited high," he explained. "One round knocked out the main servo and hydraulic fluid was all over the place . . . I knew that we needed to land and check out the whole aircraft." Allen was able to nurse the damaged helicopter to an ARVN outpost, where it was deadlined. A crew flew in the next day and repaired it.

Major Braddon landed at an ARVN LZ about half way to Quang Ngai to check out the battle damage. "We determined that one of the .50 caliber rounds had gone through us end to end and had taken out the firewall junction box causing the electrical problems," he explained. "Another round had put a hole in the exhaust system which accounted for the new engine noise. I finally decided that except for some electrical damage and exhaust problems, I still had a bird whose engine was developing satisfactory power, the transmission and drive trains were intact and we had radios, we were ready to rejoin the mission." Meanwhile the VNAF Skyraiders resumed pounding the enemy positions as the first wave flew back to Quang Ngai, where several UH-34s were deadlined for battle damage. At 1355 the second wave of transports approached the LZ. "Before LtCol La Voy's lead division had even flared for landing, intense fire was again received," Woodmansee reported. "It came from places I had anticipated but there was one new location, the north perimeter of the zone. We were in another fire fight as intense as the first wave had experienced off-loading their troops."

The Viet Cong gunners concentrated their fire on the landing zone. According to, *U.S. Marines in Vietnam: The Advisory & Combat Assistance Era 1954-1964*, "One VNAF and several Marine helicopters were hit by enemy .50 caliber fire. The Vietnamese aircraft, which lost its tail rotor controls, spun sharply while trying to take off and crashed near the center of the zone." Major Braddon swept down through the heavy fire for the second time. The crew of the downed bird scrambled aboard and mounted their .30-caliber machine guns in the windows. "Those big guns, firing those big rounds out of the aircraft, bounced my flight helmet up and down on my head," Braddon exclaimed. "I had a devil of a time getting out of the zone because we were so heavy. We had a normal crew of two pilots, a crew chief, a gunner, plus the rescued four plus two mechanics to help retrieve a downed bird and a 500 lb. box of spare parts and tools."

Major John Rendall Braddon, United States Marine Corps, Silver Star citation:

The President of the United States of America takes pleasure in presenting the Silver Star to Major John Rendall Braddon, United States Marine Corps, for conspicuous gallantry and intrepidity in action while serving as leader of a section of helicopters, attached to and serving with Marine Medium Helicopter Squadron Three Hundred Sixty-Four (HMM-364), First Marine Aircraft Wing, charged with rescue and maintenance relative to downed aircraft as the result of enemy action on 27 April 1964. On that date, the entire squadron was committed to the mission of landing over four hundred troops of the Army of the Republic of Vietnam in an offensive action against the insurgent communist guerrillas (Viet Cong). In the course of the initial assault lift into the contested zone, one of the aircraft was fatally hit and crash landed into the zone. Major Braddon, without hesitation, departed from his position and flew into the direct opposition of the gun that had just downed the crew he was determined to rescue. In doing so, he had to fly into the contested area as a single target allowing all of the enemy automatic weapons to concentrate their fire on him. Major Braddon's aircraft was hit and seriously damaged by .50-caliber fire. This did not deter him in his mission as he landed near the dismounted crew. Subsequently, Major Braddon once again flew his aircraft into the face of enemy fire to land and evacuate the crew of another helicopter which was badly damaged and crash landed in the same area. By his selfless and daring actions and his loyal devotion to duty in the face of great personal risk, Major Braddon upheld the highest traditions of the United States Naval Service.

The fourth and final lift of the day was completed with very little enemy fire. Most of the Viet Cong had withdrawn deeper into the jungle in the face of the South Vietnamese infantry advance. *The Advisory & Combat Assistance Era* noted, "During the first day of the operation, 15 of 19 participating Marine UH-34Ds were hit. Only 11 Marine and VNAF helicopters originally assigned to support the operation remained airworthy." The following day another sixty South Vietnamese soldiers were airlifted into LZ Bravo. "Fourteen UH-34Ds, several of which had been repaired during the night, and four Army UH-1Bs lifted the remainder of the South Vietnamese battalion . . . by then the intensity of the enemy action had diminished greatly. Only one Marine helicopter was hit and it suffered only minor damage."

Major Braddon, escorted by Captain Woodmansee, returned to the LZ to pick up several wounded soldiers. Both helicopters shut down in the zone. "Jack Woodmansee walked up to me, held out his hand and said he would like to shake the hand of a brave man," Braddon recalled emotionally. "I was overwhelmed and still am. I have never seen a display of courage such as Jack put on that day. It was the greatest compliment I have ever received." After loading the casualties the two aircraft flew back to Quang Ngai. "We refueled our beat up old dog with all its holes, non-functioning electrical components and an engine sounding like a threshing machine and, with Jack on my wing, flew back to Da Nang. I still remember flying along the coast, the cockpit lit up with numerous warning lights indicating various system problems and failures, seeing Jack's Huey on my wing and hoping the beat up old Dog would get us home. It did."

Lieutenant Colonel La Voy recommended Woodmansee for the Navy Cross. Unfortunately, the award was never approved. The Marine pilots were all awarded the Distinguished Flying Cross, including Braddon's copilot. The basic citation stated:

> For heroic achievement as a Helicopter Aircraft Commander serving with Marine Medium Helicopter Squadron Three Hundred Sixty-Four, on 27 April 1964. [name of pilot] flew as a Helicopter Aircraft Commander in a troop lift operation in support of the Forces of the Republic of Vietnam into the heart of an insurgent communist guerrilla (Viet Cong) stronghold. The operation was conducted against an extremely well deployed and well armed anti-aircraft unit that brought the fire of many heavy automatic weapons to bear upon the incoming and departing waves of helicopters as well as laying down a destructive fire upon the landing zone. Exercising skillful judgment, iron determination and displaying outstanding aeronautical skill, [name of pilot] courageously maneuvered his helicopter into a safe landing while receiving serious damage during the approach and departure and utilizing all the skill at his command in saving the aircraft for further assault waves. [name of pilot] subsequently participated successfully in three additional heliborne assault landings into this very heavy fire to complete the mission which had been assigned. His courage and selfless action was in keeping with the highest traditions of the United States Naval Service.

The remaining copilots received a single mission Air Medal, while the crewmembers received the Navy and Marine Corps Commendation Medal. In addition, the South Vietnamese government awarded seventeen officers the Gallantry Cross Medal. The Do Xa Campaign lasted one month, ending on 27 May 1964. The ARVN forces lost 23 men killed in action and 87 wounded. The Viet Cong lost 62 killed, 17 captured and a large number of crew served and individual weapons captured, as well as a large quantity of ammunition.

CHAPTER THREE

DEATH ON THE FLIGHT LINE

The watch officer in the III Marine Amphibious Force (III MAF) Command Center hurriedly scanned the radio message and then picked up the handset of the EE 8 field telephone, cranked the handle, and spoke briefly to the senior officer on the other end. "Sir, we have a priority SPOTREP that you better look at. Chu Lai and Marble Mountain are under attack!"

SPOT REPORT 280115H

Chu Lai Airfield: At approximately 0001H, 28 October, a VC force estimated at 15–20 penetrated the Chu Lai Airfield and launched a well-coordinated and well-planned attack. The base received mortar fire on the runway and parking area. Two aircraft are reported burning. There are unknown Marine casualties.

Marble Mountain Air Facility: At approximately 0009H, 28 October, a VC force estimated at 90, and possibly including some personnel from North Vietnam launched a well planned and well coordinated attack on the Marble Mountain Air Facility. The enemy used mortars, small arms and automatic weapons fire. Eight helicopters are reported burning. Damage control teams are in the area putting out fires. It is reported that there are two Marine casualties.

[A spot report is a concise narrative report of essential information covering events or conditions that may have an immediate and significant effect on current planning and operations that is afforded the most expeditious means of transmission consistent with requisite security.]

A few minutes past midnight on 28 October 1965, Viet Cong sapper teams launched a coordinated attack on two locations in the III Marine

Amphibious Force (III MAF) enclave, Marble Mountain Air Facility and Chu Lai Airfield, inflicting over one hundred killed and wounded American servicemen and the damage and destruction of almost fifty aircraft. It was the most devastating attack on Americans up to that time.

VIET CONG SAPPERS

CHARACTERISTIC SAPPER ORGANIZATION

SAPPER RAIDING PARTY

SECURITY ELEMENT	RESERVE ELEMENT	FIRE SUPPORT ELEMENT
4 men, 1 B-40,	13 men, 1 B-40,	27 men, 2 82mm mortars
2 AK-47s,	9 AK-47s, 1 machine gun,	4 AK-47s, 1 K63 radio
2 mines	40 shaped charges	1 K63 radio

ASSAULT TEAM 1

CELL 1 (PENETRATION)	CELL 2 (ASSAULT)	CELL 3 (ASSAULT)
4 men, 2 AK-47s,	5 men, 2 B-40s,	4 men, 1 B-40,
3 Bangalores,	3 AK-47s, 70 shaped	2 AK-47s, 50 shaped
2 wire cutters	charges, 5 AT grenades	charges, 5 AT grenades

ASSAULT TEAM 2

CELL 1 (PENETRATION)	CELL 2 (ASSAULT)	CELL 3 (ASSAULT)	CELL 4 (FIRE SUPPORT)
4 men, 2 AK-47s,	5 men, 1 B-40,	4 men, 1 B-40, 2	2 men, 1 B-40,
4 Bangalores	2 AK-47s, 45	2 AK-47s, 35	1 AK-47
	shaped charges,	shaped charges,	
	5 AT grenades	3 AT grenades	

Sappers were elite, highly trained assault troops that targeted airfields, firebases, headquarters and other fortified positions.

Sappers, called dac cong by the North Vietnamese, were elite assault troops especially adept at infiltrating and attacking airfields, firebases, and other fortified positions. About 50,000 men served as sappers during the war. They were organized into groups of 100 to 150 men, further broken down into companies of roughly 30 to 36 men, with subdivisions into platoons, squads, and cells. Specialist troops such as radiomen, medics, and explosives experts were also attached. Many were volunteers. Sappers were often assigned to larger units (regiments, divisions, etc.), carrying out attacks and recon operations, but could also be organized as independent formations. Sappers trained and rehearsed carefully in all aspects of their craft and made use of a variety of equipment and explosive devices, including captured or abandoned American munitions. Sappers also carried out intelligence missions and could work undercover. One of the sappers in the spectacular 1968 Tet Offensive attack against the U.S. Embassy for example, was once a driver to the U.S. Ambassador.

Assault planning:

A typical assault plan began with a detailed reconnaissance of the target: pinpointing bunkers, ammo dumps, command and communications centers, barracks, power generation facilities, and other vital points. Intelligence was also gathered from local farmers, spies, and informers. A detailed mock-up of the target was then created and several rehearsals conducted to ensure the assault force was fully prepared. Assaults were usually planned to commence after nightfall. Signaling systems were sometimes devised using colored flares. A typical signal package would be red flare: area hard to get into; white flare: withdrawal; green flare: victory; green followed by white: reinforcements requested.

Assault organization and formations:

Depending on the size of the attack, sappers were usually divided into 10-20 man assault groups, which were further subdivided into 3-5 man assault teams or cells. Each team was tasked with destroying or neutralizing a specific area of the enemy defense. Generally there were four groups employed on a typical sapper operation.

- An assault group took on the main burden of the initial penetration through the wire and other defenses.
- A fire-support group would lay down covering fire via RPGs, mortars, or machine guns at key moments such as when the penetration elements cleared the wire, or at a set time, or via a prearranged signal.
- A small security group would be deployed where it could ambush any reinforcements rushing to the defense of the sappers' target.
- A reserve group would be held back to exploit success, mop up, or extract their fellow soldiers if the situation began to deteriorate.

Deployment of these elements depended on the target and available forces. In larger attacks, where the sappers were to lead the way, the fire support, exploitation, or security roles might be undertaken by bigger echelons of regular follow-on forces that would exploit breaches created by the sappers.

Initial assault movement:

Movement to the target area was typically by long, roundabout routes that served to conceal the mission and fool enemy observation. Once the sappers had reached the target, infiltrators in the advance units spread themselves around the perimeter according to their assigned tasks. Detailed prior reconnaissance helped in this effort. They strapped weapons and explosive charges to their bodies to minimize noise as they maneuvered through the outer band of fortifications and often covered their bodies in charcoal and grease to aid movement and make detection more difficult. Barbed wire was sometimes only partially cut, with the actual breaks made by hand to muffle the tell-tale "snip" of wire-cutters. Trip flares were neutralized by wrapping their triggers with cloth or strips of bamboo carried in the teeth of the vanguard fighters. Claymore mines might be turned in another direction.

A point man usually preceded each team, crawling silently through defenses and probing with his fingers to detect and neutralize obstacles, while the others followed behind. Sometimes gaps in the wire were created by tying down strands to make an assault corridor. Woven mats might be thrown over barbed wire to facilitate passage. Sappers often used Bangalore torpedoes made from blocks of TNT tied to bamboo poles to blast open assault routes. Attack routes often took unexpected avenues of approach, such as through the trash pits of U.S. Firebase Cunningham in 1969.

The main attack and withdrawal:

Based on the target and relevant military situation, some attacks proceeded mainly by stealth, with little initial covering fire until the last moment. Breaches might be created in the wire at several points, then left open while the penetration teams aligned with their objectives and hunkered down, awaiting the hour of decision. Other strikes, particularly against heavily defended U.S. targets used a barrage of covering fires to keep defenders penned in their positions, heads down, while the assault groups moved stealthily into position. Targets were usually hit in priority order, according to the level of danger they presented to the sapper units, or based on relevant military or political objectives.

If discovered, the sappers often sprang up and attacked immediately. Diversionary assaults and fires were also created to screen the main sapper effort. Once the objectives had been achieved, the pullout began. Small rearguard type elements were left in place to delay or as a diversionary force. Valuable enemy weapons and other equipment were rounded up, and the bodies of the dead and wounded were removed. Detailed after-action reports and critiques were conducted by VC/PAVN forces, absorbing lessons learned and sharpening their skills for the next assault.

CHU LAI

The two dozen highly trained Viet Cong sappers picked just the right night to infiltrate the perimeter barbed wire entanglements of the Chu Lai airfield: moonless, pitch black, with visibility down to a few feet. They were heavily laden with an assortment of Soviet and captured U.S. weapons, hand grenades, and satchel charges. Their mission was to destroy aircraft and kill as many Americans as possible in a quick hit and run raid. Timing was every-

Overhead view of the expeditionary airfield at Chu Lai. Note the C-130 on the taxiway preparing for take-off and the wreckage of another aircraft in the foreground.

thing for this type of operation. They planned to strike at midnight, giving them several hours of darkness to conduct the attack and get away before daylight. They also knew from experience that the defenders would be less alert at that hour of the night. The sappers were confident of the plan. Local guerrillas who worked for the Americans inside the compound had furnished details that allowed the sappers to construct an accurate mock-up of the base. The sappers spent several days studying the model and rehearsing every detail of the operation. Picked members of the unit had actually entered the facility as temporary laborers. They were able to verify the location of the interior and perimeter security posts, as well as to determine the best method to attack the aircraft in their protective revetments.

Every sapper had memorized his assignment. When the leader judged it was time to strike the assault group stripped down to loincloths and smeared their bodies with mud, which made them almost invisible in the darkness. They crawled up to the first strand of wire—a three foot high barbed wire fence marking the edge of the perimeter—and carefully examined it for trip wires before working their way under the lower strand. They continued, noiselessly advancing through the coils of concertina wire, until they were inside the perimeter past the outer security positions. At a point a thousand feet south of the north end of the runway they split into two groups.

One group attacked the VMA-224 flight line, setting satchel charges as they proceeded south along the aircraft revetments. "The first knowledge the Marines had of the attack was when they heard machine-gun fire and satchel charges blowing up," Col. Leslie E. Brown, commanding officer MAG-12, said. A MAG-12 sentry on Post 4 spotted four VC walking slowly toward the line of parked aircraft and challenged them. One of the VC threw a grenade but the sentry was able to get to cover before it exploded. The sentry spotted another intruder and tried to shoot him with his shotgun, but it misfired. In return, the VC threw a satchel charge, which failed to detonate. The lucky sentry then took cover behind a piece of ground support equipment and fired two shots at a sapper who was firing an automatic weapon into an aircraft. He missed and the enemy disappeared behind an aircraft.

The sentry at Post 5, alerted by Post 4's challenge ran to the front of the plane he was guarding and saw a VC running toward him firing an automatic weapon at the line of aircraft. The sentry fired two shots and saw the man stagger. The sentry took cover, reloaded, and prepared to defend his position. A third sentry at Post 6 was surprised by a sapper who suddenly appeared.

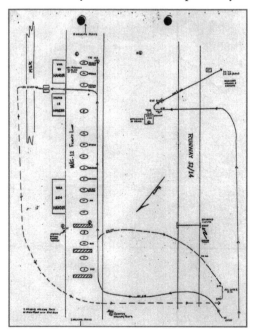

The sentry fired twice, hitting the man in the face and chest, and shot him again when he attempted to get up. The sergeant of the guard and several Marines from the crash crew took four of the sappers under fire, mortally wounding one and hitting two others. The two were later found dead just west of the runway. Another

Viet Cong sapper attack on the flight line at Chu Lai airfield on the night of 28 October 1965. The sappers succeeded in wounding a Marine, destroying two A-4 fighter bombers and damaging six others.

guard saw two more VC run east between the tents toward the runway. It appeared he was joining the wounded VC who had retreated earlier. All three were later killed trying to escape.

By this time, automatic weapons fire and explosions were occurring all along the flight line. "A couple of airplanes were on fire, and the sappers had gotten through intact," Colonel Brown recalled. "They had Thompson sub-machine guns and they were spraying the airplanes with automatic weapons fire and . . . throwing satchel charges into tail pipes. Some went off and some didn't, but the net effect was that the machine-gun fire caused leaks in the fuel tanks . . . and in the middle of that, the airplanes were on fire." A sentry spotted a sapper crouching behind a jet engine, pointing an automatic weap-on at him. For some reason the sapper did not fire and instead ran away, dis-appearing behind several maintenance tents. The sentry later identified the man as a worker in the camp that he saw a few days before the attack.

The second group of sappers attacked south along the west side of the runway and, as the first explosion took place, they threw a grenade against the back of a personnel tent with several Marines inside. Fortunately a wooden box absorbed the blast and no one was injured. The sappers then crossed the runway and ran toward the crash crew tents where, due to an alert NCO, the men had set up a hasty defense. Just as they got into position, four VC suddenly appeared only a few feet away. One threw a hand grenade, which bounced off a truck and exploded. One Marine was hit in the leg by shrapnel and another was knocked down by the blast. The crash crew opened fire, killing one of the assailants and wounding another. The surviving VC were seen heading south over the sand dunes.

Within minutes of the start of the attack, members of the crash crew rushed to the flight line to fight the fires. Despite the gunfire and explosions the men tried to contain the damage. At one point a 250-pound bomb ex-ploded, knocking one man to the ground. Fortunately it was a low order ex-plosion or it could have killed several men. Another bomb exploded, sending fragments through the roof of the hanger. Fuel from damaged fuel tanks had saturated the ground under the runway matting and under adjacent aircraft but timely damage control prevented further destruction. Ordnance person-nel braved the fire to defuse bombs that were loaded on the aircraft. Several of them were too hot to handle and had to be continuously sprayed with foam before they were cool enough to be defused. A detailed search of the flight line turned up five unexploded satchel charges on the aircraft, while six explosive charges and hand grenades were discovered on the taxiway. Just before daybreak, a patrol found two dead and one wounded VC about two thousand feet northwest of the runway. As the searchers cautiously approached them, the wounded man threw a grenade and was killed by return fire. By 0730 that morning MAG-12 was ready to conduct normal flight operations.

Brigadier General Frederick J. Karch, Chu Lai Base Coordinator, remembered, "[Col.] Les Brown was on the scene [and] the armament crews were going up and down the flight line disarming bombs . . . I couldn't give Brown too much credit for the job he and his crews did there that night—it was fabulous."

Colonel Leslie Brown received the Silver Star for his conduct during a sapper attack on the Chu Lai airfield.

Colonel Leslie Eugene Brown, United States Marine Corps, Silver Star citation:
The President of the United States of America takes pleasure in presenting a Gold Star in lieu of a Second Award of the Silver Star to Colonel Leslie Eugene Brown, United States Marine Corps, for conspicuous gallantry and intrepidity in action against insurgent communist (Viet Cong) forces while serving as Commanding Officer, Marine Aircraft Group Twelve (MAG-12), First Marine Aircraft Wing, in the Republic of Vietnam. During the early morning hours of 28 October 1965, Viet Cong suicide squads suddenly and violently attacked and infiltrated Chu Lai Airfield in a determined effort to destroy aircraft. Proceeding immediately to the center of action on the flight line, Colonel Brown, defying the hazards involved, directed the entire Group counteraction. With fires raging from bombed aircraft, and with guerrilla infiltrators dispersed throughout the area, he fearlessly moved from position to position, directing explosive ordnance disposal teams, firefighting efforts, searches for bombs, and other defensive operations. Ignoring the low order detonation of two 250-pound bombs, and the danger from further explosions or the possible conflagration of the jet fuel which

flooded the area, Colonel Brown fearlessly moved through the area supervising and personally assisting his Marines in their hazardous tasks. Displaying remarkable presence of mind and attention to detail, he was always the master of the situation, making his presence strongly felt everywhere and thereby establishing order from the potential chaos. By his selfless courage, inspiring leadership and loyal devotion to duty throughout, Colonel Brown upheld the highest traditions of the United States Naval Service.

*Sergeant Andrew M. Schreiner, Jr., United States
Marine Corps, Silver Star citation:*
The President of the United States of America takes pleasure in presenting the Silver Star to Sergeant Andrew M. Schreiner, Jr., United States Marine Corps, for conspicuous gallantry and intrepidity in action while serving as an Ordnance Noncommissioned Officer with Marine Attack Squadron Two Hundred Fourteen (VMA-214), in connection with combat operations against the enemy in the Republic of Vietnam. In the early morning hours of 28 October 1965, Marine Aircraft Group Twelve, based at the Marine Corps Expeditionary Airfield at Chu Lai, was suddenly attacked by insurgent communist (Viet Cong) suicide squads in a vicious and determined attempt to destroy aircraft on the flight line. Hearing an explosion on the flight line, Sergeant Schreiner rushed to the vicinity, where a second explosion had caused an aircraft carrying heavy ordnance to be engulfed in flames. Disregarding the small arms fire and satchel charges exploding throughout the area, Sergeant Schreiner helped direct a crash crew in keeping the fire away from the wing bombs. While the crash crew was spraying the ordnance as directed, two bombs exploded in low order detonations. After the fire had been extinguished and with complete disregard for his personal safety, he courageously assisted in removing the fuses from the two remaining overheated, unstable bombs and in their removal from the flight line. Repeating his heroic actions, Sergeant Schreiner then assisted in the removal of the fuses of four other bombs from an adjacent aircraft. His acts were accomplished with the full knowledge that the bombs could explode at any time. Due to the slick foam under the aircraft, movement was treacherous; and in addition, fuel from the destroyed and damaged aircraft, if ignited, could have caused an instantaneous

conflagration. By his prompt and courageous actions at the risk of his own life, Sergeant Schreiner assisted in the prevention of further damage to the aircraft and thereby upheld the highest traditions of the United States Naval Service.

U.S./VC LOSSES

1. *Casualties:*

	KIA	WIA
VC	15	2
U.S.	0	1

2. *U.S. Aircraft and Equipment:*

Aircraft	Destroyed	Major Damage	Minor Damage
A-4	2	3	3

Equipment 1 Crash Truck damaged / 1 Aerology Van damaged

MARBLE MOUNTAIN AIR FACILITY

On 24 October, 140 men of the 278th Sapper (Special Operations) Company left their base camp and moved by motorized junks from the vicinity of the Hai Van Pass to an assembly area on the eastern slope of high ground six hundred meters north-northwest of the Mobile Construction Battalion 9 (MCB-9, Seabees) compound. A second enemy company, the 275th, crossed the bridge just east of Marble Mountain and prepared to launch a coordinated two-pronged attack.

The 278th Sapper Company was divided into five teams for the attack:

- Team One: 1st Platoon (forty-five men) was assigned to break into the western side of the airbase and pin down the Seabee defenders with mortar and automatic weapons fire.
- Teams Two and Three: 2nd and 3rd platoons (sixty men) were assigned to break into the helicopter parking area and destroy aircraft with Bangalore torpedoes and hand grenades.
- Team Four: Mortar Platoon (two 60mm mortars) was assigned to bombard the defenders with fifty rounds of ammunition. Two squads of the Mortar Platoon were also assigned to lay mines at the two ends of the road into the objective area to check the advance of South Vietnamese reinforcements.

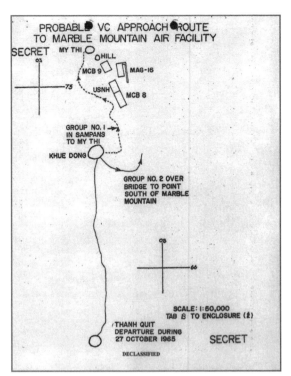

PROBABLE VC APPROACH ROUTE
TO MARBLE MOUNTAIN AIR FACILITY

Classified overlay of the route that the 278th Sapper Company used to attack MAG-16's Marble Mountain base.

- Team Five: Ten sappers were assigned to harass the 1st Battalion, 9th Marines, with small-arms fire from positions north and west.

The signal to attack was to be the explosion of mortar rounds inside the American perimeter. Staff Sergeant Richard Shamrell noted, "all the Viet Cong sappers were in the nude, except for the loin cloths covering their private parts in an effort to blend in with the sand during darkness. The area was like one big beach with tan colored sand." They were almost impossible to spot in the darkness.

Colonel Thomas J. O'Connor, the MAG-16 commander, remembered, "I awoke to the sound of explosions shortly after midnight." Mortar rounds were impacting behind the group's tent lines and on the pierced steel runway matting. "Several of us ran out of the tent, and looking east," Captain Bob Stoffey wrote in *Cleared Hot, A Marine Combat Pilot's Vietnam Diary*, "we saw a burning truck off the road between our western perimeter wire and the village just north of the Seabee camp. I knew immediately that it was our MAB's [Marine Air Base] two-thousand-gallon water truck . . . the VC obviously had laid a mine on the road and blew up the truck." Three mechanics, Cpl. Eugene Mortimer, LCpl. Leonard O'Shannon, and Cpl. Lawrence Brule had just left the hanger when "we heard three explosions, which sounded like mortars. We grabbed our weapons and headed for a sand-bagged hole. We'd been in the hole only about twenty seconds when we saw [several] people, all armed, running towards us," O'Shannon said. "They were about thirty to forty feet away. We saw they were Viet Cong. When they got within fifteen feet of us, we opened fire with our rifles." The three Marines killed seven of the VC and wounded four others, whom they captured. Colonel O'Connor reached his command post just in time to receive a call from the wing commander, Maj. Gen. Keith McCutcheon. "He was warning me that the airfield at Chu Lai had been attacked and to be on the alert. I told him no one was asleep at Marble Mountain, as we had also been under attack for about fifteen minutes."

Sapper Team Four unleashed a dozen mortar rounds as fast as they could drop them down the tubes. "A tremendous quantity of incoming mortar-fire impacts began pounding the area up near our flight line," Captain Stoffey said. "The sickening *woop, woop, woop* of mortar hits sounded like they were coming from across the street to the east near the Seabee camp." The 60mm mortar rounds blanketed the MCB-9 compound (Camp Adenir), primarily the officers' billeting area, for about ten minutes and then the Seabees came under intense automatic weapons fire from the north and east. Staff Sergeant Shamrell said that, "The Seabee Battalion across the roadway from the air facility was kept pinned down by a couple of .50-caliber machine guns throughout the attack." The heavy fire kept the reaction force from fully manning all the security posts for over twenty minutes. When they were able to reach their posts, the Seabees returned the enemy fire on four Viet Cong positions in the village to the west with a vengeance. The next day patrols determined from bloody drag marks in the sand that at least five VC had been wounded in the exchange.

Commander Richard E. Anderson,
United States Navy, Silver Star citation:
The President of the United States of America takes pleasure in pre-senting the Silver Star to Commander (CEC) Richard E. Anderson, United States Navy, for conspicuous gallantry and intrepidity in action while serving as Commanding Officer, U.S. Naval Mobile Construction Battalion Nine (USNMCB-9) near Da Nang, Repub-lic of Vietnam, against the Viet Cong during the night of 27 and 28 October 1965. When his Battalion's camp was suddenly struck by intense enemy mortar and automatic weapons fire, Commander An-

derson courageously moved from his covered position at his living area to the Battalion Command Post, and in so doing, was wounded in the leg by fragments from a mortar explosion. Ignoring his painful wounds and the incessant fire, he continued on to the Command Post and took direct control of the execution of his effective defensive plan. As the battle progressed, he boldly moved about the camp, directing the care and evacuation of the wounded, and encouraging his men. He resolutely rejected treatment of his wounds until all other known wounded had been treated. By his heroic actions and inspiring devotion to duty in the face of grave personal risk, Commander Anderson upheld the highest traditions of the United States Naval Service.

Several sappers from Teams One and Two worked their way through the perimeter barbed wire and attacked a key machine-gun bunker on the west side of the MAG-16 aircraft parking mat. The three Marines occupying the bunker took the Viet Cong under fire until all three were wounded and put out of action. About this time Captain Stoffey "grabbed my grease gun [.45-caliber machine gun] and threw two bags of .45 ammo clips over my shoulder. I had to get down to the command post fast. I was the officer in charge of the MABS [Marine Air Base Squadron] mobile alert platoon." Sergeant William E. Cassada recalled, "We quickly grabbed our gear and poured outside of our ten-man general purpose tents [and] were met with a towering inferno of white magnesium smoke and flames rising from the flight line. We were all scared shitless . . . even though the philosophy of the Corps is that every Marine is a basic rifleman—we were all armed with M-14s [rifles]—even so we were air-wingers, not jungle combat veterans."

Major Randall Wallace Duphiney, United States Marine Corps, Silver Star citation:

The President of the United States of America takes pleasure in presenting the Silver Star to Major Randall Wallace Duphiney, United States Marine Corps, for conspicuous gallantry and intrepidity in action while serving as a Helicopter Aircraft Commander with Marine Medium Helicopter Squadron Three Hundred Sixty-One (HMM-361), Marine Aircraft Group Thirty-Six (MAG-36), First Marine Aircraft Wing, in connection with operations against insurgent communist (Viet Cong) forces in the Republic of Vietnam, on 28 October 1965. On this occasion, Major Duphiney exhibited unusual courage and devotion to duty on a medical evacuation mission. Shortly after midnight, Marble Mountain Airfield and adjacent Camp Adenir came under a strong and determined Viet Cong attack, delivered with vicious fanaticism. Besides inflicting many Marine casualties, the attack damaged and destroyed many aircraft. When a call from Camp Adenir was received asking for immediate evacuation of wounded personnel, Major Duphiney volunteered to fly the wounded to the nearest medical facility. With utter disregard for his personal safety, he proceeded on foot through intense automatic weapons fire to the aircraft parking area. There he was met by violent explosions and raging fires generated by the attack. Ignoring the conflagration, the incessant enemy fire and bodies of slain suicidal attackers with demolition charges still strapped to them, Major Duphiney finally found an apparently undamaged aircraft. With no opportunity to determine whether the helicopter had been prepared for demolition by the enemy, he took off into the intense fire and headed for Camp Adenir. Forced to land in a small area, guided only by flashlights and a truck's headlights, he called upon his experience and superior skill to land in spite of hits from enemy fire. Major Duphiney evacuated as many wounded as his helicopter would carry and delivered them to the nearest medical facility. Repeatedly hit by enemy fire, he heroically continued to evacuate casualties until informed that the mission was complete. He was successful in evacuating twenty seriously wounded men, many of whom would not have survived without his courageous and determined efforts. By his initiative, skill and selfless devotion to duty, Major Duphiney upheld the highest traditions of the Marine Corps and of the United States Naval Service.

Sapper Team One proceeded north through the VMO-2 tent area throwing grenades. Sergeant Ray Reinders, a VMO-2 crew chief, was an interior guard. "We heard the explosions from the VMO-2 maintenance area and then we came under fire as the VC swept up the line of VMO-2 aircraft. There were four Hueys parked on the runway adjacent to our bunker and we commandeered the internal M-60s [machine guns]. We initially established a defensive line along the runway and engaged the VC attempting to get to the fuel farm located between the east edge of the mat and the runway. There was a lot of firing to and from the mat area with most of the perimeter fire ricocheting off the steel matting." By this time Captain Stoffey and his thirty-man reaction force had mustered and were heading toward the sound of "several loud explosions coming from the flight line." The sappers reached the helicopter parking area where they commenced a methodical attack on each aircraft. Chief Hospital Corpsman Walter J. Gelien, U.S. Navy, had volunteered to take the medevac watch in the ready helicopter on the flight line. He was killed as the VC attacked down the line of aircraft. Captain Stoffey recalled, "I heard about our chief Corpsman [Walter Gelien]. He had volunteered for the night medevac chopper and had been sleeping inside the

Marines clean up the debris after the sapper attack on the Marble Mountain Air Facility.

Huey when the attack started. Apparently when the mortars began impacting, he had decided to stay in the chopper, probably thinking that the ready crew would be out rapidly to crank up the helo and to take any wounded to Charlie Med [medical aid station]. Instead of a flight crew, he was greeted by an attacking VC with a satchel charge that got him and destroyed the Huey." Staff Sergeant Shamrell said, "as the sappers reached and planted their explosives in and around the helicopters positioned on the flight line, the explosions and the activity created by the Viet Cong could be heard and seen many miles. It was the first real attack by them on U.S. forces deployed around Da Nang City and showed just how vulnerable we were."

The sappers worked their way east across the parking ramp just as Captain Stoffey and the reaction force reached the flight line. "I had my troops spread out so we could cover all the aircraft parking areas as we counterattacked. As we charged across the open runway, numerous helicopters were exploding and burning, particularly along the VMO-2 flight line." The light of the burning helicopters assisted the reaction force. "We could see the VC running up and down the lines of the parked aircraft . . . I screamed, 'Fire at will!'" One sapper was seen running through a tent ripping out communications wire and then he ran back to the ramp under fire the entire time. Private First Class Edward E. Graboskey, a member of the crash crew, was killed trying to stop the attackers. "As we closed with the VC, between the aircraft, some of them continued to try to drop satchel charges into the remaining VMO-2 UH-1E gunships and also down the exhaust stacks of the UH-34Ds and larger CH-37s. We were now all between the lines of parked aircraft, feeling the immense heat of the fires."

An aerial view of the damage caused by the Viet Cong attack. Nearly one third of the Marine helicopters were destroyed or damaged during the attack.

The fighting was at close quarters. "As I ran along the taxiway . . . two VC came directly in front of me from between two UH-34Ds," Captain Stoffey recalled. "They were clad only in black shorts or swimsuits and were barefooted. Each had satchel charges, grenades and an AK-47 automatic assault weapon. They both raised their AK-47s while pushing their shoulder-hung satchel charges aside. Only one was fast enough to crank off some rounds in my direction. I gave them both a steady burst from the grease gun and they both buckled to the steel matting. I felt a searing pain in my inside right wrist. The one bastard had hit me. I looked at my wrist and the flaming helicopter near me gave me ample light to show me that I was bleeding a fair amount, but the wound was simply a big scratch below the inside of my palm on the wrist." The VC pushed farther along the flight line where they ran into several members of the crash crew who were trying to save the aircraft. Lance Corporal Thomas P. Rowland was killed in the ensuring firefight. The surviving enemy sappers split up and went south placing grenades and explosive charges as they went through the rows of parked UH-34Ds of HMM-263 and HMM-361. Sergeant Reinders said, "one group of VC swung through the [UH]-34s dropping grenades into the exhaust stacks not covered and randomly spraying the tent areas with small arms as they exited the base using a line of parked earthmoving equipment as cover."

Captain Stoffey recalled, "We charged up to the west wire and we spread out on both sides of the M-60 machine gun bunker. Out in front of it lay four dead VC, apparently gunned down by the mechanic assigned there. He obviously killed them when they first came over the wire from the hospital . . . which the Seabees had been building." The half-constructed hospital was unoccupied at the time, except for a six-member roving patrol and a doctor and twenty-three hospital Corpsmen, who were billeted south of the construction site. The VC pinned down both groups with a heavy volume of small arms while they systematically placed explosives in critical buildings, which were either completely destroyed or heavily damaged. At 0150, the surviving sappers withdrew through the village west of the hospital site. The Seabees reported the movement to the MAG-16 defenders, who poured a heavy volume of automatic weapons fire into the village. "As fast as it began," Captain Stoffey said, "it was over. The enemy hit us fast and hard." Seven UH-1Es that were line up beside the hanger were destroyed, as well as six on the parking ramp. Two others received major damage and two suffered minor damage. Six UH-34s were destroyed, nine suffered major and seventeen minor damage.

U.S./VC LOSSES

1. *Casualties*:

	KIA	WIA	Missing
VC	20	34 *(4 captured)**	25
U.S.	4	108	
	(3 MAG-16,	(24 MAG-16,	
	1 MCB-9)	84 MCB-9)	

2. *U.S. Aircraft and equipment losses:*

a. Aircraft:**

	Destroyed	Major Damage	Minor Damage
UH-1E	3	2	2
UH-34	6	9	17
CH-37	0	0	5

b. Vehicles

150-gal Water Truck	1	0	0
M422 Truck	1	0	1
MB5 Crash Truck	0	1	2
M63 Gas	0	1	0

c. Miscellaneous:

   15,000 square feet of matting destroyed.

Captain Stoffey survived the onslaught and as he made his way back through the rubble and charred helicopters to the command post. After reaching the command post Stoffey helped line up the VC dead. "Our Vietnamese interpreter shouted, 'This one is a North Vietnamese. Look see. He have NVA belt buckle. Also look at hands: no callus like local VC farmer

---

*The four wounded captives were evacuated to a Vietnamese Hospital and interrogated after treatment. All four were enlisted men from nearby villages in Quang Nam Province. They indicated that the 278th Sapper Company was activated within the past 5 months. This was their first operation.

**Colonel O'Connor remarked that, "Helicopters were burning all over . . . VMO-2 was practically wiped out. The helicopter losses resulted in "a 43% loss of division mobility," and that it "put a crimp in division plans for several months afterward," he said.

A Viet Cong prisoner.

hands with thick skin. Him city man from North Vietnam.' We all looked, and sure enough the so-called VC had smooth palms and he was wearing a black belt with a silver buckle with a Communist Star on it." While the initial SPOTREP mentioned the possibility of North Vietnamese involvement in the attack, it was never conclusively proven. The last victim of the attack was Lt. Cmdr. Robert J. Fay, the commanding officer of the Naval Advisory Detachment and the first Navy "frogman" killed in Vietnam. Staff Sergeant Shamrell recalled, "After the attack, the commander's jeep was found a couple miles from NAD Headquarters. He had been shot during the attack and subsequently died of wounds as he was heading for the camp site near My Khe."

A VMO-2 UH-1E Huey that was destroyed by enemy sappers.

CHAPTER FOUR

ONE VERY BAD AFTERNOON

Little was known in the United States about the deployment of U.S. Marine Corps helicopter squadrons to Vietnam until a thirty-six-year-old British photographer named Larry Burrows climbed aboard a UH-34D helicopter named Yankee Papa 13 (YP-13) and began taking photos. The resulting photo essay, which appeared in the 16 April 1965 issue of *Life Magazine*, documented the traumatic death of a Marine Corps pilot. It also captured the bravery, sacrifice, and devotion to duty of the helicopter crews. For most Americans, it was the first time they became aware of the country's involvement in Vietnam. After taking several photographs of the crew (Capt. Peter J. Vogel, 1st Lt. O. M. Sherrer, Lance Corporal James C. Farley, and Pfc. Wayne L. Hoilien) Burrows climbed aboard Yankee Papa 13 and took a seat among the nine South Vietnamese paratroopers in the cramped troop compartment. He positioned himself to take photos of the crew chief, Lance Corporal Farley, who was manning the starboard M-60 7.62mm machine gun.

The mission on this last day of March 1965 was to airlift 465 troops of the ARVN 5th Airborne Battalion from the vicinity of Tam Ky in Quang Tin Province to a landing zone about twenty-five miles south of Da Nang. Intelligence reports indicated the landing zone was a Viet Cong assembly area. The assault force was to be carried in three waves by 17 UH-34Ds from Marine Medium Helicopter Squadron 163 (HMM-163), 2 UH-34Ds from Marine Helicopter Squadron 162 (HMM-162) and 7 U.S. Army Bell UH-1B Huey gunships belonging to the Utility Tactical Transport Detachment, 68th Aviation Company.

As YP-13 touched down in the dry rice paddy Burrows photographed the Vietnamese paratroopers scrambling out of the hatch to join their comrades running toward a bamboo-and-scrub-growth lined hedgerow. Suddenly their objective exploded with gunfire. "The Viet Cong [were] dug in along the tree line," Burrows wrote. "They were just waiting for us to come into the landing zone." Heavy automatic weapons fire repeatedly hit the stationary helicopters. "We were like sitting ducks and their raking crossfire was murderous," he said. Radios came alive with reports of aircraft damage and enemy sightings. Lieutenant Colonel Norman Ewers, the squadron commander in the lead aircraft responded, "We're all being hit, if your aircraft is flyable, press on." Ewers thought they had "landed in the middle of the Viet Cong . . . maybe a trap." The number two aircraft in Ewers division

A UH-34 door gunner mans an M60 7.62mm machine gun. The door-mounted machine gun improved the helicopter's firepower protection.

was hit several times. The pilot, 1st Lt. Wendell T. Eliason, was killed and copilot 1st Lt. Donald R. Wilson was wounded. Despite the injury, Wilson managed to fly the badly-damaged helo back to Da Nang. Four other helicopters in the first wave suffered battle damage and had to be flown back for repairs.

Lieutenant Colonel Norman G. Ewers, Silver Star citation:
The President of the United States takes pleasure in presenting the Silver Star Medal to Norman G. Ewers (0-28152), Lieutenant Colonel, U.S. Marine Corps, for conspicuous gallantry and intrepidity in action while serving with Marine Medium Helicopter Squadron 163 (HMM-163), 1st Marine Aircraft Wing, in connection with combat operations against the enemy in the Republic of Vietnam on March 31, 1965. By his courage, aggressive fighting spirit and steadfast devotion to duty in the face of extreme personal danger, Lieutenant Colonel Ewers upheld the highest traditions of the Marine Corps and the United States Naval Service.

The remaining helicopters flew back to Tam Ky to pick up the second wave. Photographer Burrows recalled that YP-13 was able to lift off and "[hurried] back to a pickup point for another load of troops." Intense fire damaged several more aircraft when they returned to the landing zone. Many of them were so badly damaged that they could not complete the third lift. First Lieutenant Paul Gregoire said, "Only six or seven of us made the third and last trip because of battle damage and wounded crew on the two previous trips." Captain Vogel's YP-13 reached the landing zone for the third time. He spotted YP-3 still on the ground with its rotors turning "Why don't they lift off," he mumbled over the intercom and brought his ship down close by to see if the crew needed help. "One of the crew came lurching across the field towards us, followed by another," Burrows said. "They were the copilot and the gunner. Both had been wounded and had to be helped aboard." Crew Chief Farley pulled them inside the cabin. Sergeant Billie Owens slumped against the bulkhead bleeding severely from a shoulder wound. First Lieutenant James E. Magel collapsed on the deck and lay in a pool of blood.

Captain Peter Jerome Vogel, United States Marine Corps, Silver Star citation:

The President of the United States of America takes pleasure in presenting the Silver Star to Captain Peter Jerome Vogel, United States Marine Corps for conspicuous gallantry and intrepidity in action while serving as a Pilot of a UH-34D with Marine Medium Helicopter Squadron One Hundred Sixty-Three (HMM-163). First Marine Aircraft Wing, in connection with combat operations against the enemy in the Republic of Vietnam. On 31 March 1965, Captain Vogel participated in a seventeen helicopter flight transporting troops of the Fifth Vietnamese Airborne Battalion in an airborne assault in Quang Tin Province. Each of the three assault landings was met by intense fire from an estimated two insurgent communist (Viet Cong) companies armed with automatic weapons, mortars and recoilless rifles. Upon lifting off after debarking the third load of troops, Captain Vogel observed a companion aircraft which had failed to become airborne. Although his own aircraft had taken many damaging hits, and he had suffered a painful neck wound, Captain Vogel courageously landed adjacent to the stricken aircraft in order to effect a rescue of the crewmen. Realizing fully the hazardous position he was in, he fearlessly remained in the fire-swept landing zone and, ignoring the bullets hitting the aircraft, directed the rescue efforts until the two crewmen were successfully rescued. Only after it was determined that further rescue attempts would be to no avail did Captain Vogel leave the landing zone. Despite his painful wound and severely damaged aircraft, he successfully flew his aircraft back to his home base. By his courageous actions, inspiring devotion to duty and exceptional aeronautical skill in the face of grave personal risk, Captain Vogel upheld the highest traditions of the Marine Corps and of the United States Naval Service.

Captain Vogel could see the pilot of the downed aircraft slumped over the controls. "Farley," he said, "See what you can do for that other pilot." The crew chief unhooked his radio cord, jumped to the ground, and sprinted to the assist the wounded officer. "I chased after him," Burrows said. "From a stone building some seventy yards away a Viet Cong machine gun was spraying the area." Despite the heavy automatic weapons fire, Farley climbed up to the cockpit in full view of the enemy and attempted to drag the severely wounded man out. "Farley hastily examined the pilot," Burrows explained. "Through the blood around his face and throat, Farley could see a bullet hole in his neck. That, plus the fact that the man had not moved at all, led him to believe the pilot was dead." Machine-gun bullets continued to strike all around him. "It would have been certain death to hang around any longer," Burrows related. "So, crouching low, we ran back to Yankee Papa 13."

Corporal James C. Farley Jr., United States Marine Corps, Silver Star citation:

The President of the United States of America takes pleasure in presenting the Silver Star to Corporal James C. Farley, Jr. (MCSN: 1937825), United States Marine Corps, for conspicuous gallantry and intrepidity in action while serving as a Crew Chief of a UH-34D helicopter with Marine Medium Helicopter Squadron One Hundred Sixty-Three (HMM-163), in the Republic of Vietnam. On 31 March 1965, Corporal Farley participated in an airborne assault in Quang Tin Province. Each of the three assault landings was met by intense fire from an estimated two insurgent communist (Viet Cong) companies armed with automatic weapons, mortars and recoilless rifles. Throughout the landings, he remained resolutely at his battle station delivering suppressive fire upon the enemy. After lifting off following the third landing, a damaged aircraft was sighted in the landing zone. Corporal Farley's aircraft immediately returned to the zone to rescue the crewmen of the stricken helicopter. Upon landing, without hesitation and seemingly oblivious to the intense fire of an enemy machine gun located seventy-five yards away, Corporal Farley left his helicopter, ran through the enemy fire to the downed aircraft and assisted two wounded members aboard his aircraft. Again, with total disregard for his own safety, he boldly raced to the downed aircraft in an attempt to rescue the pilot who was trapped in the cockpit. He repeatedly exposed himself in an effort to accomplish this task. Unable to free the pilot without assistance and believing him to be dead, Corporal Farley returned to his aircraft and rendered first aid to those already aboard. By his daring and courageous actions and inspiring devotion to duty in the face of grave personal risk, Corporal Farley upheld the highest traditions of the United States Naval Service.

As Farley struggled to free the severely wounded pilot, YP-3's remaining crewman, Sergeant Cecil A. Garner, dismounted one of the aircraft's M-60 machine guns, crawled away from the disabled craft, and took the enemy under fire. Despite being badly wounded in the leg, he continued to engage the enemy machine gun.

Sergeant Cecil Aubrey Garner, United States Marine Corps, Silver Star citation:

The President of the United States of America takes pleasure in presenting the Silver Star to Sergeant Cecil Aubrey Garner, United States Marine Corps for conspicuous gallantry and intrepidity in action while serving with Marine Medium Helicopter Squadron One Hundred Sixty-Three (HMM-163) in the Republic of Vietnam, on 31 March 1965. Sergeant Garner was acting as crew chief aboard a Marine helicopter. This aircraft was part of a seventeen plane flight whose mission was to transport Republic of Vietnam forces in an assault landing. After three successive assault landings in a zone subjected to intense and accurate enemy anti-aircraft fire, the aircraft was shot down. Sergeant Garner, although suffering from serious leg wounds, dismounted his M-60 machine gun, crawled away from the aircraft and began firing on Viet Cong positions. Through his efforts, an enemy machine gun nest was neutralized, aiding rescuers to reach and evacuate, under fire, the wounded pilot from his downed aircraft. When Sergeant Garner was evacuated by rescue personnel and placed inside another helicopter, he continued to engage the enemy by manning an M-60 machine gun until he collapsed from exhaustion and the effects of his wounds. By his daring actions and loyal devotion to duty in the face of personal risk, Sergeant Garner upheld the highest traditions of the United States Naval Service.

Major Bennie Mann had just lifted his damaged aircraft out of the zone when he spotted the downed helicopter. He immediately banked around and landed to assist in a rescue attempt.

Major Bennie Mann, United States Marine Corps, Navy Cross citation:

For extraordinary heroism as a Helicopter Aircraft Commander and Division Flight Leader with Marine Medium Helicopter Squadron One Hundred Sixty-Three (HMM-163) in Quang Tin Province, Republic of Vietnam, on 31 March 1965. Participating in a seventeen-aircraft flight transporting assault troops of the Fifth Vietnamese Airborne Battalion, Major Mann along with the entire mission,

Major Bernie Mann, shown here as a colonel, displayed exceptional gallantry in action by evacuating wounded aircrewmen under intense fire.

was scheduled to make three assault landings into an area defended by an estimated force of two companies of insurgent communist (Viet Cong) guerrillas. During the first landing, his aircraft was hit in the engine compartment by intense enemy automatic weapons fire. Although he was experiencing aircraft power and control malfunctions, he continued to lead the attack a second and third time into ever increasing hostile fire. When, after lifting off from the third assault landing, he saw a downed aircraft and wounded crewmen under enemy attack in the landing zone, he unhesitatingly turned his aircraft around and braved the intense enemy onslaught for a fourth time in order to rescue the crew of a stricken helicopter. Displaying exceptional leadership and courage, he directed the rescue efforts, and when his crewmen and copilot were taken under fire by the nearby enemy, he fearlessly hovered his helicopter between the enemy and the crewmen in order to shield their rescue efforts. As a result of his courageous actions, inspiring leadership, and extraordinary airmanship, Major Mann contributed significantly to the successful assault mission and to saving the lives of several of his fellow Marines. His heroic conduct and selfless devotion to duty reflected great credit upon himself and the Marine Corps and were in keeping with the highest traditions of the United States Naval Service."

As Mann maneuvered the helicopter, SSgt. Stanley J. Novotny braved the intense fire in an attempt to pull the immobile pilot from the cockpit. He had to climb the outside of the aircraft to reach the wounded officer, under fire the entire time. "Somehow [he] found the strength singlehandedly to lift the conscious but paralyzed six-foot, 200-pound Eddy out of the downed craft," Ewers noted in an after-action report. By this time Eddy was loaded, Sergeant Garner had made his way to the aircraft and Mann was able to take off.

Staff Sergeant Stanley J. Novotny, United States Marine Corps, Silver Star citation:

The President of the United States of America takes pleasure in presenting the Silver Star to Staff Sergeant Stanley J. Novotny, United States Marine Corps, for conspicuous gallantry and intrepidity in action while serving with Marine Medium Helicopter Squadron One Hundred Sixty-Three (HMM-163), First Marine Aircraft Wing, in connection with combat operations against the enemy in the Republic of Vietnam on 31 March 1965. Staff Sergeant Novotny was acting as aerial gunner aboard a Marine helicopter. This aircraft was part of a seventeen plane fight whose mission was to transport Republic of Vietnam forces in an assault landing. He manned his aerial gunners' position on three successive assault landings in a zone subject to intense and accurate enemy anti-aircraft fire. The aircraft made a fourth landing to rescue a downed aircraft crew. Immediately, without thought of personal safety, Staff Sergeant Novotny left his aircraft and ascended the port side of the downed aircraft in an attempt to free the pilot. Unable to do this, he descended, circled the aircraft and ascended the starboard side. Although constantly exposed to enemy fire, Staff Sergeant Novotny successfully freed the paralyzed pilot. By his daring actions and loyal devotion to duty in the face of personal risk, Staff Sergeant Novotny upheld the highest traditions of the United States Naval Service.

With YP-13 out of small-arms-fire range, the two gunners had an opportunity to help the two wounded men. Lieutenant Magel was the most seriously wounded. When Farley and Hoilien eased off his flak vest, they exposed a major wound just below his right armpit. Burrows noted, "Magel's face registered pain, and his lips moved slightly. But if he said anything it was drowned out by the noise of the copter." Farley desperately attempted to stop the bleeding. "The wind from the doorway kept whipping the bandage across his face," Burrows wrote. "The blood started to come from his [Magel's] nose and mouth and a glazed look come into his eyes. Farley tried mouth-to-mouth resuscitation, but Magel was dead. Nobody said a word." Attention shifted to Owens, whose left shoulder was smashed by a bullet. "[He] lay in shock against the bulkhead. He was watching, but his sunglasses hid any expression his eyes might have shown," Burrows said. "Farley poured some water into an empty ammunition can and gave it to Owens. Hoilien took out a cigarette for him, but Owens waved it aside. We were all left with our own drained thoughts." In all, twenty-five Marine and ten Army helicopters took part in the operation. Nineteen of the aircraft suffered battle damage and three were shot down, including two of the Army helicopters. Two Marines were killed and nineteen Marines and two Army crewmen were wounded.

CHAPTER FIVE

ASHAU VALLEY RESCUE

The Marine Medium Helicopter Squadron 163 (HMM-163) mess tent was filled to overflowing with pilots and aircrews. They had been summoned to get the latest word on the status of the Special Forces camp in the Ashau Valley from squadron commander Lt. Col. Charles A. "Chuck" House. "A great sense of urgency pervaded the atmosphere," 1st Lt. Shepard Spink recalled. Early reports indicated that the base was in danger of being overrun by NVA regulars and the garrison was urgently requesting evacuation. "We could hear them begging over the radio for MedEvacs, ammo and water . . . ," Private First Class George Twardzik said. One radio message was particularly poignant. "Need reinforcements—without them, kiss us goodbye." The tent buzzed with everyone's take on whether the squadron

Ashau Valley Special Forces camp in western Thua Thien Province before the assault on the camp by the NVA 95th Regiment. The isolated camp was surrounded by mountains that combined with heavy clouds to hinder relief and evacuation efforts.—*U.S. Air Force*

would be tasked with the mission. Most of the men thought it would be a no-go. "The weather was lousy and there was not too much daylight left for an evacuation attempt into the heavily defended valley," Colonel Roy C. Gray, Jr., the First Marine Aircraft Wing operations officer remembered.

The flight crews came to attention as Lieutenant Colonel House strode into the tent. All eyes were on him as he quickly gave them a rundown on the latest information on the camp. The defenders were physically exhausted—most were wounded—almost out of ammunition and about to be overrun. He told them the decision had been made to launch a rescue effort. "Everything considered, it was decided to have HMM-163 make an attempt to get under the weather into the valley for one last attempt," Colonel Gray said. "As I recall we merely called the Phu Bai squadron [HMM-163] on the land line phone and asked them to give it a try. . . ." Lieutenant Colonel House remembered it differently. "I was told to 'go' by the Wing G-3 but [I] said I would only go if ordered by the wing commander. Later I received another call—'It's an order.'" According to several of the assembled crews, Squadron Commander House finished the brief and then casually remarked, "I'm going to the Ashau to take a look, and if anyone wants to follow me, that's OK by me." First Lieutenant Norm Urban exclaimed, "Fifteen minutes later, there were no operable H-34s [helicopters] left on the ramp at Phu Bai!"

HMM-163 Vietnam-era squadron insignia.

ASHAU SPECIAL FORCES CAMP

The Special Forces Camp was located in the Ashau Valley, approximately two miles from the Laotian border in the southwest corner of South Vietnam's Thua Thien Province. It was one of the wildest, most inaccessible valleys in the country. Steep, jungle-covered mountains, some seven thousand feet high, were shrouded by rain-swollen clouds of the monsoon season, creating extremely difficult flying conditions and severely limiting resupply and reinforcement. The camp was a typical Special Forces triangular-shaped fort with walls about two hundred yards long, surrounded by barbed wire entanglements and an old minefield that was overgrown by dense, eight- to twelve-foot-high elephant grass that covered the entire valley floor. First Lieutenant Spink recalled that it "had a few small hut-like structures and a short dirt or perforated steel plank airstrip." The camp's importance lay in the fact that it sat astride three major NVA infiltration routes. One route ran westward to

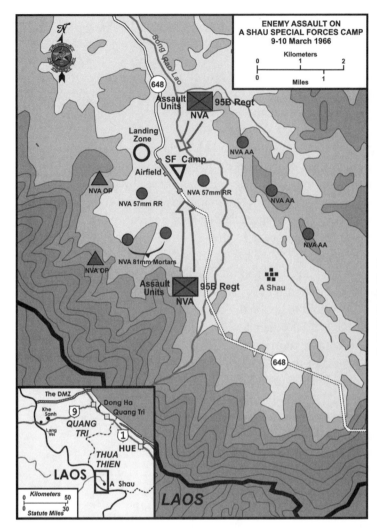

NVA assault on the U.S. Army Special Forces camp on 9–10 March 1966 in the Ashau Valley.

join the Ho Chi Minh Trail, the main terminus for troops and supplies entering the country from North Vietnam. The other two routes ran eastward through the mountains into the heavily populated areas around Hue and Phu Bai. The camp was defended by seventeen Army Special Forces (SF) advisors from Operational Detachment Alpha (A Team) 102 and 503 (SFODA-102 and -503) and just over four hundred South Vietnamese and Montagnard Civilian Irregular Defense Group (CIDG) paramilitary soldiers and Nung (ethnic Chinese descent) mercenaries.

In late February and early March 1966, intelligence reports indicated that the NVA 95B Regiment, 325th Division, was moving into the area. A CIDG patrol captured an enemy soldier's diary in which it was recorded that he "had crawled through the first row of barbed wire surrounding the camp" on a reconnaissance mission. On 5 March, two NVA defectors claimed that a four-battalion attack was planned for 11 or 12 March. Reconnaissance aircraft detected numerous weapons positions, freshly dug personnel bunkers and even more ominously, antiaircraft emplacements in the mountains ringing the camp. "The enemy had set up an aircraft trap by humping 37mm anti-aircraft weapons to the top of the surrounding hills and mountains," according to First Lieutenant Urban. Just before 0400 on 9 March, "the 325th gave us one heck of a mortar bombardment, inflicting heavy casualties, while their sappers blew gaps in our defensive wire off our south wall and half of our east wall parallel to the airstrip, and their machine guns teams completed the investment against the north wall," Capt. John D. Blair IV, the Special Forces commander, recalled. Casualties from the initial mortar attack were heavy: two American advisors and eight CIDG soldiers were killed and forty-seven wounded. In addition, the team house, supply room, and the water storage tank were heavily damaged. "A red star went up and that signaled the start of the [infantry] attack," according to Capt. Tennis "Sam" Carter, ODA 102. "They charged the wall one company at a time. Our guys were blowing the wire with claymores and stuff."

Captain Blair requested air support but poor weather prevented any assistance until midmorning when an Air Force AC-47 gunship, call sign Spooky 70, from the 4th Air Commando Squadron arrived. The aircraft made two passes in an attempt to get below the 400-foot ceiling. On its third attempt at tree top level, it succeeded and made a firing pass on the enemy troops. Circling back, it started a second pass when the right engine was hit by heavy-caliber automatic weapons fire and torn from its mount. The other engine was knocked out seconds later and the aircraft crash-landed on a mountain slope, sliding to rest at the base. The crew members survived and prepared to defend themselves. In the ensuing fire fight, three of the six-man crew were killed and three rescued. Two of Spooky 70's crewmen, Capt. Willard M. Collins and 1st Lt. Delbert R. Peterson, were posthumously awarded the Air Force Cross for extraordinary heroism in defending the crash site, which gave time for three of the crew to be rescued.

Two Cessna L-19 Bird Dog light observation aircraft attempted to evacuate the most seriously wounded from the compound but intense enemy fire forced them to take off with only one casualty, the badly wounded team sergeant who "was literally dragged to the airstrip by two SF soldiers and thrown head first into the aircraft," according to Sgt. John Bradford. At 1700, the clearing weather allowed two UH-34Ds from HMM-363 to skim under the overcast and attempt another evacuation. One, piloted by 1st Lt. Richard A. Vasdias, was hit in an oil line and crashed inside the compound. The crew was picked up by the other helicopter and safely evacuated. Just prior to darkness, an Air Force CH-3 helicopter managed to get in. "[It] landed in the camp with a roar of turbines and in a cloud of dust and debris. I remember a solitary airman firing an M-16 from the door as it touched down," Sergeant Bradford recalled. "Despite taking fire, the SF NCOs lifted the wounded, including me, over a mob of panicked Vietnamese irregulars trying to board the aircraft. The pilot held steady and lifted off only after we were safely on board." The CH-3 was able to evacuate twenty-six casualties. The camp's defenders were barely holding on. "Our casualties were heavy and mounting," Capt. Blair recalled. As darkness fell, they worked hard to repair defensive positions, anticipating another NVA assault. A U.S. Air Force C-123 flare ship provided continuous illumination throughout the long night.

At 0400 10 March the NVA attack began. "Under heavy supporting mortar fire, the [enemy] launched a massive ground assault against our south and southeast walls," Blair said. Sergeant First Class Victor Underwood remembered the NVA attacked the south wall in wave after wave. When one

Cessna 0-1 Bird Dog observation aircraft checking out the terrain for advancing troops. Note the three tanks in the foreground.

was shot down, another would come." At the same time, "Our CIDG Company holding the apex area of our south and east walls crumbled ... and rallied to the NVA ...," Blair explained. Underwood recalled, "The Nung recon platoon killed most all of them." However, the NVA took advantage of the treachery and secured a foothold in the perimeter. "The enemy achieved a significant penetration through our weakened south wall," Blair said. "The battle subsequently became a slugging match within the camp." Captain Carter recalled, "We called in tac-air [tactical-air] and the fighter pilots bombed and strafed the [NVA] trenches." A two-plane flight of Marine A-4 Skyhawks responded. As his wingman orbited the camp in the predawn darkness, 1st Lt. Augusto M. "Gus" Xavier maneuvered his aircraft around the mountains in the dense cloud cover and made a low-level bombing pass. In the face of heavy ground fire, he made a second pass, a strafing run with his 20mm cannon. He failed to pull out and crashed into the side of a mountain. First Lieutenant Xavier was awarded a posthumous Silver Star.

First Lieutenant Augusto M. Xavier, United States Marine Corps, Silver Star citation:

The President of the United States takes pleasure in presenting the Silver Star Medal to Augusto M. Xavier, First Lieutenant, U.S. Marine Corps, for conspicuous gallantry and intrepidity in action while serving with Marine Attack Squadron 311 (VMA-311), Marine Aircraft Group 311 (MAG-311), 1st Marine Aircraft Wing, in connection with combat operations against the enemy in the Republic of Vietnam on March 10, 1966. By his courage, aggressive fighting spirit and steadfast devotion to duty in the face of extreme personal danger, First Lieutenant Xavier upheld the highest traditions of the Marine Corps and the United States Naval Service.

ABOVE AND BEYOND THE CALL OF DUTY

At 1115, U.S. Air Force Maj. Bernard F. Fisher led a flight of Douglas A-1E Skyraiders on a strafing mission against the areas of the compound held by the NVA. "His wingman, Capt. Hubert King, took several hits, including one in the canopy, and had to return to base due to limited visibility from the cockpit," according to the HQ PACAF Tactical Evaluation Center. "Another A-1E flight, led by Major Dafford W. "Jump" Myers ... arrived on the scene and joined in the strafing passes." On Myers third pass, his aircraft was hit in the engine by ground fire and started burning. "I've been hit and hit hard," he radioed. Unable to see because his windscreen was covered with oil, Myers elected to crash land on the debris covered runway. Fisher followed alongside Myers, giving directions. He elected to make a "wheels up" landing and as soon as the aircraft touched down it burst into flames. "He had tried to release his belly tank, but couldn't, so it blew as soon as he touched," Fisher recalled. Myers was able to get out of the furiously burning aircraft seconds before it exploded and took cover in a weed-covered ditch.

Sergeant First Class Underwood led an ill-fated rescue attempt. "I led four Nungs to try and get him inside the camp but when we got through the main gate, we were pinned down. All four Nungs were killed and I was in a shallow hole and couldn't move." After learning that a rescue helicopter would take fifteen to twenty minutes to arrive, Fisher elected to try and pick up the downed airman, while two other A-1E's covered his landing. "I'm going in," he radioed. One pilot said later, "It was like flying inside Yankee Stadium with the people in the bleachers firing at you with machine guns." Underwood saw him coming in. "[An] A-1E came in with his wheels down. I thought, 'Oh shit!' Not another one." Fisher aborted his first attempt, swung around to the south, touched down, dodging empty oil drums, parts of Myers

USAF Majors Bernard F. Fisher and D.W. "Jump" Myers. The photo was taken after Fisher's rescue of Myers from the Ashau Valley. Fisher was awarded the Medal of Honor for the action.—*U.S. Air Force*

plane, and came to a stop just off the edge of the runway. Major Fisher turned around and taxied full speed down the runway searching desperately for Myers. "I watched enemy tracers coming at me and heard the plunk of bullets in the fuselage [a total of 19 bullet holes were discovered]," Fisher recalled in a March 1966 interview. "I saw Myers waving at me from the ditch and brought the plane to a halt. I thought he was wounded, so I started to unharness to go after him."

Myers was not only unwounded, but probably set a

record for the fifty-yard dash under enemy fire. "I pulled him into the plane head first," Fisher said. "It was hard on his head, but he didn't complain." As Myers tumbled into the cockpit he yelled, "You dumb S.O.B. now neither of us will get out of here!" Fisher ignored the comment and, "turned the plane around, and took off, flying at tree top level up the valley until I got enough air speed to go up through the overcast." Underwood watched the entire episode. "While the [NVA] were concentrating on the airplane, I got up and ran back into camp. This act not only earned Major Fisher the Medal of Honor . . . but it also saved my ass."

Major Bernard F. Fisher, United States Air Force, Medal of Honor citation:

For conspicuous gallantry and intrepidity at the risk of his life above and beyond the call of duty. . . . On that date [10 March], the Special Forces camp at Ashau was under attack by 2,000 North Vietnamese Army regulars. Hostile troops had positioned themselves between the airstrip and the camp. Other hostile troops had surrounded the camp and were continuously raking it with automatic-weapons fire from the surrounding hills. The tops of the 1,500-foot hills were obscured by an 800 foot ceiling, limiting aircraft maneuverability and forcing pilots to operate within range of hostile gun positions, which often were able to fire down on attacking aircraft. During the battle, Maj. Fisher observed a fellow airman crash land on the battle torn airstrip. In the belief that the downed pilot was seriously injured and in imminent danger of capture, Maj. Fisher announced his intention to land on the airstrip to affect a rescue. Although aware of the extreme danger and likely failure of such an attempt, he elected to continue. Directing his own air cover, he landed his aircraft and taxied almost the full length of the runway, which was littered with battle debris and parts of an exploded aircraft. While affecting a successful rescue of the downed pilot, heavy ground fire was observed, with 19 bullets striking his aircraft. In the face of withering ground fire, he applied power and gained enough speed to lift-off at the overrun airstrip. Maj. Fisher's profound concern for his fellow airman, at the risk of his life above and beyond the call of duty, are in the highest traditions of the U.S. Air Force and reflect great credit upon himself and the Armed Forces of his country.

MACV BRIEFING

CBS correspondent John Laurence wrote in *The Cat from Hue, A Vietnam War Story*, "Something was happening and everyone knew. The word went around Saigon early Thursday . . . a major battle was underway. A Special Forces "A" camp was in trouble in I Corps." By late afternoon, the Joint United States Public Affairs Office (JUSPAO) was crowded with reporters. All the seats in the briefing room were filled. "A MACV sergeant hurried into the room carrying a stack of mimeographed sheets . . . the one-page summary outlined the day's action at [the] remote camp." The summary contained radio situation reports from the camp starting early on the morning of the 10th.

- 0136 — Friendly forces report they can hear VC digging in a hundred meters from the perimeter and that they expect a heavy assault. They are under a heavy mortar attack at this time.
- 0335 — Ashau report it is under full scale attack but that the perimeter is holding.
- 0400 — The camp reports it is badly cut up.
- 0425 — Radio operator at Ashau reports he believes he is the only one left alive. Reports that the camp wall is destroyed.
- 0435 — Flare ship overhead reports it appears camp has been overrun however some people may be alive in the communication bunker.
- 0505 — Communication still exists with a man on the ground at Ashau. The man says that everything he sees is destroyed or burning. Immediate air strikes on the camp are requested.
- 0530 — Radio operator at Ashau says he hears a friendly mortar fire from somewhere.
- 0615 — Radio operator at Ashau is still adjusting rocket fire from aircraft overhead.
- 0730 — Bombing of the camp area continues through cloud cover although the camp can't be seen. Ceiling is two hundred feet scattered clouds. Two hundred to seven thousand feet solid cloud layers.
- 0807 — FAC over the area reports he still has radio contact with Ashau.
- 0840 — FAC says north section of camp is still intact.
- 0930 — Communication continues with Ashau.

Laurence noted that the briefing officer tried to downplay the incident but the reporters were in no mood to be "gaffed" off. They badgered him for more information until a senior officer took over and reminded the assembly, " . . . lives are at stake here and . . . you are bound not to reveal specific details of friendly casualties or operations in progress," according to Laurence. "On background," the officer continued, "I can tell you that an intensive search and rescue mission is under way at this time and it could be compromised by press reports. . . . "

DECISION TIME

Late in the afternoon of the 10th, Lt. Gen. Lewis W. "Lew" Walt, III Marine Amphibious Force (MAF) commander, chaired an emergency meeting at his headquarters on the Ashau situation. "There were six generals involved in the conference, including Westmoreland's deputy, Lt. Gen. John A. Heintges," Marine Brig. Gen. Marion Carl reported. First Marine Aircraft Wing ops officer, Col. Roy C. Gray, recalled, "The Special Forces reps were in contact with their advisors at Ashau, who reported the situation was deteriorating rapidly. The weather was lousy and there was not much daylight left for an evacuation attempt. It looked like the Special Forces advisors might have to leave the communication bunker at any time because of the heavy mortar and recoilless rifle fire." Brigadier General Carl, who had earlier that day had flown over the valley said, "I'd gone in there myself in a Huey and caught hell from Lew [Lieutenant General Walt] for being up there all by my lonesome." Carl urged approval. "Yes, you can get in there, and you should go in there. I estimate you're going to lose one out of every four choppers that you put in there . . . but nevertheless, I don't think we can abandon those people. We'd never live it down." Colonel Gray said, "Everything considered, it was decided to have HMM-163 make an attempt to get under the weather into the valley for one last attempt."

U.S. Army Special Forces Captain Blair received word to evacuate the camp: "Almost all friendly crew-served weapons were destroyed. Very little ammunition remained. No food or water had been available for 36 hours," he reported. Sergeant First Class Underwood recalled, "At 1700 headquarters gave us the word to abandon the camp." Underwood and another Special Forces soldier were told to set up a helicopter landing zone three to four hundred meters north of the camp so the wounded could be evacuated. "When the [South] Vietnamese [soldiers] saw us and the Nungs head for the landing zone, they lost complete control and swarmed out of the camp in a mob, led by the Vietnamese camp commander. . . . I tried to shoot him [the camp commander] but someone always kept getting in the way." Blair had intended to use all able-bodied Special Forces and irregulars to fight a rearguard action while the wounded were placed first on the aircraft. The rout left him with only a few Americans and Nungs to hold off the NVA.

RESCUE MISSION

Shortly after 1730, Lieutenant Colonel House led sixteen UH-34s from his squadron, supported by six UH-1Es from VMO-2 and fighter bombers from the 1st Marine Air Wing (1st MAW) into the valley. The squadron was organized into two flights of eight. House led one and Capt. Wyman Blakeman, the operations officer, led the other. "The weather deteriorated rapidly and I detached my second flight of four and left them east of the valley," Blakeman explained. "I put my first four into trail position and sneaked through a crotch in the mountains just below the clouds . . . the weather in the valley to the south was zero-zero so we returned to base. House continued to lead his flight toward the camp. "It was a suicide mission," House later exclaimed. First Lieutenant Urban recalled, "Ashau was socked in with an overcast sitting on top of the mountains . . . we approached the valley north of the camp by following a mountain stream, crossing the tops [of the mountains] with our rotors in the soup, then down into the valley under the overcast, which was about 200 feet above the terrain. We then turned left towards the camp about 15 miles south." House recalled, "There were tracer bullets going through our flight up, down and sideways—just a blizzard of incoming fire. I don't know how we got through all that alive." Army Captain Carter echoed his thoughts. "The ground-to-air was unbelievable," he said. "If I'd been flying those choppers, I wouldn't have gone in." First Lieutenant Spink exclaimed, "The incoming automatic weapons fire was so thick it looked as if you could get out and walk on the path of the tracers."

First Lieutenant Urban followed House's lead. "As we approached the camp, the good guys were coming out through the north barricade gate, while the bad guys came in and over the southwest wall." The helicopters swept in, flared, and settled in the fifteen-foot high elephant grass. "Some H-34s, mine included, were immediately overloaded," Urban explained. House later stated in a television interview, "So many people wanted to get out, they hung on the cables, almost pulled the helicopters into the zone . . . there were fifty of 'em hanging on one of the birds, holding onto the sides, grabbing on the wheels. We tried to drag 'em off, beat 'em off, kick 'em off—but they just came back. It was mass panic. Finally, we had to shoot 'em off. Boom! Boom! Boom!. To make 'em obey . . . We hated to do that but no one would have gotten out if we didn't." Captain Blakeman supported the decision. "To this day I think this was the right decision. The choice was to lose 30 or shoot 3 off the landing gear and save 27." First Lieutenant Urban's helicopter was mobbed. "My bird had way too much weight to lift off . . . we had perhaps 25 soldiers in the cabin and 3 or 4 hanging on the struts. I started yelling to the crew to get them off, shoot if necessary . . . we weren't going anywhere the way we were. Finally, we managed to lift off, trailing barbed wire from the tail wheel, and rose into the soup above."

Sergeant First Class Underwood hobbled—he had been wounded in the legs—to House's aircraft. "There were 20 to 30 Vietnamese trying to get in his helicopter," he recalled. "His crew chief and gunner were trying to beat them off. . . . I was on the ground trying to calm them down but they wouldn't listen and shoved me out of the way. Some of them were shot; the others backed away. The helicopter lifted off about 10 feet and the NVA shot the tail rotor off and it crashed." The crew bailed out of the stricken aircraft as it had quickly become a bullet magnet. Lieutenant Colonel House realized immediately that rescue was out of the picture and started planning to escape and evade (E&E). At one point he asked Underwood, "Have you got a compass, I've got a map." Major Blakeman pointed out, "House took charge of all the friendlies, including 7 Green Berets and 190 Vietnamese and led them north-northwest [because] it was the only logical way out." Colonel Gray noted, "They had a hairy night scrambling away and infiltrating to the north around the hills. Chuck [Lieutenant Colonel House] assumed control under very difficult conditions."

Lieutenant Colonel Charles A. House,
United States Marine Corps, Navy Cross citation:

For extraordinary heroism as Commanding Officer, Marine Medium Helicopter Squadron One Hundred Sixty-Three, in action in the Republic of Vietnam on 9 and 10 March 1966. Colonel House's helicopter was disabled by intense enemy fire in the landing zone at Ashau, where the garrison had been under siege for several days. After ensuring that all personnel had abandoned the aircraft, Colonel House immediately rallied his crew members and joined a group of seventy survivors of the garrison. With inspiring leadership and dogged determination, he skillfully led the group into the jungle to escape capture. Chopping a trail thorough the dense underbrush, he moved into the hills which surrounded the outpost, cleverly maneuvering between hostile positions and successfully evading enemy search patrols. Although the group was subjected to harassing fire throughout the march, Colonel House managed to overcome the language barrier and instill in the Vietnamese a sense of confidence and encouragement which sustained them through the ordeal. With constant concern for the welfare of the survivors, many of whom were wounded, he halted the march several times to allow them to rest, stalwartly standing watch while others slept. When the helicopters were sighted and signaled on the following afternoon, Colonel House's brilliant leadership motivated all who were able to help clear a position from which the rescue was subsequently effected. His valiant effort and determination throughout contributed in large measure to saving the members of his crew and many Special Forces and Vietnamese defenders from capture or death at the hands of the Viet Cong [NVA]. By his intrepid fighting spirit, extraordinary ability as a leader, and unswerving dedication to duty, Colonel House upheld the highest traditions of the Marine Corps and the United States Naval Service.

Enemy fire also shot down House's wingman, 1st Lt. William J. Gregory, who along with his copilot and crew chief made their way to another aircraft. Private First Class George Twardzik said that the gunner, Sergeant Puckett [first name unknown], "grabbed his M-60 machine gun, leaped out of the helo and dived into a bunker while under enemy fire. He then set up his M-60 and joined the other "grunts," who had a mortar and another machine gun blazing away. Puckett was later rescued, the only one to get out of the bunker alive." In addition to the two downed aircraft, three Marine F-4B Phantom fighter-bombers, two A-4 Skyhawks, two UH-1E Iroquois helicopters and three other UH-34s sustained damage. With the approaching darkness and deteriorating weather conditions, the rescue mission was halted. At the end of the day, four Special Forces advisors and sixty-five Vietnamese and Nungs had been rescued.

On the following morning, as soon as the weather permitted, Major Blakeman led a search and rescue mission: seven aircraft from HMM-163 and two from VMO-2. Private First Class Twardzik was in one of the rescue birds as they swept in toward the camp. "Americans were dispersed all over the zone, singly and in groups," he remembered. "We sighted three or four running near the old runway, so we spiraled on in to pick them up. We could hear a .50 cal. machine gun popping away at us on our approach. It missed us as we scooped up the soldiers and spiraled up and away. The .50 was shooting at us all the while but once again, we were very lucky and flew out of trouble. We had a lump in our throats when we spotted some of our aircrews in the zone. We went on in and hoisted them aboard into the cabin. An M-60 machine gun came up on the hoist first. I grabbed it and set it up out the aft escape hatch where a rescued gunner put it into action."

Lieutenant Colonel Charles A. House, commander of HMM-163, poses with U.S. Army Special Forces soldiers and South Vietnamese irregulars shortly after their evacuation from the Ashau Valley.

Major Blakeman recalled, "At approximately 1330 I found Chuck [House] and his entourage about 3 Klicks [kilometers] north-northwest of Camp Ashau." Lieutenant Colonel House ignited a red smoke grenade to mark the small landing zone. "Red smoke normally marked an enemy position, but Chuck popped one knowing that I would understand his reasoning . . . he knew no enemy would have the guts to pop a red smoke on himself." The situation on the ground remained desperate. The CIDG panicked and fought among themselves. One of the South Vietnamese threw a grenade, killing ten of his fellow soldiers. In another instance, Colonel Gray said, "one of the U.S. Army advisors ordered a CIDG soldier to get out of the area which they were clearing for the rescue and when he refused the advisor shot him on the spot. It was a desperate situation complicated by diluted command authority." Finally control was established and the rescue completed. Thirty-four more survivors, including House, his crew and five Special Forces advisors were evacuated. All the helicopters sustained damage: one H-34 struggled back with 126 bullet holes.

Private First Class Twardzik had a near death experience. "I had on an Army flak jacket since we were short of the USMC regulation ones, and secured to the cabin by a 'gunner's belt' hooked to a 'D' ring on the deck. Our luck ran out when the enemy .50 caliber found our helo and I was hit squarely in the chest. I lost it! I was told later by the crew chief that the force of the blow drove me completely out of the cabin doorway and into space. When the safety belt reached the end of its travel, it snapped me right back into the cabin!" Another bullet tore through the radio compartment and struck a five-gallon can of engine oil and set it on fire, which filled the aircraft with acrid smoke. "The pilot secured the engine and auto-rotated to a safe landing," Twardzik explained. "We pitched the can out and put out the remains of the fire." The pilot restarted the engine, "engaged the rotors and took off, dragging the main landing gear through the tree tops," he said. "I must have smoked a whole pack of cigarettes on the twenty minute flight. After we landed and secured, I got out of the '34 to view the battle damage. The aircraft was sieved with bullet holes. My flak jacket had a burn mark in the center where the bullet hit . . . thank God for small miracles!"

HMM-163 needed to have twenty-one of its twenty-four helicopters replaced as a result of the evacuation operation. Twardzik said the squadron area, "looked like an aircraft parking lot by the time we finished the mission . . . but the squadron brought out 161 of the 186 survivors, including 10 of the 12 Special Forces advisors." Captain Blair indicated there were seven Distinguished Service Crosses awarded to his men for heroic action during the three-day battle, including himself and Sergeant First Class Underwood. It was estimated that three hundred North Vietnamese were killed by the defenders and another five hundred killed by air strikes. "The special forces presented HMM-163 with a special award for their extraordinary efforts to rescue the beleaguered troopers from their precarious zone at Ashau," Twardzik said. "I personally received an award of a special patch which was sewn onto my flight jacket and remains there to this day."

AFTERMATH, CONTROVERSY AND PUNISHMENT

Correspondent Laurence conducted an interview with Lieutenant Colonel

House immediately after the squadron commander's rescue that appeared on national television. In the interview House described the mass panic during the evacuation and how the helicopter door gunners first fired their machine guns into the ground in an attempt to force the CIDG to back off. When that didn't work, House said he ordered his men to fire at the Vietnamese who wouldn't obey. Laurence was taken by surprise. "Colonel House was giving us the big story. For Americans to shoot their South Vietnamese allies deliberately, for whatever reason, was extraordinary news. But I doubted he would say it on film. Officers' careers had been ruined by public admissions far less controversial than this." He asked House if he would repeat what he had said on camera. "Yeah," House replied after a long pause. "I've been passed over for promotion twice, so I'm on my way out anyway." Colonel Thomas J. O'Connor, House's immediate commanding officer stated, " . . . he [House] made some rather emotionally charged statements to authority about the wisdom and futility of the mission. . . . " Colonel Gray was of the same opinion. "Unfortunately, upon his return from Ashau, he [House] made some rather emotionally charge statements to authority about the wisdom and futility of the mission—thus the anomalous results of both a citation [Navy Cross] and disciplinary action."

The release of the interview caused quite a sensation. Correspondent Laurence was criticized and Lieutenant Colonel House was investigated. Brigadier General Carl was assigned to head the investigative board. "I received a Navy Cross, a Letter of Reprimand and [was] relieved," House said bitingly. The incident was not over. "Carl was the senior member of my promotion board that passed me over," he wrote. "I am not bitter but I feel bad that the gallant men under my command did not receive the recognition they deserved."

CHAPTER SIX

HELICOPTER VALLEY

OPERATION HASTINGS

At 0540 hours 9 July 1966, four UH-1Es (two gunships and two slicks, unarmed helicopters) from VMO-2 inserted a five-man Marine detachment from Detachment "A," Reconnaissance Group Bravo on a rolling hill covered with high elephant grass. The team quickly established an ambush position on a well-used trail that ran alongside the hill. A short time later, four NVA soldiers wearing camouflage uniforms and rain hats walked into the kill zone. The recon team opened fire, killing all four. Before the Marines could thoroughly search the remains, they were taken under fire and nearly surrounded by another large group of the enemy. The detachment requested an emergency extract. The VMO-2 July after-action report stated, "The situation was becoming desperate. . . . 1st Lt. William Kirby decided to go into the zone, while the gunship provided suppressive fire. He had to hover with the nose of his aircraft against a hill. His rotor blade was cutting elephant grass above him, his tail rotor was cutting bushes and grass behind him, and his skids had to remain off the ground due to the poor location of the landing zone. The Huey began taking fire but Lt Kirby kept it in the zone until all five members of the team could climb onto the skids and into the aircraft. As he lifted out of the zone, the intensity of the enemy fire against the aircraft increased and the five men of the recon team were leaning out of the sides of the A/C firing back at the enemy."

The next day First Lieutenant Kirby inserted another team at the bottom of a steep narrow canyon while it was still dark . . . without landing lights. VMO-2's Command Chronology stated, "After an hour and half on station, the reconnaissance team called for an immediate emergency extraction. They reported having one company of enemy on each side of them, with about 25 more in front of them . . . and closing in on the LZ. Lt Kirby landed his plane and embarked the recon team while the enemy were visibly firing and moving

Marines from 3rd Platoon, Company A, 3rd Reconnaissance Battalion, pose at Dong Ha after a patrol extraction in July 1966. During this period fourteen of eighteen patrols in the DMZ had to be withdrawn because of enemy contact.

into the zone. The gunship above brought suppressive fire on the enemy while Lt Kirby lifted his plane out over the heads of the NVA and/or VC troops and received heavy automatic and small arms fire but was able to complete the extraction successfully." For the next several days, the reconnaissance teams operating south of the Demilitarized Zone (DMZ) made contact with numerous groups of uniformed enemy soldiers. Major Dwain A. Colby, Recon Group Bravo's commander said, " . . . no patrol was able to stay in the field for more than a few hours, many for only a few minutes." In a ten-day period, fourteen of eighteen patrols had to be withdrawn early because of enemy contact. The reconnaissance teams sighted more than three hundred NVA troops, verifying intelligence reports that elements of the NVA 324B Division had moved into the area.

BELL UH-1 IROQUOIS

The Bell UH-1 Iroquois was developed to meet the U.S. Army's requirement for a medical evacuation and utility helicopter. It first flew on 20 October 1956 but was not ordered into production until March 1960. Originally designated the HU-1, which led to its nickname, Huey, it was the first turbine-powered helicopter to enter the military's rotary-wing inventory. In 1962, the Marine Corps choose a modified Huey for its assault support helicopter and designated it the UH-1E. The major changes included the use of all-aluminum construction to be corrosive resistant for shipboard use, radios compatible with ground frequencies, a rotor brake for shipboard use to stop the rotor quickly on shutdown, and a roof-mounted rescue hoist.

The Huey was an enduring symbol of U.S. involvement in Vietnam, and as a result became one of the world's most recognized helicopters. The UH-1E was used initially for command and control, medevac, visual reconnaissance and observation, and most other light utility roles. Initially, however, it was not armed, but even before the first aircraft was delivered, suggestions were made to equip it as an armed helicopter. At first Marine Corps Headquarters resisted its use in a gunship role. Eventually, however, the Corps approved the development of armed gunship configurations because "Tactical doctrine requires these helicopters to perform observation, reconnaissance, and rescue missions forward of friendly lines without armed escort. There is no present system of self defense against ground fire for these helicopters." In May 1965, the first armed UH-1E joined VMO-2 for duty.

A captured NVA soldier was identified as being from a two-hundred-man advance party of the PAVN 5th Battalion, 812th Regiment, 324B Division, and stated that the other regiments of the division, the 90th and 803rd, had also entered South Vietnam. A few days later a lieutenant from the 812th Regiment surrendered. He stated that the mission of the division was to liberate Quang Tri Province and destroy U.S. and ARVN forces in the area. General Westmoreland, Commander, U.S. Military Assistance Command Vietnam (COMUSMACV), thought that the NVA might attempt to seize the northern provinces to set up a Viet Cong government.

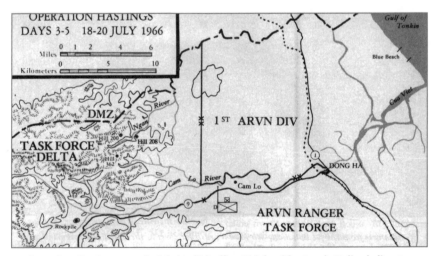

Operations Hastings was scheduled to kick off on 15 July with a two-battalion helicopter assault into the Song Ngan River Valley, about one to three miles south of the DMZ.

The commanding general of the 3rd Marine Division, Maj. Gen. Wood B. Kyle, requested to "move troops north to get them [the North Vietnamese] out of there and drive them back." He was given approval on 13 July. The operation, codenamed Hastings (Vietnamese designation Lam Son 289), was to be commanded by Brig. Gen. Lowell English, the division's assistant commander, and consisted of seven Marine infantry battalions (1st Battalion and 2nd battalions, 1st Marines; 1st Battalion, 3rd Marines; 2nd and 3rd battalions, 4th Marines; 3rd Battalion, 5th Marines; and 2nd Battalion, 9th Marines) and one artillery battalion (3rd Battalion, 12th Marines) as well as elements of the 1st ARVN Division and four ARVN airborne battalions, which would operate south of the Marines. Brigadier General Kyle's force was designated Task Force Delta. The 1st Marine Air Wing (MAG-11 and MAG 12) was tasked to support Task Force Delta with both fixed-wing and helicopters from bases at Da Nang and Phu Bai. The mission of Task Force Delta was to conduct multi-battalion search and destroy operations in Quang Tri Province in conjunction with the ARVN forces. Its specific mission was to search out enemy build-up and strong points, to stop infiltration to the south, and to destroy the enemy, his supplies, and his will to resist.

Operations Hastings was scheduled to kick off on 15 July with a two-battalion helicopter assault into the Song Ngan River Valley, six miles north-west of Cam Lo and about one to three miles south of the DMZ. The terrain was composed of a series of ridges and steep hills rising to an elevation of 550 meters. Heavy foliage and rough terrain made all ground movement difficult and reduced the number of possible helicopter landing zones. *U.S. Marines in Vietnam, An Expanding War 1966* noted, "Lt. Col. Summer A. Vale's 3rd Battalion, 4th Marines was to land in LZ *Crow* in the southwestern sector of the valley and establish blocking positions below the bend of the river to prevent enemy movement. Three miles further to the northeast, the 2nd Battalion, 4th Marine, commanded by Lt. Col. Arnold E. Bench, was to land in LZ *Dove* near the mouth of the valley and attack southwest along the high ground toward Hill 208 and the 3rd Battalion's blocking position." The operation kicked off early in the morning with a briefing for the helicopter pilots. "At Dong Ha, the entire flight was briefed . . . on the approach and retirement routes, pick-up coordinates and condition of the landing zones," according to Capt. Richard C. Harper.

While the brief was going on, A-4 Skyhawks from MAG-12 and F-4B Phantoms from MAG-11 bombed and napalmed the two landing zones. As the aircraft cleared the area, the artillery of 3rd Battalion, 12th Marines, took over, pounding the two zones for twenty minutes with almost eight hundred rounds of 105mm and 155mm artillery ammunition. At 0745, the Tactical Air Controller Airborne (TAC-A), call sign Deadlock, piloted by Lieutenant Colonel Barden, radioed that the zone was clear for the 0800 L-Hour. Five minutes after receiving the information, helicopters from HMM-164 and HMM-265 lifted off from the runway, climbed on course to 2,000 feet, and preceded directly to the landing zones. Each successive division lifted off with a two minute interval. The HMM-164 July Command Chronology noted, "LtCol W.C. Watson with 27 CH-46-As, 4 CH-37s* and 10 UH-1Es transported approximately 550 troops into Landing Zone Crow and the same into Landing Zone Dove." The transports were escorted by 4 Huey gunships from VMO-2.

BOEING VERTOL CH-46 SEA KNIGHT

The Boeing Vertol CH-46 Sea Knight is a medium-lift tandem rotor transport helicopter used to provide all-weather, day-or-night assault transport of combat troops, supplies and equipment. Assault Support is its primary function, and the movement of supplies and equipment is secondary. Additional tasks include combat support, search and rescue, support for forward refueling and rearming points (FARP), casualty evacuation and Tactical Recovery of Aircraft and Personnel (TRAP). Known colloquially as the Phrog, the CH-46 has two 50-foot, contrarotating rotors mounted on pylons, directly over the cockpit and the extreme rear of the aircraft. The rotors overlap each other at the center of the aircraft for a distance of 16 feet. To prevent the blades from striking each other in this overlap area, the two rotors were interconnected by a carefully geared drive shaft. With the blades folded for movement on the deck of a large helicopter carrier (LPH), the aircraft measures slightly less than 45 feet long and 15 feet wide. The cargo compartment has no obstructions throughout its 24-foot length to hinder the entry of vehicles and troops. The six foot square clean cabin was made possible by the use of small stub wings or sponsons attached to the outside of the fuselage. They double as fuel tanks and mounting points for the main landing gear. The sponsons also add stability if the aircraft is landed in the water. Empty, the CH 46 weighs 11,641 pounds and with 2,400 pounds of fuel and a crew of three is designed to carry either 4,000 pounds of cargo or seventeen combat-equipped Marines. Under emergency overload condition, the cargo capacity can be increased to almost 7,000 pounds. Its top speed is 137 knots.

---

* Former Marine pilot Michael Fiorillo stated in an email to the author that only two CH-37s were available.

The twenty-four CH-46s assigned to LZ Crow were divided into six divisions of four aircraft each because the landing zone appeared large enough to allow four aircraft to land together. Each aircraft carried a fourteen-man heliteam in addition to a crew of four (two pilots, a gunner and a crew chief). Lieutenant Colonel Vale said, "We picked the landing site from a helicopter flying at several thousand feet to avoid ground fire and also not to give away that we were scouting out possible sites." Even so the squadron's command chronology noted, "Small arms fire was received in both zones during the troop buildup phase with one aircraft taking two hits, one in the cabin section (which caused a fatal injury to a Marine) and one in the aft pylon which caused sufficient damage to require the aircraft to return to Dong Ha."

Private First Class John Harris was in one of the heliteams. "The first indication of trouble that I can remember was the little light holes appearing in the fuselage. I remember just seeing them appear, but really not associating any danger with this strange phenomenon. You see, the aircraft made so much noise that you could hardly hear yourself think. Any type of exterior noise was masked by the noise of the huge engines. When those light holes started to appear, the door gunner started firing his weapon and cursing at the top of his lungs. The chopper began to lurch heavily one way, then another. I don't think that it was because of the bullets hitting it. I think the pilot was doing everything that he could to lessen the profile of the chopper, and make it less of a target." As the helicopter neared the landing zone, 1st Lt. Edward P. Conti saw, "The terrain grew progressively steeper and greener. It became obvious that the terrain was drastically different than anything we had been in so far. The low, steep hills surrounding LZ Crow were covered with dense, dark green vegetation. The LZ itself, about half the size of a football field, was fairly flat and grassy, probably used for cultivation of some sort not many years past."

Private First Class Harris remembered that Lieutenant Conti "sat on the seat nearest the door, next to the crew chief/door gunner. After a flight of about ten minutes, we started to orbit downward toward the landing zone in a spiraling pattern. The engine noise drowned out any attempts at speech. The crew chief glanced over at me, silently tapped his flight helmet twice with his right hand, indicating radio traffic on his headset. He pointed down toward the ground, then grasped the firing handles of his M-60 machine gun with both hands. It didn't take much for me to figure out what he meant . . . Hot LZ! . . . The gunner turned and screamed at us to get out, 'OUT!' 'OUT!' 'OUT!' 'NOW!' Being closest to the ramp, I could plainly see that we had not landed. We weren't even close to the ground. But, the gunner grabbed my arm and shoved me, physically, out the hatchway. I was off balance as I hit the ground, and tucked and rolled to one side, trying to regain my footing."

Marines from 3rd Battalion, 4th Marines, escaping from a crashed helicopter in landing zone Crow. Note the helicopter's aft pylon is sheared off.

Lieutenant Conti recalled, "As our heliteam jumped from our chopper and headed for the edge of the clearing for cover and to allow the choppers to depart, I was faintly aware of popping noises overhead. It dawned on me moments later that the popping noise was enemy small arms fire, probably directed at the choppers more so than at us. Later, other people told me we were under heavy automatic weapons fire in the LZ. Fortunately, no one was hit." Lieutenant Conti explained, "A hot LZ [landing zone under enemy fire] is utter chaos. You land in a clearing of high elephant grass encircled by trees. The visibility is poor, and you don't have a clue as to which way to go. If you take too much time to figure out where the hostile fire is coming from, it's too late. The helicopter crew knew what was going on before we did. I don't think any of the choppers actually landed. Instead, troops departed the copters at varying heights. I can't blame the helicopter crew. Their job was to get us in and get out alive, and with all the automatic weapons fire coming in their direction, they didn't waste any time."

Landing Zone Crow was marked with yellow smoke, which was drifting northeast at about 5 knots. The flight leader commenced a 180 degree right descending turn from the southeast into the small (roughly three hundred feet on a side), pasture-like LZ located on the west bank of a stream. According to the official report "On the western edge there was an embankment approximately 15 feet high with one or two trees located at the edge. . . . In

An aerial view of landing zone Crow which was later called Helicopter Valley because of the downed helicopters. Three badly damaged birds can be seen in the photo.

the zone itself there was a single tree about 25 to 30 feet tall. The ground sloped downhill to the zone." The first two divisions landed without incident. However, a helicopter from HMM-265, call sign Roseann 1-14, in the third division overshot the landing point and hit a tree line, resulting in the loss of the aircraft and minor injuries to the passengers and crew. The squadron's command chronology noted, "Roseann 1-14 was lost in a small downhill zone with tall trees on the approach end and fences and trees all along the departure end of the zone." The fifth division approached the landing zone just as the fourth division touched down. Captain Harper (Roseann 1-19) received a radio call that a CH-46 had crashed. "I could see the helicopter [Roseann 1-14] smoking forward and to the right of the landing zone," he said. "I decided to continue my approach based on the information I received."

The fourth division completed its drop off without any difficulty and departed the area. However, two helicopters from HMM-164 in the fifth division slightly overshot the zone, landed in close proximity, and intermeshed their aft rotor blades. A Marine NCO and a Navy Corpsman were killed as they ran from the downed bird when fragments from the rotor blade hit them. Seven other Marines were injured, one seriously. Major T. S. Reap described the incident. "As the lead aircraft of four CH-46As, the fifth division of a strike flight, I commenced my approach at approximately 0810. I signaled the flight for a free cruise trail by wagging the aft section of my aircraft from left to right as in normal procedure. As I approached the zone, I was in hover aft and indicating approximately 30 knots. It appeared I was going to land long so rather than make an exaggerated maneuver to stop, I elected to land in a smaller field about 30 yards straight forward. It was fairly small so I came to a hover and proceeded to land. We were on the deck for approximately six seconds, the ramp was down and some of the troops had already debarked when an immediate gyration commenced. I had no idea what was happening so I shut down the engines and rotor blades and vacated the aircraft. Upon debarking I saw the aircraft had broken in two. Both engines had fallen through the aft ramp."

Captain W. J. Sellers piloted the second helicopter involved in the accident. "I sat the aircraft down near some bamboo standing about 20 feet tall," Capt. Sellers recalled. "The downwash from the rotors bent the bamboo over and kept it out of the rotor blades. Just prior to landing, I had to move the tail of the aircraft to the right towards Major Reap to keep from landing on some troops." His plane was only on the ground for a few seconds when, "the aircraft began to shake and vibrate violently." Private First Class Jerry

Corpsmen administering aid to an injured Marine after two helicopters collided.

Dust and debris fly when the two CH-46s collide. The aft pylons collided, flew apart and killed two men as they ran from the helicopters.

A. Ensign, aerial gunner aboard Sellers's aircraft recalled, " . . . there was a loud noise and the aircraft started violent gyrations. I looked back and saw the upper aft section of the aircraft break down on the ramp and heard Captain Sellers on the ICS [intercom] shout, 'Get out of here!'." Sellers evacuated along with the crew. "I went outside [and] saw that the aft rotor blades of both aircraft were gone and they were broken just forward of the aft pylon." Lance Corporal Gary L. Bailey, the crew chief, stated, "My gunner and I were thrown to the floor . . . I saw the aft pylon collapse . . . and started hollering to the troops to get out of the plane. When I went around the aft end, I noticed two bodies lying on the ground." Private First Class John Harris remembered seeing "a chopper in the distance hit the ground sideways and crash. It erupted into heavy flames as soon as it splintered against the deck, and pieces of it went flying into another chopper close by."

Captain Harper, flying the number three aircraft in the division recalled seeing "parts [begin] to fly in all directions and in the next instant both aircraft rotor systems contacted each other, creating a large amount of dust and breaking both fuselages in several places. At this point both my copilot and myself were not sure if they had hit each other or if they had landed on mines or received mortar fire." A fire started in the number 2 engine of Sellers aircraft. "I got the fire bottle after finally locating it outside by the ramp and sprayed the CO2 into the engine exhaust. I then gave the bottle to the crew chief and he sprayed the intake until the fire . . . was extinguished. Meanwhile Captain Harper landed, off-loaded his heliteam and directed his crew chief to assist the downed crews. "He made repeated trips to all three aircraft taking stretchers for the wounded and organizing the other crew members to get out all useable guns, ammo and equipment." Private First Class Ensign recalled, " . . . the two aircraft started receiving sniper fire in the zone and had to get down." Harper and his wingman evacuated the crews and the two dead men to Dong Ha.

Later in the afternoon, a security force was flown into the area to guard the three downed helicopters. The HMM-265 CH-46 flown by Capt. T. C. McAllister was approximately fifteen hundred feet high when it was hit in

Helicopter crewmen carry a casualty from the damaged aircraft.

the fuel cell by enemy12.7mm fire. As the cockpit and passenger compartment filled with smoke, the aircraft's fuel system continued to pump jet fuel into the flames. The aircraft lost an engine forcing Captain McAllister and First Lieutenant Richey to put it into auto-rotation in an attempt to land. The USMC Combat Helicopter Association's (Pop-A-Smoke) KIA database states, "Photos taken from the ground show smoke coming from the cockpit windows and flames from the rear of the aircraft. When they tried landing on [LZ] Crow, smoke filled the cockpit so no one could see. They overshot the LZ and crashed on the edge of the battalion CP and 81mm mortars." Thirteen Marines died and three were injured in this incident. Thereafter, the Marines referred to the Song Ngan River Valley as "Helicopter Valley." Lieutenant Colonel Vale said when McAllister's aircraft "came under ground fire from the ridge on the south side of the valley . . . the pilot tried to land in the landing zone but as he slowed down and hovered the smoke got into the flight compartment and he had to move forward to keep the smoke out. As a result he overshot the landing zone and after moving over the CP tried to set down again. By this time the helo was rolling and barely remaining airborne. The pilot had to move forward again and then crashed on the edge of the area in which our CP and 81mm mortars were set up."

Corporal Keith Miller observed the crash. "There were a bunch of us that watched as the helicopter was hit on its inbound run. We watched it go into a nose high attitude roll and crash. We felt helpless as we ran toward the flaming crash site to try and do something, but small arms, grenades, and other ammo was cooking off. Our leaders ordered us away from the site because of the danger." Crew Chief Bunnie McCosar saw it go down. "Expressions on the ICS were to the pilot going down was 'Get it down!' 'Get it down!' 'Get it down!' It was heavily smoking and wavering through the air and finally went over a small hill. Thereafter, we saw a huge plume of smoke rising from the general site where the a/c went in." Corporal William M. Ebersbach recalled, "The '46 struck the ground on its right side. The pilots and flight crew escaped . . . one crewman through the open gunner's hatch. The helicopter was totally destroyed by fire after crashing."

Operation Hastings lasted from 15 July to 3 August and was the largest and most violent operation of the war up to that point. During the operation three regiments of the 324th B Division opposed the Marines. The NVA suffered more than sixteen hundred killed, another nine hundred probably killed, and seventeen captured, with tons of equipment, weapons, and ammunition destroyed. In addition some six thousand enemy documents were captured with "some of the most meaningful information found in South Vietnam up to this time," according to Brigadier General English.

Marine casualties were 126 killed in action and 448 wounded with dozens of helicopters damaged or destroyed. Lieutenant General Walt, III MAF commander, said, "We found them [the NVA] well equipped, well trained, and aggressive to the point of fanaticism. They attacked in mass formations and died by the hundreds. Their leaders had misjudged the fighting ability of U.S. Marines . . . our superiority in artillery and total command of the air. They had vastly underestimated . . . our [helicopter] mobility."

PART II:

HEAVY COMBAT, 1967–1969

CHAPTER SEVEN

SPECIAL LANDING FORCE

OPERATION BEAU CHARGER

On 18 May 1967 Special Landing Force Alpha (SLF-A) commenced Operation Beau Charger, in the eastern area of the southern half of the Demilitarized Zone in northern Quang Tri Province. The multi-battalion U.S. and ARVN operation was a search and destroy mission to foil enemy attacks against Marine outposts below the Ben Hai River along the southern boundary of the DMZ. SLF-A consisted of Battalion Landing Team, 1st Battalion, 3rd Marines (BLT 1/3) and Marine Medium Helicopter Squadron 263 (HMM-263) aboard four ships of Amphibious Ready Group Alpha (ARG-A): USS *Okinawa* (LPH-3), USS *Point Defiance* (LSD-31), USS *Bayfield* (APA-33), and USS *Whitfield Country* (LST-1169).— The BLT's concept of operation called for Company D to land across the beach by tracked landing vehicles (LVTs) and Company A and Company C to helilift in. Intelligence reports indicated the presence in the area of an unidentified NVA battalion and a Viet Cong local force company, which combined had an estimated strength of over six hundred men. Due to the proximity of known enemy coastal defense batteries located in the Cap Mui Lay coastal area near the DMZ, the operation was to be supported by the largest concentration of naval gunfire support ships since the Korean War: a light cruiser and a guided-missile cruiser (USS *Saint Paul* CA-73 and USS *Boston* CAG-1), three destroyers (USS *Fechtler* DD870, USS *Edson* DD 945 and HMAS *Hobart* D-39) and one guided missile destroyer (USS *Joseph Strauss* DDG-16).

SPECIAL LANDING FORCE

A special landing force (SLF) consisted of a Marine battalion landing team (BLT) of approximately 1,100 men and a 350-man Marine medium helicopter squadron (HMM). The SLF was located aboard a U.S. Navy amphibious ready group (ARG) comprised of five ships: a landing ship tank (LST), an amphibious assault ship (LPH), a dock landing ship (LSD), an attack transport (APA), and an amphibious transport dock (LPD). The composition of the SLF gave it the capability of both heliborne and waterborne assaults. In 1967, the Seventh Fleet's SLF (Alpha) was the Pacific Command's strategic reserve for all of Southeast Asia, including Vietnam. Early in 1967 the Joint Chiefs of Staff authorized the formation of a second SLF (Bravo) and directed that both be used for extended operations in Vietnam, primarily in I Corps Tactical Zone as an emergency reinforcement to counter North Vietnamese operations. Over two dozen SLF operations were conducted during 1967.

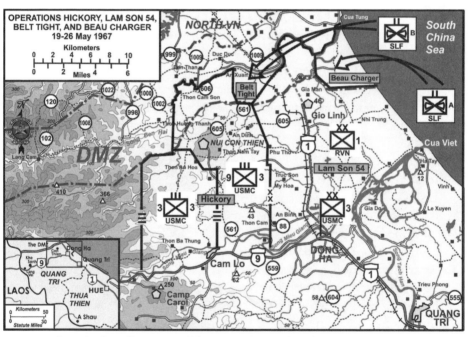

Operation Beau Charger, one of three operations conducted along South Vietnam's Demilitarized Zone involving Marines from the Special Landing Force.

1st Battalion, 3rd Marines, Concept of Operations:
Commencing at H and L hours one company will conduct waterborne assault over Green Beach seize and secure the beach area and approaches thereto. Simultaneously one company will conduct helicopterborne attack into landing zone Goose, seize and secure the landing zone, and commence destruction of enemy forces/military facilities and withdrawal of non-combatants from the area. Subse-

quently a second company will conduct a helicopterborne attack in landing zone Duck and conduct similar operations within their area. One company will be established as SLF reserve aboard the LPH to include Sparrow Hawk [reaction force] platoon size force until released to the control of BLT 1/3. On order or upon completion of their mission the BLT will conduct an amphibious withdrawal.

At 0400, the World War II light cruiser USS *Saint Paul* (CA-73) maneuvered into position to support the landing with her 5- and 8-inch naval guns. As the ship came into range, it was targeted by shore batteries in the Cap Mui Lay. The *Saint Paul* returned fire but was unable to determine the results. Two hours later, the USS *Summer* (DD-692) reported that at 0652, she and the Australian destroyer HMAS *Hobart* received sixteen rounds of heavy-caliber artillery fire. Two of the rounds landed within a hundred yards of the *Summer*. The two destroyers turned seaward at high speed, then turned parallel to the beach, and commenced counterbattery fire. The dock landing ship USS *Point Defiance* (LSD-31) was in the midst of launching the troop-carrying amphibious tractors (LVTs) when she was blanketed by ten salvos of 130mm artillery fire. The rounds hit within fifty meters of the LVTs and within two hundred yards of the *Point Defiance*. The LSD cranked on 20 knots and took immediate evasive action, while the cruiser and destroyers returned fire. Several fixed wing sorties were also called in. The shore batteries were knocked out under the concentrated bombardment.

Aboard the amphibious assault ship USS *Okinawa* (LPH-3), the flight

USS *Saint Paul* firing her 8/55 guns in support of ground troops during Operation Beau Charger.

crews and infantrymen were up well before dawn. Private First Class Joseph C. Connelly recalled, "At 0330 reveille was sounded and we gathered and checked our gear. I had cleaned my weapon the previous night, filled my two canteens and grabbed an extra pair of socks." The men wolfed down a quick breakfast on the mess decks before assembling for a last minute briefing on the operation. "As we filed into the chow hall at 0430, I couldn't believe what I was seeing or smelling," Private First Class Connelly said. "My God they were serving steak and eggs . . . real steak and real eggs, not those powdered green eggs as usual. When they serve steak and eggs in the Marine Corps, it's the equivalent of the Last Supper! I couldn't even eat for the tightening in my stomach. From the looks we were getting from the Navy food servers, it was clear that they knew more about the upcoming assault than we did."

The battalion's logisticians laid out open cases of "C"-rations, cloth bandoliers of small arms ammunition, mortar rounds in black cardboard tubes, green fiber-encased anti-tank missiles and a variety of grenades (fragmentation, smoke and white phosphorus (WP)) in one corner of the hanger deck for issue to the heliteams. Word was passed over the ship's intercom that the "smoking lamp" was out, a standard announcement whenever ammunition was being handled. When all was ready, the heliteams passed along the line under the watchful eye of the company gunnery sergeant, who brooked no horse play now that live ammunition was in their hands. Private First Class Connelly drew "three days of C-Rations, 1,000 rounds of M-16 ammunition [and] our issue of frags [hand grenades] and WP [white phosphorus grenade]." After the Marines loaded their rifle magazines and stored the grenades and missiles in their web gear, a guide led the heliteams to ready positions in sheltered areas adjacent to the flight deck where they waited to board the helicopters. "Our squad leaders gathered us around and told us that we lucked out, we were assigned the second wave," Private First Class Connelly said.

Helicopter crew chiefs busied themselves with last minute checks of their aircraft and weapons systems, while the gunners mounted the M60 machine guns and checked the linked 7.62mm ammunition to ensure they were free of kinks that could jam the guns. Pilots gathered in the squadron's ready room where Lt. Col. Edward K. Kirby and his staff reviewed the flight information and the enemy situation. Much of the brief dealt with the approach and retirement lanes that were to be used. Intelligence sources reported many enemy antiaircraft machine guns in the area. The routes had been selected based on aerial photographs; overflights had not been conducted so as not to alert the NVA. The pilots also learned that the landing zone had not been prepped by supporting arms for the same reason.

Following the briefings, the pilots headed for their aircraft and commenced a final preflight inspection with the crew chief. Satisfied that all was ready, they climbed into the cockpit and went through the start-up procedures. The flight deck came alive with the roar of the big 1,525-horsepower Wright engines. On signal, the five-man heliteams left the deck shelters and double-timed to the aircraft. For many of the heavily-burdened infantrymen the climb into the cabin required a boost, all the while trying to juggle a weapon, pack, and helmet. The unwary invariably hit their helmet on the hatch frame, driving their head into their shoulders, much to the amusement of their more seasoned buddies. Once aboard, the Marines settled uncomfortably in the jump seats—a thin pieces of nylon fabric stretched between aluminum tubes—and buckled their seat belts, a difficult chore even in the best of times. The ends of the belts were often jammed underneath the adjacent man, who was also trying to find his own belt. By the time the aircraft launched, the members of the heliteams were hot, sweaty, and extremely uncomfortable.

At 0730, fifteen UH-34s from HMM-263 carrying the assault elements of Company A lifted off from the flight deck of the USS *Okinawa* and headed for Landing Zone Goose. The flight was escorted by two gunships from VMO-2, call sign Deadlock. *U.S. Marines in Vietnam, Fighting the North Vietnamese, 1967* states that, "Flying lead, LtCol Kirby [Edward K.] led his '34s toward the potentially dangerous zone, flying at altitudes of less than 50 feet to reduce the enemy gunners' effectiveness. A maximum speed

Marine heliteams from BLT 2/3, part of the special landing force (SLF) on the carrier USS *Valley Forge* (LPH-8), run to board helicopters for movement ashore. Some of the troop-laden helicopters are already airborne and can be see flying above the ship.

approach, about 80 knots, lack of prominent landmarks, and the tenseness of the situation made navigation difficult at best." As Lieutenant Colonel Kirby came in to the north end of the zone for a landing, machine gun fire tore into his aircraft, destroying his radio and wounding his copilot, crew chief, gunner and three infantrymen. A fourth infantryman standing in the hatch was mortally wounded and pitched to the ground. The wounded gunner returned fire and ... "saved our bacon!" according to Kirby. The gunships swept in with machine gun and rockets trying to knock out the NVA weapons positions. One aircraft, Deadlock 2-5 expended four thousand rounds of ammunition and thirty rockets suppressing the enemy's fire.

Four other UH-34s in the wave were hit but managed to land their infantrymen under covering fire from the escorting UH-1E gunships, two of which were hit and suffered extensive damage. Despite the heavy fire, the first assault wave, 2nd Platoon, Company A, landed but was in serious trouble from a well-entrenched enemy force, estimated to be in battalion strength. The platoon, commanded by Second Lieutenant Dwight G. Faylor, was spread out over eight hundred yards in the landing zone and was under heavy enemy pressure, mainly from the northwest. He requested air and naval gunfire support. Ensign John W. McCormick, the BLT's naval gunfire liaison officer was killed while trying to call in support; his efforts were in vain. He states: "The ships denied his requests; no one was certain of the exact location of friendly positions and in many cases the enemy was too close to use naval gunfire without endangering the Marines." (*Fighting the North Vietnamese*) The battalion after-action report stated that "Heavy fighting ensued ... [with] the enemy engaging friendly forces at extremely close range (20-200 meters), reducing friendly capabilities to withdraw and fully utilize supporting arms ... it was obvious the enemy was thoroughly schooled to concentrate their fires on friendly machine gun teams and other key personnel and elements."

Ensign John W. McCormick Jr., United States Navy, Silver Star citation:

The President of the United States of America takes pride in presenting the Silver Star (Posthumously) to Ensign John W. McCormick, Jr., United States Navy, for conspicuous gallantry and intrepidity in action while serving as Naval Gunfire Liaison Officer with the First Battalion, Third Marines, Third Marine Amphibious Force, in connection with operations against insurgent communist (Viet Cong) forces in the Republic of Vietnam. On 18 May 1967, during Operation BEAU CHARGER, while his unit was under a heavy enemy mortar attack, Ensign McCormick fearlessly exposed himself to intense fire to direct and adjust supporting fires against enemy entrenchments. Maneuvering his gunfire-spotting team into more advantageous positions from which to observe friendly fires, he courageously disregarded his own safety while he moved from one position to another, encouraging his men and adjusting supporting fires with exceptional accuracy. As enemy fire intensified, Ensign Mc-Cormick directed his men to covered positions while he continued to expose himself to the hostile fire to adjust friendly artillery missions. Although he sustained severe fragmentation wounds, he refused assistance and, urging his men to remain in their relatively secure positions, maintained radio contact with friendly artillery units, directing their fires until he was no longer able to move. His indomitable fighting spirit and steadfast determination were an inspiration to all with whom he served, and contributed significantly to the accomplishment of his unit's mission. By his extraordinary courage, bold initiative, and selfless devotion to duty, Ensign McCormick upheld the highest traditions of the United States Naval Service.

Lieutenant Colonel Kirby was able to nurse his crippled aircraft back to the *Okinawa* where, according to *Fighting the North Vietnamese,* he briefed "Colonel Gallo [James A.], the SLF commander, on the bad situation at LZ Goose. Gallo immediately ordered the cancellation of all further lifts into Goose and the substitution of the alternate LZ Owl, 800 meters south...." The second wave of Marines was standing by to board the returning helicopters. "There were ten of us, each enveloped in our own thoughts," Private First Class Connelly recalled. "The hatch was opened to the ocean breeze, and the sun looked beautiful as it broke the horizon in a red sky." The helicopters returned. "As they set down," he said, "it was clear that they were all shot to s——-! We watched in horror as they unloaded body after body on to stretchers...." The Marines boarded and the helicopters lifted off. "As I looked around the chopper, I was amazed we were in flight. At least a dozen bullet holes were visible in the side fuselage ... it looked like transmission fluid was running from the overhead, and pools of blood and discarded bandages were strewn about the deck."

HMM-164's helicopters landed the second wave in LZ Owl, which linked up with Company D that had landed unopposed across Green Beach,

UH-34s dropping off troops in a hilltop landing zone. Note the barrel of the M60 machine gun protruding from the helo in the foreground. Also note that the Marines are armed with M14 rifles.

900 meters south of Owl. *Fighting the North Vietnamese* noted that, "By 0855, the remainder of Company A had landed in Owl. Overland reinforcements arrived at Owl in the form of one platoon from Company D and a section of tanks. At 0930 the lead elements of Company B began landing. The force at Owl then moved out to rescue the beleaguered platoon at LZ Goose ... and by 1100 the rescue force had regained contact with Faylor's platoon, but the enemy showed no signs of breaking off the engagement." Company A and B moved against an extensive NVA trench line but was stymied by heavy automatic weapons fire. The assault force pulled back and hit the entrenchments with air, resulting in a large secondary explosion. The after-action report noted, "After eleven aircraft, of four different models, had hit the enemy positions, friendly elements advanced with minimal resistance." The battalion suffered fourteen killed in action and fifty-five wounded on the first day of the operation., while the NVA lost sixty confirmed dead and a further twenty-two probable, and one captured.

Operation Beau Charger continued for seven more days (18–26 May) before the battalion withdrew. The after-action report stated, "At 0200 Company A withdrew followed by Company C [Company B had withdrawn on the 25th]. Company D covered the withdrawal and was itself extracted at 1010. No incidents or enemy contact occurred during the withdrawal." The battalion suffered a total of twenty-three men killed in action and another ninety-nine wounded during the week-long operation. HMM-263 flew a total of

1,237 UH-34 sorties, 75 UH-1E gunship sorties, and 132 CH-46 sorties.

OPERATION BELT TIGHT/HICKORY

Flight quarters sounded early aboard the *Princeton*; six CH-46s from HMM-164 (White Knights), augmented by four HMM-165 (Buffalo City) aircraft based at Ky Ha, were scheduled to lift off at 0630. They would be escorted to the landing zone by two gunships from VMO-2. The pilots and flight crews had rolled out of their racks several hours earlier for the usual preflight brief. They learned that 2nd Battalion, 3rd Marines, was scheduled to be lifted into two landing zones (LZ Parrot and LZ Mockingbird) to join their sister battalion 1/3, which was then completing a sweep of NVA forces in the eastern part of the DMZ during Operation Beau Charger. Although 2/3 was going to be employed in the same general area, the operation code name had been changed from Beau Charger to Belt Tight and Hickory.

At 0714 on 20 May, HMM-164 lifted Company's F, H, and the BLT command group into LZ Parrot. The squadron's command chronology cataloged problems with the initial lift. "Due to the limited aircraft availability [maintenance problems] of the SLF helicopter squadron, a request was submitted and approved for four additional CH-46 aircraft from HMM-165. The late arrival of these aircraft plus mechanical failures on two of the SLF squadron's helicopters caused the first wave of troops landing in the primary landing zone to be only half of the planned number of troops. One of the SLF squadron's aircraft was repaired in time for the second wave, and HMM-165's four CH-46s arrived in time to join the third wave." In addition, the two UH-1Es "arrived on the morning of D-Day, allowing only a minimum briefing of the pilots prior to launch of the first wave." During the landing in LZ Parrot, the VMO-2 gunships expended over five thousand rounds of 7.62mm and seventy-seven rockets.

At 0850, Company's E, G, and another command group were landed in LZ Mockingbird. Even though both zones had been prepped with artillery and air strikes, they were still being hit by enemy fire. HMM-164's command chronology noted, "Mortars and small arms fire was received by the strike aircraft [CH-46] coming into the LZs. YT-13 received two hits on the third trip into landing zone Parrot; there was negative injury to personnel, and damage to the aircraft was minor. No other aircraft were hit." The BLT reported that "enemy fire was light, consisting of an estimated 5-20 NVA employing automatic weapons and sniper fire. . . ." However, late that afternoon, "Company E had two listening posts overrun by an estimated 10 enemy and

A Navy flight-deck crewman signals the pilot of a UH-1E that he is cleared to take off in support of Operation Beau Charger. Note the M60 machine gun protruding from the starboard hatch.

Company F received probing attacks ... [and] the BLT command post was hit by three 82mm mortar rounds. ... " HMM-164 launched two medevac aircraft, which evacuated sixteen casualties. Both helicopters received fire in the zone but were not hit. The BLT reported "enemy casualties were one confirmed and twelve probable KIAs. One NVA soldier was captured. Enemy bunkers, and caches containing ammunition, equipment and other miscellaneous items were destroyed."

Throughout the next day, the BLT reported scattered enemy contact.

TIME	INCIDENT
0001:	CP and Company F received 15 rounds enemy mortar fire.
0020:	Company F probed. No casualties.
1010:	Company E engaged three VC by fire. VC fled, Company E pursued them. During the pursuit Company E discovered a large enemy ordnance cache. One enemy KIA (probable).
1050:	CP received three rounds enemy artillery fire from NW direction across the Ben Hai River.
1125:	Company G discovered hole 10'X10'X10' filled with 60mm mortar rounds (1,164) and other miscellaneous ordnance.
1310:	Company F artillery FO fired on six enemy carrying mortar tube. Fifty-six rounds 105mm fired. Four enemy probable KIA; one 82mm mortar destroyed.

1515:   Company F discovered sophisticated enemy bunker reinforced with steel Overhead and walls. Discovered two 82mm mortars and medical supplies including morphine in a five gallon can.

1755:   CP and all companies less Company E received 169 rounds of mixed 82mm and 105mm artillery. Fire lasted 35 minutes. Unable to get counter-battery cleared. Battalion sustained 3 KIA, 48 WIA.

1930:   Captain R. Culver temporarily took command of Company F when Captain S. Vaughn became a casualty.

The artillery attack was particularly galling as the BLT commander noted, "The [lack of] timely response to immediate requests, particularly counter-battery missions, on several occasions, virtually halted the forward movement of the battalion and prevented the immediate suppression of enemy fires . . . the delays were the result of failure to receive positive clearance. On one particular occasion, the battalion took 169 rounds of enemy mortar and artillery fire over a period of 35 minutes. Suspected enemy firing positions were reported within 10 minutes, but clearance could not be obtained. The battalion sustained a total of 51 casualties." HMM-164 launched two CH-46s to pick up the wounded, several of whom were classified as *emergency* medevacs (in danger of losing life or limb). Two gunships from VMO-2 fired over ten thousand rounds of 7.62mm and sixty rockets in an attempt to suppress the enemy fire.

Aircraft availability continued to plague HMM-162 during the remainder of the operation and HMM-165 was tasked to augment the hard pressed SLF squadron. On 21 May, Capt. R. W. Byrd launched minutes prior to sunset with two Buffalo City aircraft on an emergency mission to resupply ammunition. The squadron command chronology noted, "Both helicopters received fire going into and coming out of the zone, but Capt Byrd's gunners returned the fire and the aircraft departed unscathed." The resupply mission was escorted by two VMO-2 gunships that expended over five thousand rounds of machinegun ammunition and thirty-two rockets.

Operation Belt Tight and Hickory officially ended on 28 May. "SLF casualties were light during the nine days of Belt Tight/Hickory considering the fact that the battalion was either in contact or under artillery attack during most of the period. SLF Bravo had 17 Marines killed and 152 wounded. North Vietnamese losses totaled a confirmed 58 killed and one prisoner taken by the Marines."(*Fighting the North Vietnamese*)

CHAPTER EIGHT

A MONTH IN THE TOUR OF HMM-165

Squadron insignia of HMM-165 known as the White Knights. Its radio call sign in Vietnam was Buffalo City.

The month of May did not bode well for HMM-165, call sign Buffalo City. Two of its aircraft, Buffalo City 2-1 and 2-2, were returning to base when the lead pilot received a radio call from the First Hospital Company asking if he would accept a mission to transport several sick and wounded men from the hospital to the USS *Sanctuary* (AH-17). After accepting the mission the two helicopters landed at the hospital's helipad and loaded the patients; 2-1 loaded eleven litter cases, while thirteen ambulatory patients boarded 2-2. At approximately 2300, the flight approached the *Sanctuary*. In accordance with standard operating procedure, 2-1 jettisoned its extra fuel before landing on the ship's helipad. While the litter patients were being unloaded, 2-2 circled overhead. As 2-1 cleared the landing pad, 2-2 started jettisoning excess fuel and turned on final approach to the ship. Suddenly the aircraft's number one engine quit, the flight controls got sluggish, and the helicopter started to sink. Seconds later the second engine quit, forcing the pilot to auto-rotate into the sea. "I'm going in," he radioed, declaring an in-flight emergency.

When the pilot declared the emergency, the crew chief worked his way through the cabin shouting ditching instructions to the passengers. Just as he returned to his position by the door, the helicopter hit the water. It was a good water landing. The helicopter hit flat, in a nose-high attitude with no forward air speed, but within a few seconds the 8 to 10 foot swells tipped the helicopter on its right side. Within 30 seconds the aircraft went down, trapping several men. The crew chief was able to get out of his door but the pilot could not open his escape hatch and had to climb through the space between his seat and the copilot's. He found an air pocket and was able then to squeeze out the left side door and swim twenty feet to the surface. At this point there were several survivors in the water trying to stay afloat. The pilot in 2-1 circled overhead illuminating the men with his searchlight and had his crew toss them life vests. He also attempted to use his hoist but it jammed after lifting one man out of the water. The *Sanctuary* launched several small boats, which picked up ten survivors. Unfortunately six men were unaccounted for and were listed as killed in action/body not recovered.

The next day, a Buffalo City aircraft was hit by intense small arms fire as it climbed out of a landing zone in the Que Son Valley. A round hit a fuel line causing highly flammable JP4 to spray all over the cabin. To make matters worse, the number one engine started smoking, which the pilot had to quickly shut down. With only one engine, the aircraft started to lose altitude. The pilot ordered the crew to throw out the cargo to lighten the load. At the same time, the copilot began to jettison fuel. It wasn't enough; the aircraft was going down and the only secure zone was the Special Forces camp at Thien Phouc, a long five miles away. With one eye on the gauges and the other on the ground, the pilot nursed the crippled helicopter toward safety. The two big questions in his mind were "would the helicopter stay in the air long enough and would a spark set off an explosion." Finally, after several very long anxious minutes, the camp appeared on the horizon. A few more minutes and the pilot set the bird down on the landing pad. The downed crew was picked up by another aircraft. The next morning helicopter was repaired and flown back to Ky Ha."

By May 1967 the war was rapidly heating up. North Vietnamese Army regulars were infiltrating across the DMZ in battalion and regimental strength. I Corps Tactical Zone, the northern most region of South Vietnam, became a major battle ground. Its terrain favored the enemy: rugged, jungle-covered mountains in the west hid NVA base camps and supply areas, while the more populated piedmont and coastal lowlands concealed Viet Cong guerrillas. The hard-pressed Marine forces were spread thin and depended on helicopters for airlifting troops, insertion and extraction of reconnaissance teams, resupply, and medevac. The overworked squadrons frequently supported more than a dozen major ground operations during a given month. The 1st Marine Air Wing's eleven helicopter squadrons, eight transport and three observation squadrons, that were tasked to support I Corps operations were simply not enough lift to meet all the requirements. The aircrews were tired and their birds worn out.

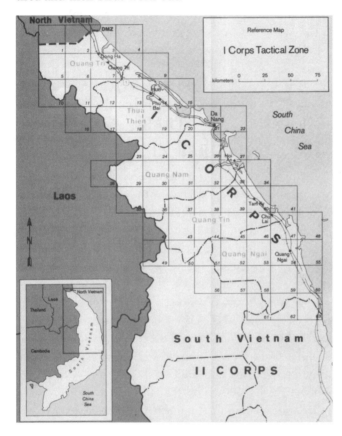

The northernmost military region of South Vietnam, I Corps Tactical Zone, was the scene of bloody fighting in 1967–1968 as the North Vietnamese in battalion and regimental strength infiltrated across the DMZ.

HMM-165 was typical of 1st MAW's over-taxed helicopter squadrons. In May 1967 the squadron supported five separate operations—Union I, Union II, Hickory, Shawnee, and Beau Charger—in I Corps between the DMZ and the Marine Corps air facility (MCAF) at Ky Ha where it was based. During the month, the squadron flew over fourteen hundred hours, despite a three-day shutdown due to a suspected mechanical defect in the aircraft and the continued lack of spare parts. The maintenance department struggled heroically to maintain an average of twelve *up* aircraft a day out of the nineteen that were in the squadron's inventory. The squadron's May 1967 command chronology documented its tempo of support operations for, "a month in the life of HMM-165."

The pilots normally started their day with an early morning brief by the squadron's operations officer, who would go through the what, where, and when of the day's flight schedule. His brief included radio call signs and frequencies and a host of other details that the pilots noted on their knee pads. A large blackboard in the ready room noted the flight assignments: who was flying with whom, airplane number, and the "frag" number (mission assignment). Of all the missions assigned, medevac reconnaissance insertion-and-extraction were the most likely to draw enemy fire because friendly forces were in close contact with the enemy. In many cases, ground fire in the landing zone was almost a certainty because the NVA had become adept at counterreconnaissance techniques. James W. McCoy in *Secrets of the Viet Cong* noted, "In the bush, the enemy stationed landing zone watchers near areas where American helicopters might land. Trail watchers were assigned trails to observe, along with any traffic moving along them. Stream crossing points were also closely observed . . . all major NVA bases . . . were surrounded by counter-reconnaissance screens. That picket of infantry troops intensely patrolled the bush seeking enemy reconnaissance units to destroy or drive back."

HMM-165's May command chronology cited several missions that highlighted the danger. On 2 May, Capt. W. D. Kalas, mission number 67, was assigned to extract Canal Zone, an eleven-man Marine reconnaissance team that had been fighting all night against a large force of enemy soldiers. The team had been in a night laager when it heard movement. Fifteen minutes later, it was attacked by an unknown number of NVA using hand grenades and small arms. The Marines responded with an M-79, rifles, hand grenades and claymore mines. They also called in artillery. The movement continued and it appeared the enemy was attempting to surround them. At dawn the team requested air support and an emergency extract. The call for help brought an immediate response. Several flights of fixed wing pounded the area around the team and two Huey gunships from VMO-6 arrived to support the Buffalo City mission. As Captain Kalas began his approach to the landing zone, enemy gunners opened fire. The helicopter's gunners fired back, enabling the aircraft to escape without damage. With the zone too hot to land, the NVA positions were hit again with bombs and rockets. After several bombing runs, the rescue bird was able to land and extract the team. The recon team reported seven enemy confirmed and ten probable KIAs. Two Marines were slightly wounded by grenade fragments.

On the same day, two Buffalo City aircraft led by Maj. D. N. Anderson were assigned to insert reconnaissance team Duckbill. The first landing zone

Reconnaissance team jumping off the ramp of a CH-46. These small teams were used to gather intelligence and strike the North Vietnamese with artillery and air support.

was covered with punji sticks and he was forced to land in an alternate LZ. As he lifted from the zone, his wingman, Capt. J. F. Pleva came in on final. Just as Pleva landed, the enemy opened fire, hitting the aircraft in the right fuel tank, igniting it and spreading flames all over the helicopter. A section of UH-1Es swept in to provide suppressive fire, enabling the damaged CH-46 to lift off. In a remarkable feat of airmanship, Captain Pleva lifted out of the zone and landed in a nearby river, which extinguished the fire. His quick actions saved the aircraft and crew.

A maintenance team from HMM-165 rigs a hoist sling to a CH-46A sitting in a mountain stream northwest of Chu Lai on 12 May 1967. Enemy ground fire had set the aircraft on fire and the pilot, Capt James F. Pleva, force-landed in the stream, dousing the flames.—*Department of Defense*

INSERTION AND EXTRACTION OFFICER

Captain Marty Higgins, 1st Reconnaissance Battalion was assigned as the insertion and extraction Officer (I&E) during his tour in 1970–1971. It was the battalion's standard operating procedure (SOP) to have the I&E officer accompany every mission in the reconnaissance team's helo. He was to be the first man off the helicopter on insertion and the last man on during the extraction. For one mission the battalion commander, Lt. Col. William G. Leftwich Jr., took Higgins's place on an emergency extraction in order to give him a well-deserved rest. Captain Higgins related that the team had to be extracted using a Spie Rig because of the dense jungle. The helicopter failed to gain enough altitude and dragged the team into the trees. The subsequent drag on the aircraft caused it to crash, killing everyone on board, including the battalion commander.

On 7 May, 1st Lt. R. M. Dalbey, leading a flight of two was assigned to extract recon team Duckbill, which was under heavy enemy pressure. Two VMO-6 (Klondike) gunships and several flights of F-4 Phantoms were working over the area surrounding the landing zone. Dalbey was first in the zone and managed to pick up half the team without receiving fire. As his wingman, Maj. R. E. Romine, set down, the enemy opened fire with a .50-caliber machine gun. An armor piecing tracer punched through the copilot's windshield, barely missing his head and causing minor wounds to his arms from glass fragments. The round lodged in the back of his armored seat. The cockpit immediately filled with flame and smoke, momentarily blinding both pilots and slightly burning the copilot on the neck. Major Romine had the presence of mind to get the aircraft into the air where the crew quickly checked for damage. They did not find any serious damage to the flight systems, so Major Romine went back to recover the recon team. He received fire again but managed to recover the team without further damage.

Three days later, reconnaissance team Bennington was surrounded by NVA regulars and needed help badly. They requested an emergency extraction after having fought their way to a low tree covered hill, but were still under heavy pressure by a large enemy force. Their emergency request was passed to HMM-165, which assigned it to a flight of two CH-46s led by Capt. Nesmith. VMO-6 assigned two gunships, Klondike 4-5 and 4-6, as escort. Upon arriving in the area, the flight discovered that the team was pinned down and had a badly wounded man who could not be moved. They were going to have to be hoisted through the trees. As Captain Nesmith began his approach, the Klondike gunships and fixed-wing aircraft prepped the area around the team. It was not good enough; the helicopter was hit by small arms fire on final and had to wave off. The enemy positions were pounded again. Nesmith attempted a second pickup, but had to abort because of the intense ground fire. On the third attempt, two A-4 fighter bombers delivered their ordnance within a hundred meters of the Marines, while the Klondikers provided suppressive fire on all sides. Captain Nesmith hovered over the team and hoisted out the wounded Marine despite intense small arms fire. As a second team member was being hoisted, the helicopter was hit and lost all the oil in the aft transmission line, forcing it to terminate the extraction and head for the nearest secure area. With the wounded man out of harm's way, the team was able to move to a more secure landing zone, where they were picked up by another Buffalo City flight.

HMM-165 pilot Captain Rocky Darger recalled a particularly dangerous extraction. "I remember sitting in an LZ while we were trying to load on a Force Recon team of about five or six Marines, three of whom were trying to carry two dead fellow Marines and all their equipment. I knew we weren't going to get out of there because we were taking all of this fire from fifty to one hundred yards away. You could see these flashing lights from a tree line. We were sitting in this little glass cockpit and the crew were in the back with only a thin aluminum between us and death. I accepted the fact that we were going to die. We weren't going to leave until all those Marines were on board. Somehow we got everyone on board without being hit. I still don't understand it to this day. . . . I have a different attitude about death today because of that incident."

On 22 May, HMM-165 was tasked to support Project Delta, a MACV Special Forces hunter-killer operation. Major D. C. Heim led a flight of four Buffalo City, two Bonnie Sue (HMM-265), and two Mohair (HMM-262) aircraft to insert 65 ARVN and 5 U.S. Special Forces advisers into western Quang Nam Province, a notoriously hostile area. The first section safely dropped off its troops and departed the zone. As the second section landed, the enemy opened fire and shot down a Buffalo City aircraft flown by Capt. L. R. Medlin. The heavily damaged helicopter caught on fire and was forced down near the landing zone. The hard landing injured the copilot and shook up the rest of the crew. The search-and-rescue (SAR) bird immediately flew in to pick up the downed airmen. As it came in range, the enemy gunners opened an intense fire. A crewman aboard the helicopter saw several enemy soldiers moving toward the downed aircraft and immediately opened fire with his .50-caliber machine gun. The pilot of the rescue aircraft landed next to Medlin's helicopter, loaded the four-man crew aboard, and lifted off. The downed aircraft was napalmed to prevent it from falling into enemy hands. Late the next afternoon, the Project Delta force was extracted under heavy fire. Six Army and two VMO-6 gunships along with several flights of fixed wing provided suppressive fire.

The Project Delta force experience was not uncommon. James McCoy wrote, "Calling upon both Soviet advisers and Algerians who had fought against a French helicopter war in North Africa, the NVA rapidly developed an anti-airmobile doctrine."(*Secrets of the Viet Cong*) By 1967, the NVA were adept at responding to American helicopter mobility. They learned from hard-won experience to develop tactical plans that incorporated identification of potential landing zones, early warning systems to alert nearby units, and implementation of counterlanding operations. McCoy noted, "The first Chu Luc [NVA] tactical priority was to place potential landing zones under surveillance [and] rig them with obstacles, mines, trip devices, punji stakes and pits and long poles. The reds [NVA] refrained from attacking enemy aircraft conducting prep fires, in order to prevent unnecessary casualties to themselves. If they fired at helicopters, poorly armed troop transports were their favorite targets."

On 25 and 26 May, the squadron was involved in two large troop lifts. The first lift was in support of a Korean Marine Corps battalion. Eight Buffalo City aircraft, escorted by two Klondike (VMO-6) gunships, shuttled 250 Korean Marines organized in three waves. The first two lifts into the zone encountered enemy fire. The lead aircraft was hit but not seriously damaged. The gunships began extensive fire suppression and, as a result, no enemy fire was encountered on the third and last waves. The next day, eight Buffalo City aircraft together with twelve helicopters from Dogma (HMM-362) and Tarbush (HMM-361) were tasked to support Operation Union II, a search and destroy operation in the Que Son Valley. The landing zone was prepped by several flights of fixed-wing aircraft controlled by two VMO-6 gunships acting as the airborne tactical air controller. The landing plan called for the first wave of 150 Marines to be inserted simultaneously, with the remaining troops to be inserted by aircraft division until the lift was completed. The first birds in the zone stirred up a hornet's nest. Five Buffalo City aircraft were hit and one pilot wounded, HMM-361 escaped damage, but HMM-362 had three aircraft hit before the lift was completed.

On the last three days of the month, HMM-165 conducted one reconnaissance insert and an extraction, and participated in a major troop lift. On 29 May two Buffalo City aircraft were shot out of a hilltop landing zone while attempting a recon insert. The next day, ten HMM-165 and six HMM-262 (Mohair) aircraft escorted by six VMO-6 gunships lifted two battalions of the 5th Marines deep into hostile territory. The flights experienced scattered enemy sniper and mortar fire in and around the landing zone but no aircraft was damaged nor crewmen hurt. Finally, on the last day of the month, two squadron aircraft extracted recon team Hong Kong. On the lift out the flight received small arms fire but cleared the zone without damage.

During the "month in the life of . . . ," HMM-165 lost one CH-46, three officers and two enlisted men were wounded and one enlisted gunner, Sgt. S. L. Corfield was lost at sea. The squadron flew over 3,500 sorties, carried 525 tons of cargo and 8,857 passengers.

CHAPTER NINE

THE BEACH RESCUE

*I still have four men on the ground, the VC are trying to take
them prisoner or kill them; God, can somebody help them!*
—Unknown Army pilot

Late in the afternoon of 19 August 1967, a U.S. Army CH-47
Chinook helicopter enroute to Chu Lai with a load of injured
American soldiers was hit by small arms fire. The pilot set the aircraft down
on the beach one mile north of the mouth of the Song Tra Khuc River to
determine the extent of the damage. Staff Sergeant Lawrence H. Allen recalled, "The crew chief and myself, along with two other NCOs climbed out
to check the extent of the damage. Three of us set up a security guard between
the helicopter and the inland position of the beach, while the crew chief
checked out the damage. At this time, a grenade thrown by a Viet Cong exploded near the front of the aircraft. We attempted to withdraw to the helicopter, but the pilot had already lifted off."

Captain Stephen W. Pless was flying a UH-1E gunship, call sign Cherry
Six on a medevac escort mission when he heard a plaintive call for help over
the aircraft emergency frequency, "Guard" channel: "My aircraft is all shot
up and I have a lot of wounded aboard. I'm going to try to make it to Duc
Pho." After a slight pause, the unknown pilot radioed, "I still have four men
on the ground, the VC are trying to take them prisoner or kill them; God,
can somebody help them!" The transmission was electrifying . . . Americans
were in grave danger! Captain Pless continued toward where he thought the
men were located while his copilot, Captain Rupert E. Fairfield, "ascertained
that our original mission, the evacuation of one wounded Korean Marine,
could be accomplished without our escort." By this time, Pless had determined that the four trapped Americans were located approximately one mile
north of the Song Tra Khuc River and, " . . . they were under attack by mortars

and automatic weapons, and that a CH-47 had been driven off by severe automatic weapons fire." Staff Sergeant Allen recalled, "We began to receive a barrage of grenades; we returned fire, but soon ran out of ammo. The Viet Cong then moved in close and threw more grenades. Everyone was wounded by this time."

Pless learned that other aircraft were in the area. "There were three jets overhead and four Army UH-1Es orbiting about a mile to sea. None of these aircraft could get in close enough to the four besieged Americans due to the mortar and severe automatic weapons fire. I made two transmissions offering to help, but received no reply. Since the other aircraft seemed reluctant to aid the downed men and unable to get organized, I decided to go in alone and hoped they would follow me and help." Captain Pless asked the crew, "How do you feel about going down?" Captain Fairfield recalled, "I turned to give the thumbs-up signal to Gunnery Sergeant Poulson [Leroy N.]. He and Lance Corporal Phelps [John G.] quickly returned the signal, and we began preparing our ordnance. . . ."

As the Marine gunship neared the action, "I could see the mortars exploding on the beach," Pless said. "Then, the mortars quit and I saw a large group of people swarm the beach from a tree line about 100 meters from the beach." Captain Fairfield remembered, "As we passed directly over the top of the Viet Cong at an altitude of less than fifty feet, we saw four American prisoners lying on the sand." At this point, Staff Sergeant Allen "saw a Viet Cong appear on the flank with an automatic weapon. His fire struck everyone but me. I crawled next to the sand dune and tried to pass as dead. I could hear the Viet Cong move among us, removing our weapons." Pless remembered seeing "a Viet Cong standing over one man crushing his head with a rifle stock, and other people seemed to be in the process of butchering the others." Lance Corporal Phelps remembered "one of the men waved to us, and for his efforts got a rifle butt in the face. The V.C. were too close to the Americans to safely fire at them, but the V.C. were killing them anyway, so Captain Pless ordered Gunnery Sergeant Poulson to fire."

Poulson pointed his M60 machine gun and "fired close to the perimeter at the Viet Cong and they all took off in a group for a tree line near a village." Pless immediately "pulled the aircraft into a near wingover to the right and fired fourteen rockets into the mass of Viet Cong," Copilot Fairfield explained. "Our white phosphorus rockets scored direct hits on the V.C., but the smoke obscured the trees and the enemy." Lance Corporal Phelps said, "Captain Pless continued to fire into the smoke, displaying the most remarkable airmanship I have ever seen in my eighteen months in country as an air crewman. I couldn't believe what he was making the helo do. . . ." Staff Sergeant Allen, "looked up and saw a Huey gunship making rocket and gun runs on the Viet Cong, who were returning the fire as they attempted to flee into the brush along the beach. At this time, several Hueys were orbiting the area, but Capt Pless's aircraft was the only one to come to our aid." Pless made continued runs on the VC, some of whom were dressed in Khaki or green uniforms. "Several of the V.C. ran out of the smoke area, and I shot at point blank range, firing from so low that my own ordnance was spraying mud on the windscreen," he said.

With his ammunition almost exhausted Pless decided that something drastic had to be done. "I'm going to land," he transmitted to the crew. Fairfield recalled that "He flared the aircraft to a spot on the beach directly between the four Americans and the V.C. and continued firing from a hover. Then he kicked the aircraft around, pointed the nose seaward, and landed, utilizing the aircraft itself as a shield for the four Americans. Lance Corporal Phelps fired his M-60 at several V.C. who attempted to close with us from our left rear." Gunnery Sergeant Poulson, said, "[I] unplugged my head set, unhooked my gunner's belt and jumped out of the aircraft to get to the wounded. The first medevac [Staff Sergeant Allen] was fairly easy to get to the airplane because he could walk with my aid." Poulson then ran to the next man. "The second man was a large man, and was down in a gully or tide-line type of place. I was having a hard time with him. As I bent over . . . a round hit right

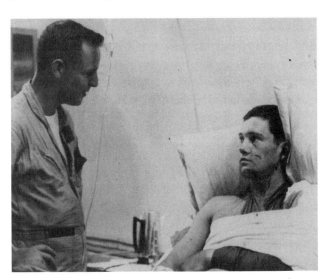

Major Stephen Pless visits SSgt. Lawrence H. Allen in the Chu Lai hospital. Pless rescued Allen from an overwhelming Viet Cong assault.

above me. I waved for help, because every time I tried to pick the man up, I would sink into the sand." During this time, enemy fire was "spraying sand around the helicopter and splashing in the water," Pless recalled.

Captain Fairfield unstrapped and climbed out the right rear door to assist with the casualty. "As I came out, I suddenly saw three V.C. with rifles less than ten feet from the rear of the helicopter. I removed the right door machine gun and killed them." The two men dragged the soldier back to the helicopter while Lance Corporal Phelps provided covering fire. Two soldiers still remained. "Captain Fairfield and I went out to get the third man. He was heavier than the second man, so Lance Corporal Phelps came out to help us," Poulson explained. Phelps turned over his gun to Staff Sergeant Allen, who was propped up against the copilot's seat. Allen cradled the gun in his injured arm, while pulling the trigger with his good hand. The three crewmen lifted the casualty, "Lance Corporal Phelps and Captain Fairfield were at each arm and I had the man by his legs." At the same time they were carrying the man, they were firing at the enemy with their revolvers. "We were about twenty feet from the aircraft, when a lone V.C. with a hand grenade of some kind came running from behind the plane," Phelps said. "I let go of the wounded man and drew my pistol, firing all six rounds into the V.C. He was only about ten or fifteen feet away, so I knew I was hitting him." They finally managed to carry the man to the helicopter and load him aboard.

One soldier remained. "I ran to the fourth man, but failed to detect heartbeat or pulse," Captain Fairfield observed. "I became certain he was dead. He had been badly mutilated and his throat was slashed. I looked for his dog tags but found none. I ran back to the helicopter and noticed that the small arms fire had intensified. I jumped in and told Captain Pless that the fourth man was dead." Poulson confirmed his diagnosis, having checked the corpse himself. Pless saw no reason to remain in the zone any longer and lifted off. "The only route of departure was over the water," he said. "I knew I was well over the maximum payload for the aircraft; I also thought we had been hit, but had no idea as to the extent of the damages." The aircraft was at least five hundred pounds over maximum take-off weight according to Captain Fairfield. "When I first lifted, it appeared that I had over-committed myself. After about a mile of straightaway and bouncing off the waves four times, I finally started picking up airspeed and built up my RPM back up. I jettisoned my rocket pods and told the crew to throw anything else over the side to lighten the load so we could get more airspeed." Once up to speed, Pless set a direct course for the nearest medical facility. During the flight to the 1st

Hospital Company at Chu Lai, Phelps and Poulson tried their best to keep the wounded men alive.

During the rescue an Army Huey, flown by WO Ronald L. Redeker made several strafing runs. "We gave them as much cover as our couple of door gunners could give," he said. "We emptied both guns before the ship left the beach." Gunnery Sergeant Poulson believed that, "Without their support, we would have been unable to complete our mission." Redeker was unequivocal in his admiration of the rescue. He stated that, "Without communications and without protection that he knew of, Captain Pless took a gunship down twenty-five meters from hostile fire and performed the most outstanding medevac I have ever witnessed.

On 26 August 1967, the commanding officer VMO-6, Lt. Col. Joseph A. Nelson, forwarded a letter through the chain of command to the Secretary of the Navy recommending Pless for the Medal of Honor. On the same date, he also recommended Captain Fairfield, Gunnery Sergeant Poulson and Lance Corporal Phelps for the Navy Cross. The awards were approved, making them the most highly decorated flight crew in history.

The photo was taken at the Da Nang press center during a new conference on 26 August 1967 following the dramatic flight that earned VMO-6's Capt. Stephen W. Pless (second from left) a Medal of Honor. Others of the crew from left to right are LCpl. John G. Phelps, Capt. Rupert E. Fairfield, and GySgt. Leroy N. Poulson.—*Department of Defense*

MEDAL OF HONOR AWARD CRITERIA

The Medal of Honor is awarded by the President in the name of Congress to members of the naval service, who distinguish themselves conspicuously by gallantry and intrepidity at the risk of his life above and beyond the call of duty

- while engaged in an action against an enemy of the United States;
- while engaged in military operations involving conflict with an opposing foreign force;
- while serving with friendly foreign forces engaged in an armed conflict against an opposing armed force in which the United States is not a belligerent party.

There must be no margin of doubt or possibility of error in awarding this honor. To justify the decoration, the individual's service must clearly be rendered conspicuous above their comrades by an act so outstanding that it clearly distinguishes their gallantry beyond the call of duty from lesser forms of bravery; and it must be the type of deed which if not done would not subject the individual to any justified criticism. The deed must be without detriment to the mission of the command or to the command to which attached.

Official photograph of Major Stephen W. Pless.

Captain Stephen W. Pless, United States Marine Corps, Medal of Honor citation: The President of the United States takes pleasure in presenting the MEDAL OF HONOR to MAJOR STEPHEN W. PLESS UNITED STATES MARINE CORPS For service as set forth in the following CITATION: For conspicuous gallantry and intrepidity at the risk of his life above and beyond the call of duty while serving as a helicopter gunship pilot attached to Marine Observation Squadron Six in action against enemy forces near Quang Ngai, Republic of Vietnam, on 19 August 1967. During as escort mission Major (then Captain) Pless monitored an emergency call that four American soldiers stranded on a nearby beach, were being overwhelmed by a large Viet Cong force. Major Pless flew to the scene and found 30 to 50 enemy soldiers in the open. Some of the enemy were bayoneting and beating the downed Americans. Major Pless displayed exceptional airmanship as he launched a devastating attack against the enemy force, killing or wounding many of the enemy and driving the remainder back into a tree line. His rocket and machine gun attacks were made at such low levels that the aircraft flew through the debris created by explosions from its rockets. Seeing one of the wounded soldiers gesture for assistance, he maneuvered his helicopter into a position between the wounded men and the enemy, providing a shield which permitted his crew to retrieve the wounded. During the rescue the enemy directed intense fire at the helicopter and rushed the aircraft again and again, closing to within a few feet before being beaten back. When the wounded men were aboard, Major Pless maneuvered the helicopter out to sea. Before it became safely airborne, the overloaded aircraft settled four times into the water. Displaying superb airmanship, he finally got the helicopter aloft. Major Pless' extraordinary heroism coupled with his outstanding flying skill prevented the annihilation of the tiny force. His courageous actions reflect great credit upon himself and uphold the highest traditions of the Marine Corps and the United States Naval Service.

Captain Rupert E. Fairfield Jr., United States Marine Corps, Navy Cross citation:

The President of the United States takes pleasure in presenting the Navy Cross to Rupert E. Fairfield, Jr., Captain, U.S. Marine Corps, for extraordinary heroism as a Copilot of a UH-1E Helicopter attached to Marine Observation Squadron SIX (VMO-6), Marine Aircraft Group SIXTEEN (MAG-16), First Marine Aircraft Wing, near Quang Ngai, Republic of Vietnam on 19 August 1967. While conducting a regularly assigned mission, Captain Fairfield's aircraft monitored a transmission giving the approximate location of four soldiers from a downed helicopter. The UH-1E diverted from its mission to this site and found the soldiers in the midst of an estimated thirty to forty Viet Cong, who were bayoneting and beating them with rifle butts. They began a series of low level attacks, and the Viet Cong scattered and withdrew to a tree line. Upon making a second low level pass, they observed one man raise his arm in a gesture for help. Immediately the helicopter landed on the beach between the men and the enemy, who were now firing furiously at the aircraft. Seeing that two men were unable to move a wounded man to the aircraft, Captain Fairfield exited the aircraft to go to their aid. As he stepped onto the ground, three Viet Cong appeared on top of a small sand dune, only ten feet from the aircraft. He quickly removed one of the machine guns from its mount and killed the enemy with a short burst of fire. Replacing the weapon, he drew his pistol and ran into the hail of fire to aid in carrying the wounded man to the aircraft. With all but one of the wounded men aboard, Captain Fairfield once again braved the enemy fire to race to the aid of the remaining soldier, only to find he had succumbed to his wounds. Returning to the aircraft, he leaped into the cockpit. The helicopter, being subjected to intense enemy fire and overloaded, was barely able to fly, as they made their way to a field hospital. By Captain Fairfield's bold initiative, indomitable fighting spirit and selfless devotion to duty, he was instrumental in saving the men's lives and thereby upheld the highest traditions of the Marine Corps and the United States Naval Service.

Gunnery Sergeant Leroy N. Poulson, United States Marine Corps, Navy Cross citation:

The President of the United States of America takes pleasure in presenting the Navy Cross to Gunnery Sergeant Leroy N. Poulson, United States Marine Corps, for extraordinary heroism while serving as a Gunner of a UH-1E Helicopter attached to Marine Observation Squadron SIX (VMO-6), Marine Aircraft Group SIXTEEN, First Marine Aircraft Wing, near Quang Ngai, Republic of Vietnam, on 19 August 1967. While conducting an assigned mission, Gunnery Sergeant Poulson's aircraft monitored an emergency transmission giving the approximate location of four Army personnel from a downed helicopter. The UH-1 E crew diverted to the site and arrived to find the soldiers in the midst of an estimated 30 to 40 Viet Cong who were bayoneting and beating them with rifle butts. They began a series of low level machine-gun and rocket attacks, and the Viet Cong scattered and withdrew to a tree line. They made another low pass over the Army personnel and observed one man raise his arm in a gesture for help. Unhesitatingly, the UH-1E landed on the beach between the wounded men and the Viet Cong, who were now firing furiously at the aircraft. Gunnery Sergeant Poulson leaped out of the aircraft and raced to the side of the nearest soldier. Unassisted, and through a hail of enemy fire, he moved the man to the helicopter. With complete disregard for his personal safety and in the midst of heavy enemy fire, he ran to the second man, and because of his weight, was unable to move him. At this time the copilot joined him, and the two of them managed to get the man safely aboard the aircraft. The Viet Cong began to appear all around the aircraft as he made another attempt to rescue the third man. Because of the man's size, it took three crew members to move him. Upon placing the wounded man in the helicopter, Gunnery Sergeant Poulson made another attempt to rescue the fourth man. Upon reaching his side, under a heavy volume of fire, he discovered the man had succumbed to his wounds, and returned to the aircraft. As the aircraft lifted, he administered first aid to the wounded until they reached a medical facility. By his daring initiative, valiant fighting spirit and selfless devotion to duty in the face of insurmountable odds, Gunnery Sergeant Poulson was responsible for saving the lives of the Army personnel and thereby upheld the highest traditions of the Marine Corps and the United States Naval Service.

Lance Corporal John G. Phelps, United States Marine Corps, Navy Cross citation:

The President of the United States of America takes pleasure in presenting the Navy Cross to Lance Corporal John G. Phelps, United States Marine Corps, for extraordinary heroism as a Crew Chief of a UH-1E Helicopter attached to Marine Observation Squadron SIX (VMO-6), Marine Aircraft Group SIXTEEN, First Marine Aircraft Wing, near Quang Ngai, Republic of Vietnam, on 19 August 1967. While conducting a regularly assigned mission, Lance Corporal Phelps' aircraft monitored a transmission giving the approximate location of four soldiers from a downed Army helicopter. The UH-1E diverted to the site and arrived to find the Army personnel in the midst of an estimated thirty to forty frenzied Viet Cong, who were bayoneting and beating them with rifle butts. As the UH-IE began a series of low level attacks, the Viet Cong scattered and withdrew to a tree line, firing frantically at the helicopter. Making another low level pass, they observed one soldier raise his hand in a gesture for help. Unhesitatingly, the UH-IE landed on the beach between the wounded men and the Viet Cong, who were now firing furiously at the aircraft. As the aircraft touched down, Lance Corporal Phelps laid down a heavy volume of fire to cover the gunner, who had leaped from the aircraft and raced to the wounded soldiers. When the gunner was unable to carry the man, because of his weight, Lance Corporal Phelps left his machine gun to help move the man. Observing the Viet Cong swarm around the helicopter, he ran back to his gun to provide protective fire, cutting down the enemy advance. Again observing problems being encountered in moving the third man, he handed his machine gun to one still conscious soldier, drew his pistol and raced to their aid. As the men moved with the wounded man, a lone Viet Cong, armed with a grenade, appeared from behind the UH-IE. Unhesitatingly, he released the wounded man, drew his pistol, and shot the Viet Cong. Once inside the helicopter, as it lifted for flight, Lance Corporal Phelps administered first aid to the wounded men until they reached a hospital. By his courageous actions, bold initiative, and unswerving devotion to duty, Lance Corporal Phelps was instrumental in saving the soldiers' lives. His great personal valor reflected great credit upon himself and the Marine Corps and enhanced the finest traditions of the United States Naval Service.

CHAPTER TEN

SUPER GAGGLE

At first light on 21 January 1968 a UH-34D resupply/medevac helicopter approached Hill 881 South near the Khe Sanh Combat Base (KSCB) to evacuate several wounded Marines. Captain William H. "Bill" Dabney, India Company commander, recalled, "We off-loaded the ammunition and immediately began loading wounded aboard. The bird had been in the zone two or three minutes when a 120mm mortar round impacted within a few feet of it. Our senior Doc [Corpsman] and two of our previously wounded Marines were killed in action. About a dozen others, including the helicopter crew were wounded. The UH-34 remained on the hill throughout the siege of Khe Sanh. The wreckage coined a phrase by air crews . . . when one inbound pilot asked how he was going to identify the landing zone when he got there. The pilot of the accompanying helo responded, 'Just look for the downed helicopter. India Company always marks its zones that way!'" Lance Corporal Walt Whitesides, a member of the Tactical Air Control Party (TACP), said, "It became apparent that the landing zone on the top of the hill was a registered target and that alternate landing zones would have to be established." Several more helicopters were shot down or damaged by NVA antiaircraft gunners who ringed the Marine hilltop positions around the base. The losses could not be sustained; something had to be done or the garrisons on the hills would have to be withdrawn, which would place the main combat base at risk.

HILL POSITIONS

Hill 881 South (881S), located 7 kilometers west-northwest of the Khe Sanh Combat Base, was one of three company sized hilltop positions—the others being Hill 861 and 861A, three kilometers east of 881S—that guarded the western approach to the combat base. The hills were garrisoned by Marines to prevent the North Vietnamese from interdicting the critical airfield. In

late December 1967, India and Mike Companies, 3rd Battalion, 26th Marine
Regiment, were helilifted to Hill 881S from which patrols were sent out to
scour the area for signs of NVA activity. Second Battalion, 26th Marines, was
positioned on Hill 558, just over a kilometer east of Hill 861, to prevent in-
trusion from the north. Echo Company, 2nd Battalion, defended 861A, five
hundred meters northeast of 861. A reinforced platoon from the regiment's
1st Battalion guarded the radio relay station on Hill 950, a tiny outpost which
was only fifty feet wide and a hundred feet long, just enough room for, "a
small landing zone, a few bunkers, and the radio relay tower," according to
John Prados and Ray Stubbe in *Valley of Decision, The Siege of Khe Sanh.*

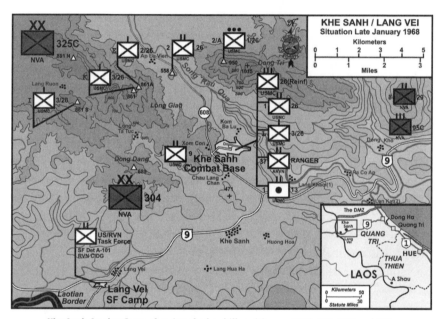

Khe Sanh Combat Base, showing the key hill positions—881S, 861, 558 and 950.

Lieutenant Colonel James B. Wilkinson, commanding officer of the 1st
Battalion, remembered a meeting in the fall of 1967 with the regimental
commander, Colonel David Lownds, to discuss whether the 881S and 861
should be evacuated " . . . the two companies could be used elsewhere in the
perimeter," he recalled. Hill 950 was never considered for abandonment
because of its importance for maintaining the regiment's communications.
However, Lieutenant Colonel Wilkinson was very concerned about its defense: "The enemy had people up on 1015 [a higher part of the same hill

complex] with a .50 caliber that could hit 950 with impunity. Additionally, the hill could not be resupplied unless the weather was really good . . . it was a pretty precarious landing zone. I was particularly concerned about water because it was simply not available there." In one nine-day period for example, clouds cloaked the hill preventing resupply. The platoon was down to less than two gallons of water before a patrol was authorized to find a water source. "They surprised a rather lethargic NVA unit and just kicked hell out of them!" Lieutenant Colonel Wilkinson exclaimed, "And brought back water . . . it sure lifted their spirits!"

Wilkinson believed that the hill positions were critical for the overall defense of Khe Sanh. "I felt that if we did receive an attack, the NVA could not take the base without controlling the hills. I also felt that the Marines

Right: Lieutenant Colonel James B. Wilkinson, commanding officer, 1st Battalion, 26th Marines, at Khe Sanh. *Left:* Colonel David Lownds, commanding officer 26th Marines, during the siege of Khe Sanh. For his leadership, Lownds was awarded the Navy Cross.

on the hills could provide an early warning if the NVA tried to attack from that direction." He felt there would be severe political ramifications if the hills were abandoned. "If you gave so many lives to take those hills back in the spring, why are you now giving them up now? If they were important then, why aren't they important now? In the end, we decided that we should not consider politics . . . but only consider the immediate situation."

On 20 January, Captain Dabney's company launched a reconnaissance-in-force toward Hill 881 North, approximately four kilometers north of their position. The company ran into a battalion-sized NVA force from the 6th Battalion, 95C Regiment, and suffered four men killed and thirty wounded in the day-long battle, while over a hundred North Vietnamese were left on the battlefield. Many of Dabney's wounded required immediate evacuation. "As the medevac aircraft [from HMM-262 and flown by Capt. Robert Ropelewski] approached the zone, it was hit by a burst from an anti-aircraft weapon and immediately caught fire," Captain Dabney recalled. "The pilot, apparently realizing the consequence of crash-landing a burning aircraft in a landing zone where several wounded men were staged, sheared off into a gully and made a controlled crash about 200 meters west of the zone." The HMM-262 command chronology stated, " . . . Captain Ropelewski took a .50 caliber hit through the main fuel line. He crash landed the burning CH-46 in a nearby zone. Two crew members were hurt seriously and the aircraft sustained strike [total loss] damage."

Following the battles of April and May 1967 for the Khe Sanh area, shell-scared Hill 881 South, shown here in an aerial view, became a combat outpost for two companies of the 26th Marine Regiment.

HMM-262, known as the Flying Tigers, built a close relationship with not only India Company, but also the other Marines garrisoning the hills. Based at Quang Tri, its mission was to provide four CH-46 aircraft for re-supply and medevac to the outposts on hills 881S, 861, 861A, 558 and 950, as well as the Khe Sanh airfield. The squadron also provided two CH-46 aircraft at night for emergency medevac and resupply missions. The squadron's command chronology noted, "Weather was a primary consideration during this period. Early in the evening the fog would roll in and the visibility and ceiling would remain zero until late the following morning. This monsoon weather hampered flight operations extensively. Squadron aircraft resupplied many days without the cover of fixed wing aircraft resulting in many hit incidents from small arms, .50-caliber and mortar fire. The majority of hit incidents were recorded while working in the vicinity of Hill 881. Thirteen aircraft sustained extensive damage on the ground at Khe Sanh during the many rocket, artillery and mortar attacks.

Just before midnight on 20 January, the North Vietnamese launched a battalion assault on Hill 861, held by Kilo Company, 3rd Battalion, 26th Marines. Sergeant Mike Stahl remembered saying to a friend, "There isn't a North Vietnamese within a hundred miles of here. Just as I said that, the first RPG slammed into the hill." The NVA quickly penetrated the perimeter barbed wire and overran several Marine positions. An RPG seriously wounded the company commander, Capt. Norman Jasper, and several members of the command group, including 1st Sgt. Bernard

Marine helicopter squadron HMM-262 squadron patch. The squadron was known as the Flying Tigers.

G. Goddard who received a serious neck wound. "The First Sergeant was holding the ends of his severed carotid artery together to keep from bleeding to death," Sergeant Stahl recalled. Goddard made his way out of the damaged bunker and collapsed against an outside wall. A passing Corpsman stopped the blood flow with a medical scissors and told the badly wounded senior NCO to hold it tight if he wanted to live. Goddard survived and was evacuated the next morning. The battle ended when Marines from the opposite side of the perimeter counterattacked and drove the NVA from the heights.

At 0530 on 21 January the NVA struck the main base with a heavy barrage of rocket, mortar and artillery fire from the 45th Artillery Regiment. According to historian John Prados, "The bombardment marked the first NVA use of the newly deployed long-barreled D74 model 122mm gun." Several rounds hit the ammunition dump, which exploded with a terrific blast, throwing unexploded ordnance high into the air. Corporal Kreig Lofton, a helicopter crew chief, on overnight duty to provide emergency support recalled, "We started receiving incoming rounds . . . and the ammo dump was hit. There was a massive explosion and the concussion almost knocked the air out of you." The resulting fire released a large stockpile of tear gas that wafted through the adjacent defensive positions, sending Marines scrambling for their gas masks. The barrage also cratered the runway and destroyed two

HMM-262 aircraft in the revetments. "We had just landed and were walking across the airstrip when enemy rockets and mortar rounds started falling all around us," Capt. Steve Dickey said. "We all managed to squeeze into a drainage pipe just along the strip. We stayed for the next 45 minutes while the enemy fired rounds into the zone."

During the incoming barrage, the word was passed for the duty helicopter to launch. "We were still receiving sporadic artillery and mortars," Corporal Lofton recalled. "We assembled the air crew and made a mad dash completely across the combat base, which was probably three football fields wide, running from hole to hole, trying to dodge the incoming. All the hills were calling for medevacs as we launched. I remember looking at 861, seeing bodies in the wires, large numbers of NVA dead, Marine dead as well. The impact from the NVA artillery and rockets was so great on that one location that the top of the hill was completely obscured by dust and debris. Tracers were flying everywhere. We circled for what seemed like an eternity until finally it died down and we went in, picked up the wounded and whatever dead they could throw on, and we pulled out of there."

Normally several helicopters laagered at the base to respond to emergency medevacs and to resupply ammunition. In January and February, Maj. Walter H. Shauer, the commander of HMM-362, a UH-34 squadron, assigned crews to stay for three or four days. "During the siege there was of course no aircraft maintenance support, only fuel," he said. "The [aircraft] were parked in Khe Sanh's revetments, while the crews bunkered underground in the 26th Marines CP." The revetments were ten-foot high metal containers filled with dirt, with the open end facing the tarmac. They were

situated on the north side of the runway, across from the regimental command post, where the flight crews stayed at night. In order to man their aircraft, the crews had to cross the runway, which was totally devoid of cover.

On 23 January, HMM-262 lost a third CH-46. The squadron's January command chronology stated, "Attempting to resupply Hill 950, Major [Anton E.] Therriault crashed near the landing zone and the aircraft was destroyed. No casualties occurred." Private First Class Robert Harrison said the day-to-day routine on Hill 950 consisted of "digging deeper trenches, laying

Marine helicopter squadron HMM-362, known as the Ugly Angels was the first operational squadron deployed in Vietnam.

concertina wire and playing cards." This all changed when a resupply helicopter came in. "The NVA would open up with heavy-caliber machine gun and mortar fire. We would usually be able to call in some close air support to suppress the enemy fire." According to the squadron's February command chronology, from the end of January to mid-February, "Twelve HMM-262 aircraft received battle damage while supporting the hill positions. It ranged from minor small arms damage to strike [total loss] damage. Several more sustained extensive damage on the ground during the many rocket, artillery and mortar attacks. Eight aircraft received serious damage while sitting in the revetments and had to be externalled [lifted out] from the field."

Sergeant Patrick Murgallis was a crewman aboard a CH-53, tail number YH-21 from Marine Heavy Helicopter Squadron 463 (HMH-463), during a resupply mission to Khe Sanh. "We did a typical cork screw into the base, dropped our cargo and picked up about 8 or 10 Marines and flew straight down the valley. I was on my M-60 pointing it down when we started taking heavy fire from all over the valley." Sergeant Murgallis instantly returned fire and, "as I looked around every Marine on board was firing their M-16s out of every opening. The NVA must have thought we were some kind of gunship! Little did they know these guys were on their way home and weren't planning on staying." The aircraft was hit several times, including some through the rotor blades. The pilot was able to nurse the plane to Dong Ha, where it remained overnight. Murgallis remarked that new blades were installed but, "they were probably cannibalized from some other bird."

On 22 February Sergeant Murgallis was aboard the repaired YH-21 when it came under heavy artillery fire during a resupply/medevac run to Khe Sanh. Both pilots (Capt. J. T. Riley and 1st Lt. C. E. Smith) were killed and all three crewmen were wounded. "Every time we got close to settling down the NVA gunners zeroed in on us and we lifted off," Sergeant Murgallis recalled. "All I can see in incoming all around us . . . then a big flash and explosion at the back of the plane . . . we took a hit in the tail." Sergeant Murgallis was knocked unconscious, "I really thought I was dead," he said when he came to. "I looked back at the helicopter and saw the pilots with most of their heads crushed . . . I'm sure I was in shock by then." Shrapnel from the explosion left Sergeant Murgallis with minor wounds in the head and leg.

A week later, HMM-262 suffered a major loss when one of its aircraft was shot down on the way to Khe Sanh. All twenty-three occupants were killed. Corporal Kellan Kyllo crew chief aboard an accompanying helicopter recalled, "My aircraft had just crossed over a ridge at tree top level that was a thick blanket of fog. When the chase plane crossed the ridge at almost the same spot, the aircraft radioed that they had taken automatic weapons fire. There were no further communications. The aircraft then banked to the right and started to descend towards the valley at a high rate of speed. There was a yellow-white fire in the aft section of the cabin that could be seen through the cabin portholes. The fire moved towards the front of the cabin and consumed it. The aircraft hit the valley floor at full speed." The squadron commander, Lt. Col. Melvin J. Steinberg, explained, "It was our practice to take a direct route to Khe Sanh but the NVA spotted this route and set up automatic weapons in strategic locations to direct large volumes of fire on our aircraft. We altered our flight plan . . . but the NVA spotted this and again set up automatic weapons to shoot at our aircraft."

Lieutenant Colonel Richard E. Romine, commanding HMM-165, remarked about the dangerous flight path. "If we stayed high and made a steep approach to Khe Sanh we were not vulnerable to the surrounding enemy anti-aircraft guns (mostly 12.7mm), which were predominantly to the west. It took only one time to realize when you'd made a bad approach and flown over the wrong position. The clatter of rounds got your attention. The guns were impossible to spot form the air. I later observed why. The ingenious little bastards had most of their anti-aircraft guns mounted on dollies or wheels at the entrances of small caves high on the hillsides. They stuck the noses of the guns outside just long enough to take potshots at us and then pulled them back into concealment before we could see where the fire was coming from." Major John A. Chancey recalled, "The aircrews of HMM-364 arose each morning before daylight, flew two to five trips into Khe Sanh and its outposts, and returned after dark. Much of this was maximum weight with external loads . . . rocking the aircraft 15 degrees from side to side and pitching the nose up and down 10 to 20 degrees . . . it was a constant fight to combat vertigo."

Chancey was awarded two Distinguished Flying Crosses "for heroism and extraordinary achievement in aerial flight.

Major John A. Chancey, United States
Marine Corps, Distinguished Flying Cross citations:

On 28 March 1968, Major CHANCEY launched as Aircraft Commander of the third aircraft in a flight of ten CH-46 helicopters assigned to resupply the Marine outpost on Hill 881 near Khe Sanh. When he learned that one of the aircraft was forced to make an emergency landing in enemy controlled terrain due to battle damage, Major CHANCEY volunteered to extract the downed crew which was heavily engaged with North Vietnamese soldiers. In an attempt to draw hostile fire from the Marines, he landed 100 meters from the damaged aircraft and directed machine gun fire against the enemy positions. Ignoring the heavy volume of hostile small arms and automatic weapons fire, he lifted from the area and maneuvered his helicopter to within twenty-five meters of the beleaguered crew. Despite the increased intensity of enemy fire that damaged his aircraft and wounded his aerial gunner, he steadfastly held his position on the ground until he was aware that he continuing heavy volume of North Vietnamese fire would prevent the downed crew from embarking. Lifting out of the hazardous zone, he orbited the area and directed armed helicopter attacks against the enemy emplacements. Realizing the urgency of extracting the Marines before their position was over- run, he courageously commenced a third approach into the fire-swept zone and landed close to the disabled aircraft, fearlessly remaining on the ground until the crew embarked. He then expeditiously departed the area for the medical facility at Dong Ha.

On 8 April 1968, Major Chancey launched as Division Leader of a flight of four CH-46 transport helicopters assigned to resupply a Marine outpost on Hill 881 South near the Khe Sanh Combat Base. Due to poor visibility resulting from deteriorating weather conditions, he maneuvered his aircraft with its external load of approximately two tons above the cloud cover and orbited the drop area until fixed wing aircraft had completed their air strikes. Undaunted by the heavy volume of hostile mortar, rocket and automatic weapons fire as he neared the landing zone, he resolutely continued his approach and led his division into the hazardous area to successfully deliver the vital supplies. After expeditiously departing the area and rendezvousing with the flight over Khe Sanh, Major Chancey was diverted to an emergency medical evacuation mission at Hill 689 southwest of the combat base. While preparing to embark the last of the Marine casualties, his CH-46 came under a heavy enemy mortar attack. Ignoring the hostile rounds impacting near his aircraft, Major Chancey steadfastly held his helicopter on the ground until the last casualty was aboard. Despite sustaining severe damage to his CH-46 from a mortar round that impacted within five feet of his aircraft, wounding two members of his crew, he displayed exceptional skill in maneuvering the helicopter out of the fire-swept area. Unable to maintain effective control of the CH-46 after flying a short distance, he skillfully executed a single engine landing on a ridge. Coordinating the orderly evacuation of all personnel from the helicopter, he assisted in carrying the casualties to another aircraft which had landed nearby.

A few minutes past 0300 on 5 February, Capt. Earle G. Breeding reported his company was under attack on Hill 861A by an estimated two hundred North Vietnamese infantrymen. "They're coming through the wire," he yelled. Sappers blew holes in the Marine protective wire, allowing the following infantry to penetrate the position. They quickly overran one platoon's position but were stopped cold by small arms fire, artillery and air support before they could take the entire hill. A B-52 strike was diverted to support the hill. "As I understand it," Captain Breeding recalled, "they ran closer than they had ever intentionally run in on friendly troops . . . all of a sudden the whole hill started shaking . . . and I thought, 'Oh, my Lord, they've tunneled underneath us.' It just rattled the hill, unbelievable." The company's surviving infantrymen launched a bold counterattack that killed many of the assailants and forced the remainder to flee. The NVA attacked a second time but it was quickly repulsed. Echo Company lost seven dead and twenty-four wounded, while the enemy left over a hundred bodies on the slope of the hill and inside the perimeter. "There were bodies everywhere," Pfc. Michael DeLaney recalled.

CH-46 with an external load approaching Hill 861. Note the lone machine gunner standing in the foreground, which was not conducive to long life.— *Dennis Manion*

At dawn, fog completely blanketed the hill. "This forced upon me the biggest decision of my life," LCpl. William Maves said. "If Da Nang sent the fleet of medevacs I had requested for 35 wounded and they couldn't get through the fog, it would be hours before they could come back again after refueling. I looked at the men lying there and told Da Nang to send the birds." Maves stood in the middle of the landing zone, "listening to the rotors circling overhead. One pilot said he would circle lower and lower until I could get a visual. I seemed like forever until I finally saw the bottom of that bird go over in the fog. I shot the red star cluster up at him, and down he came through the fog, onto the landing zone. The rest was easy. He left straight up and another bird was circling, ready to drop down in the spot where the first one came out."

On another occasion, Captain Breeding guided a night helicopter med-evac. "In total darkness, absolute total darkness, I brought one in myself. I did it by talking to him on the radio. I could hear him coming. Eventually I said, 'You're right on top of me. Don't go forward and don't go sideways. Come on down.' And I walked around with my hand in the air and I finally felt a tire. I talked to him. I said, 'You're five feet off the ground, four, three, two . . . You're one foot off the ground.' Then we got the wounded man on there, and I climbed upside the helicopter and talked to the pilot. I told him, 'When you take off, make sure you go straight up and not forward, 'cause you got a tree ten feet in front of you.' At the time I thought that was just real simple. Since then I found out that when you don't have a horizon reference it's difficult to know whether you're moving forward or not."

Navy Hospital Corpsman David "Doc" Johnson was assigned to help with the evacuation of wounded. "You'd bring somebody into Charlie Med [C Company, 3rd Medical Battalion], and you'd fix them up the best you could. Often times you had a doctor there," Doc Johnson recalled. "You might give a person come minor surgery, sew him back together, throw him on a stretcher, drag him up a ramp to a little area where we had sandbags, and wait for a helicopter." HN1 Mike Hill said, "Charlie Med was a huge bunker, a massive structure that could take a hit. You'd hear rounds going off and sometimes you'd see dirt falling . . . but you didn't stop working. If we had casualties, we had to take care of them, and we had to make sure they didn't get hurt worse from the shelling." When word was received that a medevac helicopter was inbound, stretcher bearers took the casualties to a low sandbag wall and waited. "When it came in," he said, "you'd load them aboard and just hope he didn't get blown away by incoming artillery. Because all the time the chopper was down on the tarmac, you can figure that artillery would follow. They had been shooting at that place for some time . . . and they had it exact."

The North Vietnamese attacks marked the beginning of a seventy-seven day effort to hold the hills and keep them supplied with food, ammunition and water. There was no secure ground route to the hills and their small size precluded parachute drops; the only way the isolated outposts could be sustained was by helicopter. Initially a "direct support package" of two UH-1E gunships, two to four CH-46 and two H-34 transports were assigned to support them. HMM-262, call sign Chatterbox, had the primary responsibility to support Operation Scotland, the name for Khe Sanh operation.

A typical mission consisted of one or two helicopter transports, escorted by two gunships for suppression of anti-aircraft fire, responded to a request from the hills for resupply or medevac. Unfortunately, according to Colonel Franklin E. Wilson, MAG-36 commander, "When the dense monsoon clouds rolled into the valley, the mountain tops were the first to become submerged and, as the overcast lifted, the last to reappear. During these periods the North Vietnamese took advantage of the reduced visibility and emplaced heavy automatic weapons along the neighboring peaks and waited for the ceiling to lift, which invariably heralded the arrival of helicopters. As a result, the UH-1Es, UH-34s, and CH-46s were pelted with a hail of enemy bullets during each mission."

On 25 January, Lt. Col. Melvin J. Steinberg, Commanding Officer HMM-262 was on a medevac mission to 881S. He remarked to his crew chief, LCpl. Ernesto "Gooie" Gomez that, "We're going to get bloodied on this one." Gomez recalled that, "On the way there I listened on the radios for any information that would help me complete my mission. I was told that two Marines would load the wounded. There was a lot of action on the hill. Tracers coming in and going out. . . . There were shells hitting the zone we were going to land in. The smell of powder hurt your lungs. Through the smoke I saw two men running towards my bird with the wounded Marine between them. . . . He had bandages over his eyes. I could see blood on the bandages. . . . He couldn't see. We were taking .50 caliber fire. They started shooting RPGs and mortars. They were trying to get the bird, and they were using the wounded Marine as bait. The small arms fire was very, very accurate." Lieutenant Colonel Steinberg was concerned by the length of time it was taking and asked, "What's going on Gomez?" The crew chief responded, "I have to disconnect, I have to get him.

Lance Corporal Gomez ran out of the helicopter and rushed across the fire swept ground to the side of the wounded Marine, who had been hit again. Gomez lifted the man to his shoulder and ran back toward the helicopter. "I told him, 'We're almost there, I'm gonna get you to the bird.'" The two made it to the aircraft, which had taken several hits. "Something big has hit us, Gomez," Steinberg exclaimed. "I'm going to try to make it to Khe Sanh. We've got to get out of here." The next day, Lance Corporal Gomez discovered that two zippers of his flight suit and part of the heel of his boot had been shot away.

Lance Corporal Ernesto Gomez , United States
Marine Corps, Navy Cross citation:
The President of the United States of America takes pleasure in presenting the Navy Cross to Lance Corporal Ernesto Gomez, United States Marine Corps, for extraordinary heroism while serving with Marine Medium Helicopter Squadron Two Hundred Sixty-Two (HMM-262), Marine Aircraft Group Sixteen, First Marine Aircraft Wing, in connection with operations against the enemy in the Republic of Vietnam. On 25 January 1968, Corporal Gomez was the Crew Chief aboard a CH-46 transport helicopter assigned an emergency medical evacuation mission on Hill 881 near the Khe Sanh Combat Base. The pilot preceded to the designated area and landed in the zone as two Marines began leading a casualty, whose head and eyes were covered with bandages, toward the helicopter. When the entire landing zone was subjected to intense enemy fire, the two men were forced to drop to the ground. Observing the blindfolded casualty attempting to reach the aircraft unassisted, Corporal Gomez unhesitatingly left the helicopter and rushed across 25 meters of fire-swept terrain to the side of the injured man. Quickly pulling the Marine to the ground, he selflessly used his own body to shield his comrade from the hostile fire impacting around them, and as the enemy fire continued, he took cover with the casualty in a nearby rocket crater. Corporal Gomez remained in this exposed area until another crew member rushed to his assistance. Then the two Marines, protecting their wounded comrade from further injury, carried him to the helicopter. The Pilot was quickly informed that the injured Marine was aboard, and the aircraft lifted from the hazardous area for the medical facility at Khe Sanh. Corporal Gomez's heroic

actions were instrumental in saving his companion's life and inspired all who observed him. By his courage, selfless concern for the safety of his fellow Marine, and unswerving devotion to duty at great personal risk, he upheld the highest traditions of the Marine Corps and the United States Naval Service.

First Lieutenant John Thomas Esslinger pointed out that, "We only had three places [landing zones] on the hill. One was in the saddle and two were up on the sort of gradual nose, east of India's position where we could land a helicopter." They were quickly registered by the North Vietnamese, who managed to destroy five helicopters in the zones. "They sort of decorated our landing area," Esslinger said. "It became obvious that the enemy had at least one mortar zeroed in on each of those three zones. As soon as they saw a helicopter approach and when they figured out which zone it was going to land in, they started pumping out rounds." The company tried to confuse the NVA gunners. "We would have the helicopter feint into one landing zone and then land in another . . . but they still only had thirty or forty seconds before the mortars would land," Esslinger explained. "We had a trench going out to the landing zone that we'd put the medevac in with a couple of guys. As soon as the helicopter got close to the ground, the guys would throw the medevac on board, jump back into the trench, and the helicopter would get the hell out of there."

First Lieutenant John Thomas Esslinger,
United States Marine Corps, Bronze Star citation:
For heroic achievement in connection with combat operations against the enemy in the Republic of Vietnam while serving as Executive Officer of Company M, Third Battalion, Twenty-Sixth Marines, Third Marine Division. On 15 February 1968, while occupying a defensive position on Hill 881 South near the Khe Sanh Combat Base, Company M came under intense North Vietnamese mortar and automatic weapons fire and sustained several casualties, including the commanding officer. Without hesitation, First Lieutenant ESSLINGER assumed command of the company and, after requesting a medical evacuation helicopter, rushed into the fire-swept area and directed the movement of the casualties to covered positions. Then, standing fully exposed to a heavy barrage of mortar and .50 caliber machine gun fire, he skillfully directed the medical

evacuation helicopter into the landing zone. Although sustaining painful fragmentation wounds in both legs, First Lieutenant ESSLINGER single-handedly moved three wounded Marines to the helicopter and resolutely remained in the hazardous landing zone until the evacuation was completed. His heroic actions inspired all who observed him and were instrumental in saving the lives of several Marines. First Lieutenant ESSLINGER's courage, bold initiative and selfless devotion to duty at great personal risk were in keeping with the highest traditions of the Marine Corps and of the United States Naval Service.

The hill's aerial lifeline depended on a small team of men from the helicopter support team (HST) and the tactical air control party (TACP). Together they formed backbone for directing and controlling aviation assets, both fixed and rotor wing. HST member Pfc. Michael Lee described his job as "directing the resupply and medevac birds to their respective landing zones. I would have to stand in the open to direct the aircraft." Captain Dabney praised their bravery. "Daily when the weather allowed and often several times a day, those [HST] Marines stood in the open in those zones under the helicopters and performed tasks without which we grunts and the helo crewmen could not have survived," he said. "The anti-aircraft rounds were always whipping by and the mortar rounds were often, 'on the way' and they knew it, yet they did their duty 'til the bird was gone then ran like hell and dove into the nearest hole."

Captain Dabney recalled an incident involving an HST member and a helo pickup of cargo nets. "Lance Corporal David P. Assum was crouching on the load, jumped up, slapped the sling-loop in the hook and gave the crew chief a thumbs up." Assum tried to jump from the load but his foot got tangled up in the net. "I hung on the best I could," he said emphatically, "and tried to signal the crew chief that the chopper had more than the load of nets. The chopper made a circle and dropped me and the nets back at the pickup point. It was so intense hanging upside down and watching 'Charlie' [NVA] take pot shots at me! Later that day Captain Dabney told me I earned jump [parachute] wings for that adventure."

Despite the danger, Marines continued to volunteer for the dangerous assignment. Corporals Terry L. Smith (TACP) and Robert J. Arrotta reached Hill 881S in late January after volunteering to replace wounded men. Corporal Arrotta was nicknamed "the mightiest corporal in the world" in recognition for the firepower he brought to bear on the NVA while serving as the India Company Forward Air Controller (FAC). He was awarded the Bronze Star for " . . . fearlessly exposing himself to enemy fire in order to direct Marine tactical air strikes on hostile positions and coordinate vitally needed helicopter resupply and medical evacuation missions. Corporal Smith received a Silver Star. "On 20 February 1968, on Hill 881S near Khe Sanh, Corporal Smith observed a Marine helicopter landing in a zone on which he knew North Vietnamese Army gunners had registered heavy mortars. He realized that the aircraft would almost certainly be destroyed if it remained in the landing zone, and attempted unsuccessfully to contact the pilot by radio. Aware that the enemy rounds were probably already on the way, he restrained a Marine junior to him from going out on to the zone, and leaving the safety of his bunker ran across the open ground signaling manually to the helicopter crew to take off immediately. As the helicopter took off and before Corporal Smith could reach cover, he was fatally wounded by mortar fragments, gallantly sacrificing his life so that the crew might live."

The loss of so many men and helicopters required a different approach if the hills were to be held. In mid-February Lt. Col. William J. White, commanding officer VMO-6, met with the 1st Marine Aircraft Wing staff to work out a plan. The resulting effort was dubbed Super Gaggle: "Eight to twelve CH-46 helicopters, a dozen A-4 Skyhawk fighter bombers, four UH-1E gunships, a Marine KC-130 refueler, and a TA-4F with a TAC (A) in the backseat to orchestrate the entire affair." (*U.S. Marines in Vietnam, The Defining Year 1968*) Lieutenant Colonel Richard E. Carey described the mechanics of the Super Gaggle. "Success of the effort was predicated on timing, coordination, and often times luck. The operation generally consisted as follows: (1) Softening up known enemy positions by four A-4s, generally armed with napalm and bombs; (2) Two A-4s armed with CS (tear gas) tanks saturate enemy anti-aircraft and automatic weapons positions; (3) 30–40 seconds prior to final run in by the helos two A-4s lay a smoke screen along selected avenues of approach . . . (4) while the helos make final run into the target, four A-4s with bombs, rockets, and 20mm guns provide close-in fire suppression."

The February HMM-262 command chronology stated, "The strike system consisted of an extensive area preparation with fixed wing aircraft preceded with CS gas and followed by smoke to conceal the flight of eight CH-46 helicopters going into the same zone in rapid succession. Fixed wing cover continued during approach and retirement of the transport helicopters.

Weather, again was the main consideration in attempting a strike of this nature. In some cases the transport helicopters were required to take . . . instrument flight rules (IFR) in order to reach their destination. The destination weather had to be visual flight rules (VFR) with ceilings high enough to work fixed wind aircraft."

The first Super Gaggle mission was flown on 24 February. Lieutenant Esslinger recalled, "They didn't tell us about this [Super Gaggle]. All we knew was one day we were told to stand by for something unusual. Suddenly two A-4 jets came screaming up each side of the hill!" The operation went as planned. Only one helicopter was hit, while eight CH-46s successfully dropped off a 3,000-pound external load. "Using the 'Super Gaggle' technique, groups of helicopters could resupply the hills four times per day with little danger of losses. Indeed, only two CH-46s fell to enemy fire during "Super Gaggle" missions, and in both cases, the Hueys picked up the crews immediately. During the month of March, the helicopters . . . delivered about 80,000 pounds of cargo per day to the hill outposts." (*U.S. Marines in Vietnam, The Defining Year 1968*) Captain Dabney explained, "You could get in 10 helicopter loads on the hill in one minute and get the birds the hell out of there and into smoke where the NVA couldn't see to shoot . . . it was a massive, complex, well rehearsed, gutsy and magnificent performance. . . . "

Free Lance Photographer David Powell had a bird's eye view of a Super Gaggle:

> The first thing I saw, which I had absolutely no idea what it was, was this huge trail of what looked to me like white phosphorus exploding across the sky in a long tight plume. The plume started to

Two CH-46 helicopters approaching Hill 861 through the smoke screen that had just been laid down by an A-4 fighter bomber. —*Dennis Manion*

descend like a curtain with chunks of it falling faster than the rest of it. I never even saw the jet that created this huge atmospheric effect. So it seemed like it appeared out of nowhere. Then I saw and heard, once again to my complete surprise, Huey gunships whipping around the hill shooting the place up. I remember very clearly thinking that it was not a good idea for those gunships to be flying that low over such hostile terrain. I remember after all the time I spent on 881S the only aircraft I had ever seen were the jets during the CAS missions. Well I am taking photos like mad amidst all of this sound and fury when here comes this flight of green choppers diving in and roaring away just as fast as they can. And now someone is telling me to get into the trench that was on the LZ. It was probably that incredibly brave Marine who stood totally upright with both his arms in the air guiding the choppers in. I took his picture. It was also like he was saying to the NVA here I am you little bastards do your worst.

The operation was much more orderly on paper than it actually was in the air however. Weather often created extremely hazardous flight conditions. The skies were overcast more often than not and the helicopters were not always able to use a visual approach. The helicopters flew on instruments to Khe Sanh and then let down through the overcast under control of the AN/TPQ-10 radar or on a self-devised instrument approach guiding on the Khe Sanh radar homing beacon. Once underneath they would pick up their fixed-wing escort. Major Chancey noted in his diary on 2 March, "Lousy weather . . . into inadvertent IFR. What a gaggle! But no mid-air (Don't know how we missed) . . . I had a badly swinging load (sheer terror) . . . what a way to earn a living!!" The next day it was worse. "Six planes to 881[S] today . . . worst weather in the drop zone yet encountered, all still ran the mission. 881[S] was IFR when we went in, and had to come through a hole South West of the hill, go below the ridge line and scoot up into the zone just over the ground and in the clouds the last 200-300 yards . . . unable to see the drop point and unable to see the A/C ahead for interval." Another pilot in the squadron agreed. "Sometimes to resupply the hills . . . we would actually slide over the side of the mountain, up through the fog, trying to get up to the top of the outposts. We would drop off the resupply, pick up the medevacs, and slide back down the side until we had visual flight again."

It often appeared that planes were everywhere . . . and it was well to be reminded of the adage, "Keep your eyes out of the cockpit; a mid-air collision could ruin your whole day." The lithe A-4s bore in on the flanks of the approach lanes blasting enemy gun positions and spewing protective smoke; CH-46s groped through the haze trying to find the landing zones; the hornet-like UH-1E gunships darted in from the rear in case someone was shot down; and the lone TA-4 circled overhead trying to keep his flock from running amuck. Corporal Thomas J. "TJ" Miller, a crew chief for HMM-364 remembered, "[We] had just pickled [dropping the external load] and I jumped up from the hell hole and looked out the side door to see an A-4 about 50 feet outside our rotor tips. The fixed wing had his gear down, flaps down, and speed brakes deployed. I yelled at the pilot, 'do not turn right.' The jet jock had a big smile on his face and gave me a thumbs up. I would have given a couple months flight pay to have a picture of that. Those guys were dead serious about supporting the Marines on the hills." Another crewman recalled "making spiraling IFR approaches into Khe Sanh so often with GCA talking us through the clouds it became routine, mundane, almost boring, couldn't see shit! Then came the day we broke out on the bottom just as an F-4 roared beneath our Huey. We got a little of that pendulum action, and I swear I could see the F-4 driver writing on his knee board!"

Marine Captain R. G. Lathrop flew several missions to Khe Sanh in an A-4 Skyhawk fighter bomber. "As we flew inland," he said, "the ground was battered beyond belief. There were overlapping bomb craters from the coast inland. There was almost nothing that had not been bombed. I couldn't believe that many bombs could have been dropped anywhere." As he approached the plateau, "The first thing that caught my eye was how small the Khe Sanh base was. It looked like a piece of tape, red and torn laid across a small ridge surrounded by taller mountains. There were wrecked aircraft on the mat and there were rounds impacting inside the perimeter." From his altitude, Lathrop could see the NVA trenches: " there were concentric rings

A McDonnell Douglas A-4E Skyhawk from VMA-223, as indicated by the tail code WP, is shown in flight. The Skyhawks were the backbone of Marine close air support during the Vietnam War.

of trenches, blown apart and separated from each other by almost interlocking bomb craters. The trenches went for as far as I could see to the north and west. A bombed out road ran past Khe Sanh to the west . . . there were air strikes being conducted by more than one air controller and the impact of bombs could be seen west toward Laos from where I was orbiting."

BOMBING MISSION

Captain Lathrop described his first bombing mission. "The controller [airborne] was giving us a mission. 'Hellborne 224 [A-4], I have a mission, are you ready to copy?' The voice of the controller was self assured and commanding. 'Roger,' replied Dash-1 [lead aircraft, Lathrop was Dash 2]. 'Run in heading will be zero six zero, left hand pull. Friendly forces will be at your eleven o'clock at five hundred meters at Khe Sanh. Ground fire is expected to be heavy.' Captain Trumfeller [Dash-1] read back the brief as it had been given. He was descending and maneuvering to a position so that he would be at the roll in point when permission was given. 'Do you see my mark, 224?' Fingerprint [controller airborne] had shot a smoke marker between the base of one of the mountains and Khe Sanh. I saw Dash-1 turn toward the smoke, call 'Roger, Dash-1 in hot,' and start down the chute and toward the target, with all switches armed. We were going to drop all our bombs and napalm on a single run. I was too far behind to roll in on the target as he called off. I watched as he rolled inverted, did a double half roll entry, leveled out and released over the target, the orange winking of ground fire coming from his nine o'clock position abeam of the target.

"I pulled upon the run in line, watching the napalm from the previous air strike run behind the lead aircraft, but behind him and beneath him. I turned on the run-in line and rolled inverted, holding the gunsight rings above the smoke and moving 100 meters to the right as the controller had indicated. I had turned on the master armament switch as I had pulled upon the run-in line. As I started the run down to the target, suddenly time slowed to a crawl. Dash-1 was turning back to the left, the smoke and fire of his ordnance drop was drifting toward Khe Sanh slowly. The target seemed too big to miss as I pulled the gunsight ring down below it and stared rolling back into a wings level upright position. Time seemed to crawl. The area of the smoke was so large I could never miss it as I watched it get bigger and bigger in the gunsight picture. I saw no ground fire, and never did when on a bombing run. I think I was too intensely focused on the target and hitting it. I pressed the target until it looked like it was going to impact with the aircraft, hit the button on the top of the stick and pulled up and to the left, Khe Sanh above me a hundred feet or more. I kicked my rudder heard left to see what was happening behind me, and could just catch the napalm and flame in the mirror on the right side of my canopy."

Hospital Corpsman Johnson recalled, "I flew into Khe Sanh prior to the siege . . . and the countryside was absolutely gorgeous. We flow out in a CH-53 helicopter after the battle. As we lifted off the runway, we kind of corkscrewed up into the sky to avoid any of the machine guns and anti-aircraft guns that might still be in the area. The thing that amazed me, the entire surrounding countryside was just totally denuded of trees. Everything was bomb craters. I turned and I looked at that, and I said, 'God, look what we've done to this area. We've taken a beautiful, beautiful area and we've turned it into the moon.'"

After spending almost the entire siege on Hill 881S, David Powell decided to leave:

"The so called trench was about six inches deep. It was so shallow that the three cameras around my neck made my back stick out of the trench like a camel. I distinctly remember rotating the cameras off to one side so I could get down lower in the trench. I kept thinking who the hell dug this puny little excuse for cover. As a matter of fact it wasn't really cover; the best that could be said was that it was concealment. Well as always in situations like that time slows down to a crawl. There were a few other Marines in the trench as well. As a matter of fact I was lying head to head with a Marine, and what really freaked me out was that he looked so damn calm. We were just staring at each other or I was staring at him. I thought to myself I hope I don't look as terrified as I feel. I know it sounds kind of stupid but I actually asked him, "Do I look scared because you don't." He said no that I didn't look scared. I was relieved for some strange macho ass reason. Finally the bird that I am supposed to get on lands and I am waiting for what seems like an eternity for the ramp to come down. When it does someone yells GO! GO! GO! Well, I mentally charted the shortest distance between the two points for that ramp, got up, and just like that movie Butch Cassidy and the Sundance Kid when they jumped off the cliff. I said to myself "OOOOHH SSHHIIIIIT!!!!!" and took off running as fast as I could.

As I am racing toward the helicopter this big Marine comes charging down the ramp and he decides that the way I am coming to the chopper is also the way he is going to the trench I just left. Neither one of us changed course. We smashed into each other like two billiard balls. Both bounced off each other backwards and to our respective right sides. So there we are standing out in the open stock still looking at each other. I am pissed and he is smiling at me as if to say you didn't actually think you could come through me did you puny little twerp. Hey, I was six feet and two hundred pounds, that guy must have been a football player or something. Anyway I took off again and as soon as I hit that ramp I took a flying leap into the back of that helicopter. When I hit the deck I started sliding like I was on ice. I slid all the way forward and came to rest face down between the legs of the Marine who is manning the 50 cal machine gun at the forward window on the right side. He was standing there with his legs wide apart aiming the gun. I turned over and looked up to see this Marine with this deadly serious look on his face staring down at me. I scrambled forward and sat up against the bulkhead of the flight deck of the chopper and tried to make myself into the smallest target as possible. It was then that I realized why I had slid so far forward so fast. The deck of the chopper was covered with expended shell casings and it was like the whole deck was covered with marbles or ball bearings. I was staring aft at the open ramp as it slowly started to close. I was just waiting for the sight and sound of holes being ripped through the chopper. I am saying, "Come on baby let's get the hell out of here please." The ramp closes and the engine starts whining and then there is that brief moment when the chopper is not off the ground but seems like it is in the air at the same time and then we are climbing the engines are roaring and the bird is straining for altitude. The machine guns are banging away and the shell casing are showering down on the deck and bouncing all over the place until finally I can feel that we are moving more horizontally then upward and it's getting quieter and an overwhelming sense of relief comes over me. I said to the Marine manning the gun, "Well, I guess we made it." He didn't say anything but just a slight smile came to his lips. I took that as a good sign.

CHAPTER ELEVEN

LANG VEI RESCUE ATTEMPT

Lt. Rosental, while flying as co-pilot to Capt Kufeldt was seriously wounded today. Originating out of Khe Sanh, near the Lang Vie area, Capt Kufeldt responded to a call to pick up a medevac and when he came to a hover, fire opened up on all sides. The aircraft received more than thirty hits but Capt Kufeldt managed to get it back to Khe Sanh where Lt. Rosental was treated for two broken legs and a broken left arm. He was shortly thereafter medevaced to the States.—Marine Observation Squadron 6 (VMO-6) Command Chronology

Late in the afternoon of 30 January 1968, North Vietnamese Army Pvt. Luong Dinh Du, a rifleman assigned to the 8th Battalion, 66th Regiment, 304th Division, carefully studied the dozing Montagnard guard on the main gate of the Special Forces camp at Lang Vei and decided that it was time to act. He stood up from his concealed position and, without being challenged, walked straight into the camp and headed for the Special Forces team house. Without so much as a "by your leave," he stepped through the door and surveyed the unsuspecting inhabitants. The Americans did a double take, taken aback by the sight of the green-uniformed, rifle-toting enemy soldier, and scrambled to grab their weapons. Before they could shoot, Du raised his hands in surrender. He was immediately disarmed and interrogated. During the course of the questioning, he startled his inquisitors by claiming that Lang Vei was going to be attacked within the next two weeks by infantry and "tanks!"

"TANKS IN THE WIRE!"

Just past midnight on 7 February 1968, U.S. Army SSgt. Peter Tiroch woke with a start. "Tanks in the Wire!" someone had shouted, sending him sprinting to Lang Vei's 4.2-inch mortar pit. The gun was fully manned, so he dashed over to a recoilless rifle position. Under the flickering light of a mortar illumination round he was startled to see two burning tanks and a third churning through the outer perimeter's barbed wire entanglements toward the inner compound. The armor was later identified as Soviet-made PT-76 amphibious tanks of the 3rd and 9th Companies of the NVA 198th Armored Battalion; ten of the PT-76s participated in the attack.

Captain Frank Willoughby, the Special Forces team commander radioed the 1st Battalion, 13th Marines, call sign Jacksonville, at the Khe Sanh Combat Base for artillery support. "Are you sure about the armor?" an incredulous Marine operator asked Willoughby. "Roger, roger, that is affirm," he heatedly responded. "We have tanks in the perimeter!" At the time of the request, Khe Sanh was also under heavy North Vietnamese mortar and rocket fire trying to suppress the Marine artillery and keep it from supporting Lang Vei. John Prados and Ray Stubbe in *Valley of Decision, The Siege of Khe Sanh* estimated that incoming mortar and rockets were exploding "at an average rate of six per minute and by morning the total stood at about 100 rockets and 450 rounds of mortar fire."

Russian PT-76 amphibious light tank, ten of which were used in the NVA assault on Lang Vei Special Forces camp.—*Museum of the Great Patriotic War, Kiev*

LANG VEI SPECIAL FORCES CAMP

Lang Vei Special Forces Camp, call sign Spunky Hanson, was established in 1966 near the village of Lang Vei in the extreme northwestern corner of Quang Tri Province, Republic of Vietnam. One of its primary missions was to conduct border surveillance of the infiltration routes from Laos in the west and northwest and from the DMZ in the north toward Khe Sanh Combat Base (KSCB). The other mission was to conduct area pacification in conjunction with the local indigenous population.

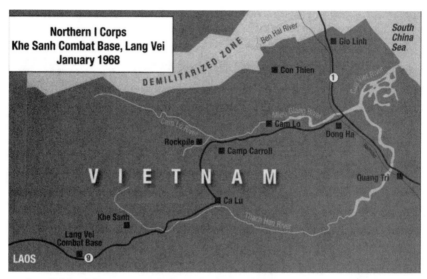

Lang Vei Special Forces camp was located in the northwestern corner of South Vietnam.
—*Jason Monroe, Leatherneck*

In May 1967, North Vietnamese regulars, aided by confederates inside the camp, penetrated its defenses, killed the Special Forces detachment commander and executive officer, and destroyed much of the compound. Since the original camp lacked good observation and fields of fire, it was moved a thousand meters west along Route 9, which placed it one and a half kilometers east of the Laotian border and eight kilometers southwest of the Marine base at Khe Sanh. In September, Naval Mobile Construction Battalion 11 (MCB-11) constructed a new camp. It was manned by Bru Montagnards and local Vietnamese called Civilian Irregular Defense Groups (CIDG), an ARVN Special Forces team, and a twenty-four man Special Forces Operational Detachment A (SFOD-A 101), a total garrison of approximately five hundred men. Their mission was to conduct surveillance of the Laotian border and the DMZ, as well as to interdict enemy infiltration routes.

The camp, which was in the shape of a dog bone, consisted of an inner and outer perimeter and corner strong points, each protected by barbed wire, trip flares, and claymore mines. A special underground, concrete-reinforced tactical operations center (TOC) was constructed in the inner compound. The camp's internal fire support consisted of one 4.2-inch mortar, seven 81mm mortars, and nineteen 60mm mortars dispersed throughout the perimeter. Lang Vei's antitank defenses consisted of two 106mm and four

Lang Vei was manned by a five-hundred-man garrison of U.S. Special Forces and Vietnamese CIDG personnel. Local CIDG strikers gather at the camp. At the left, smoking, is one of the Special Forces advisors of Detachment A-101.—*U.S. Navy*

57mm recoilless rifles and one hundred M72 LAWs (Light Anti-Armor Weapon). The camp was also supported by the 1st Battalion, 13th Marine Regiment (1/13), at Khe Sanh: three batteries of 105mm howitzers, a battery of 4.2-inch mortars, and a battery of 155mm howitzers.

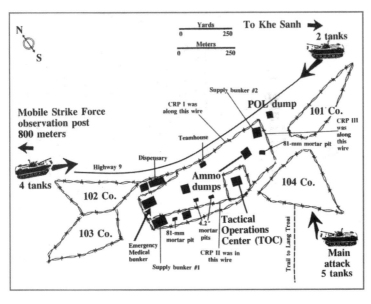

Lang Vei Special Forces camp was in the shape of a dog bone.

FIRE SUPPORT

Willoughby's emergency request for artillery support was relayed through 1/13's fire direction center (FDC) and passed to Bravo Battery. First Lieutenant Fred McGrath, the battery XO remembered, "We had Lang Vei on the radio and were providing fire support, based upon the Special Forces personnel adjusting the rounds—'repeat fire for effect on number eight [preregistered target number], left 200 [meters] and right 200 [meters]. We have tanks coming up the road, request fire number five. Keep it working up and down the road."

Willoughby called for air support. A series of U.S. Air Force forward air controllers, call sign Covey, reported in to help. Covey 232 found that "the ground fire was very heavy, extensive, making it almost impossible to stay in one position, because the minute you did they had you under fire." Covey established contact with Willoughby. "I have one tank on top of my TOC at this time," the Special Forces officer exclaimed, "there's another tank trying to enter the gate, coming into the compound, and another one coming down the road."

Covey 232 marked the target with rockets. According to a declassified report, "Yellow Bird 59 [U.S. Air Force B-57] dropped its ordnance, destroying two tanks and obtaining 15 secondary explosions." It was not enough, "Tanks and a lot of infantry are coming into the camp," Willoughby radioed and requested Jacksonville to "fire the preplanned fires right on our position."* The FAC described the situation. "Our advisors [Special Forces] were trapped in the TOC bunker in the middle of the camp, and the NVA were swarming all over it, throwing satchel charges and smoke bombs down through the [air] vents." Lieutenant McGrath noted, "The last transmission was to the effect, 'Oh hell, they have tanks. They're right on top of us.' We didn't hear anything else." Army SSgt. Harve Saal said, "There was a rushing sound and the Lang Vei radio went silent." Eight American Special Forces soldiers, including Willoughby and over a dozen Vietnamese were trapped in the TOC. They could not break out and the NVA could not get in, although they were trying their best by using satchel charges and hand grenades.

---

* From the author's position on the northwestern side of the KSCB (Red Sector) he could hear the artillery bombarding the Special Forces camp. He remarked to a nearby Marine, "It sounds like drumfire," a term used in World War I to describe a massive artillery bombardment. (At the time the author was the commander of L/3/26.)

CONTROVERSY

Controversy surrounded the Marine decision not to attempt a rescue. The decision was based on tactical considerations. In *Night of the Silver Stars, The Battle of Lang Vei* William R. Phillips wrote, "A careful study of the battle reports from Lang Vei of the tactical and strategic situations, and of the terrain . . . leads to the inevitable conclusion that any attempt to relieve Lang Vei . . . would have been an exercise in futility. The rescuers would have suffered an unacceptable level of casualties." Major Jim Stanton of the 26th Marines fire support coordination center inside the regimental command bunker said, "We were sure that the attack on Lang Vei was a ploy to get the Marine relief force outside the combat base wire, that they [the NVA] had set an ambush. . . ." Lieutenant Colonel Jim Wilkinson, CO 1/26 had tasked one of his rifle companies to determine possible routes to Lang Vei. "[The] company, avoiding well-used trails to preclude ambush, could move by foot from KSCB to Lang Vei in approximately nineteen hours." Colonel David Lownds, CO 26th Marines said, "If I thought there was a chance they could get there [relief force] I would have tried it, but I don't think there was."

RESCUE ATTEMPT

Marine Observation Squadron 6 (VMO-6), call sign Seaworthy, maintained a section (2 aircraft) of Bell UH-1E helicopter gunships at Khe Sanh to provide medical and resupply escort for a section of Boeing Vertol CH-46 Sea Knight helicopters from Marine Medium Helicopter Squadron 262 (HMM-262), call sign Chatterbox. The flight worked the daylight hours out of Khe Sanh, remained overnight and worked the next morning before returning to Quang Tri. The aircraft were laagered in specially constructed revetments on the northern side of the runway, directly across from the logistics support area. The crews stayed in the 26th Marines underground command post. On the morning of 8 February, Capt. Edward Kufeldt, VMO-6 recalled, "I was in the bunker [26th Marines] around 0600 and told to standby for the evacuation of Lang Vei. We didn't know much, except that the Special Forces camp had been overrun." First Lieutenant Charlie Crookall, a Chatterbox copilot remembered, "At one point we could hear the rumble of tanks over the radio transmission from the camp." Kufeldt noted that, "The weather was crappy, fog and low clouds, which kept us from launching."

In preparation for the launch, however, Kufeldt sent his crew chief, Cpl. Robert Crutcher to check on the gunship. Corporal Crutcher made his way across the fog-shrouded matting. "I had walked across the runway many times under rocket attack," he said. "Anytime we landed we got rocketed and mortared, it was just part of going into Khe Sanh." The NCO reported that the aircraft was OK despite the night shelling. "We continued to standby throughout the day," Kufeldt said. By late afternoon the sky had cleared and we got approval to evacuate the Special Forces." The four aircraft, led by Lt. Col. William J. White, launched after a quick preflight briefing. Kufeldt's gunship, call sign Seaworthy 4-21 was flying as the number two (dash-2) in the section led by Maj. Curt McRaney, VMO-6's maintenance officer. "We received little information on the situation, except that some of the Special Forces had been evacuated by truck and that Army Huey's might help with the remainder of the evacuation," Kufeldt said. "We were never told how bad it was, for us it was 'just another day, just another mission.'"

The flight established contact with the Air Force FAC, who directed them toward the landing zone, an elongated runway close to Old Lang Vei. "The '46s went in," Kufeldt explained, "and received ground fire, which we tried to suppress." First Lieutenant Crookall said, "It was like a flying circus. I had an A-4 roll in below me and drop napalm—scared the crap out of me—and left a big wall of fire. There was a lot of fire, everybody got hit." Kufeldt watched the transports go in. "They landed quite a distance from each other," he recalled, "and were immediately inundated by hundreds and hundreds of Laotians and Vietnamese." The crewmen attempted to establish order but were overwhelmed by the press of humanity. "I remember seeing hysterical Laotian and Vietnamese troops hanging off of anything they could get a hold of. The aircraft were so overloaded that they couldn't get off the ground," Special Forces SSgt. Dennis Thompson recalled. "There were people hanging on to the ramp, the wheels, even the VHF antenna. They were grabbing anything they could get a hold of." Kufeldt watched in astonishment. "I heard one of the pilots exclaim, 'this is not working, we're taking off.' I saw people falling of the ramp, off the wheels as the aircraft pulled out of the zone. They took some light hits from the right side of the runway. I could see the tracers, so we went in to suppress with our machine guns."

HMM-262 pilot Capt. Robert J. Richards was so overloaded that he had to fly at treetop level all the way back to Khe Sanh because the excess weight kept his aircraft from gaining altitude. As he flew over Khe Sanh village, an NVA soldier popped out of one of the abandoned huts and sprayed the low-flying helicopter with a burst of AK-47 fire. The rounds tore out a portion of his instrument panel and one bullet passed about two inches from Richard's nose before tearing through the top of the cockpit. A gunner on one of the transports killed the enemy soldier before he could get away. First Lieutenant Crookall's aircraft was also struck. "We took a hit in a hydraulic line, a pinhole leak in the forward rotor area over the cockpit," he said. "It was not enough to bleed the system but we lost some power and the gages fell off. We got down low, in case we had to set it down."

The flight headed back to Khe Sanh. "The '46s were on their final approach and we were about half a mile behind them when we got a call from Covey [call sign for the forward air controller]," Capt. Kufeldt recalled. "There is an American in the zone, will someone go back and pick him up? [Kufeldt] called Dash-1 [Major McRaney]. 'Can you pick him up?' McRaney replied that he didn't have the fuel and the CH-46 pilots said they were not going back because of aircraft damage, so I requested to go in." Captain Kufeldt asked his crew if they were up for it. "My copilot [1st Lt. George Rosental] said, 'Let's do it,' and the rest of the crew said, 'OK.'" As Kufeldt's Huey headed back to Lang Vei, the transport aircraft landed. "After we dropped off the passengers," First Lieutenant Crookall recalled, "our crew chief inspected the troop compartment and found an incendiary grenade with the pin pulled lodged between the troop seat and the bulkhead, which he carefully deactivated with a piece of wire."

While getting into position for the rescue, Kufeldt worked out a strategy with the FAC. "I circled around to the south and asked Covey to use the fixed wing on station to hit both sides of the runway with bombs to suppress NVA fire. I intended to make a high speed run, flare to bleed off airspeed and get in quick." The bombers pulled off the target and Kufeldt started his run. "As we rolled out on final approach," First Lieutenant Rosental said, "I saw a file of NVA—10 or 12—in a gully . . . at least a quarter mile away, far enough I thought that we could get in and out before they were a threat." Kufeldt alerted the crew. "I said, 'Here we go,' and crossed a tree line at maximum airspeed. As we approached the zone, I pulled back on the stick and started to flare. Suddenly the whole world lit up!" First Lieutenant Rosental recalled, "As Ed [Kufeldt] flared to land from a high hover, I looked through the chin bubble and saw an NVA directly below me on one knee. He opened fire and stitched us with his AK-47! I was hit with three rounds, one in each leg and one in the arm, which cut an artery. The bullets in the legs felt like someone had hit me with a sledge hammer." Rosental slumped in his seat, semiconscious. Several other enemy soldiers were mere yards away, blazing away with rifles and automatic weapons. "I could hear their weapons even through the flight helmet and I could feel us take hits," Kufeldt explained. Corporal Crutcher said, "I felt like my head was in a popcorn popper as the bullets cracked by my head." Kufeldt remembered, "The instrument panel lit up like a Christmas tree. Almost all the caution lights were solid yellow. The engine red fire light came on and the engine coughed. I struggled to gain control and abort the landing. I caught a glimpse of my copilot. He was slumped in his seat and I thought he was dead." Corporal Crutcher was also wounded. "I was sitting on my steel pot when the round came up through the helmet into my leg."

Kufeldt managed to keep the helicopter airborne and head for Khe Sanh. "The aircraft vibrated badly, but stayed in the air. Thank God it stayed together," he remarked with relief. He contacted the Khe Sanh control tower and declared an emergency and that he had wounded aboard. Corporal Crutcher tried to help the copilot. "He was bleeding heavily and in pain but the armored seats kept me from getting to him." A crash crew and several Corpsmen met the aircraft as it settled onto the runway. First Lieutenant Rosental was hauled out of his seat by his arm—"It hurt like hell," he exclaimed—and rushed to the aid station for initial treatment. "While they were doing that," Corporal Crutcher said, "one of the doctors told me, 'Son you better sit down, you've been hit.' Up to that time I didn't realize I had been wounded." First Lieutenant Rosental was stabilized and evacuated to the United States for further treatment and rehabilitation. Captain Kufeldt and crew chief were treated and returned to duty. Their helicopter looked like a sieve and was not in flying condition : Corporal Crutcher counted over eighty hits. The shot-up Huey was evacuated by a CH-53 heavy-lift helicopter. Unfortunately something went wrong with the lift and the Kufeldt's helicopter was jettisoned into the jungle and never recovered.

POSTSCRIPT

Corporal Crutcher was awarded a single mission Air Medal for his role in the mission. Staff Sergeant Dennis Thompson, the Special Forces soldier they had tried to rescue was captured and escaped only to be recaptured. He was repatriated during Operation Homecoming in 1973. Of the twenty-four Special Forces soldiers in Lang Vei, 14 (all but one wounded) survived to be evacuated, 3 were captured and later repatriated, and 7 were killed in action. The South Vietnamese lost 64 killed in action and 209 wounded. It is estimated that 250 North Vietnamese were killed, seven tanks destroyed, and two more tanks listed as probables.

Captain Edward Kufeldt, United States
Marine Corps, Silver Star citation:
The President of the United States takes pleasure in presenting the

Silver Star to Captain Edward Kufeldt for conspicuous gallantry and intrepidity in action while serving as a pilot with Marine Observation Squadron Six (VMO-6), Marine Aircraft Group Sixteen, First Marine Aircraft Wing, in connection with combat operations against the enemy in the Republic of Vietnam. On the afternoon of 7 February 1968, Captain Kufeldt launched as an Aircraft Commander aboard an armed UH-1E helicopter assigned to support the extraction of a friendly unit from the Lang Vei Special Forces Camp. Upon completing the mission, he was preparing to land at Khe Sanh Combat Base when he learned that additional friendly troops remained at Lang Vei. Realizing that his helicopter was the only escort aircraft available, he unhesitantly accompanied two transport helicopters back to the landing zone and skillfully directed rocket and machine gun fire on numerous North Vietnamese Army anti-aircraft emplacements. While on the ground, the two evacuation aircraft were damaged by a heavy volume of fire and forced to become airborne before a U.S. Army Advisor had been embarked. Realizing the seriousness of the situation, Captain Kufeldt elected to land and extract the advisor. Completely disregarding his own safety, he skillfully commenced an approach to the designated area and immediately received accurate enemy fire which he quickly suppressed with rocket and machine gun fire. As the helicopter neared the landing zone, it suddenly came under intense hostile fire wounding three crew members. Despite sustaining extensive damage, which resulted in a loss of power, he skillfully maneuvered his aircraft to Khe Sanh and safely landed. By his courage, superb airmanship and unwavering devotion to duty in the face of great personal danger, Captain Kufeldt inspired all who served with him and upheld the highest traditions of the Marine Corps and of the United States Naval Service.

TEAM BOX SCORE

On 16 February 1968, Seaworthy 4-20 and 4-21 were launched from Khe Sanh to assist in the emergency extraction of reconnaissance team Box Score. The transports went in to pull out the team but as they were lifting out two of the team members jumped out to help one other member who did not get aboard. The transport could not go back into the zone because of extensive battle damage. Seaworthy 4-21 elected to go into the zone to pick up the remaining three members and as he was lifting out of the zone he was shot down and crashed. Killed immediately were the pilot 1st Lt. B.F. Galbreath, the copilot 1st Lt. P.A. Jensen, and the gunner SSgt J.E. Tolliver. The crew-chief, Cpl H.W. Schneider, died of injuries enroute to Da Nang the following day. One of the team members died in the crash, one died later of injuries, and the last received medical treatment in time to be the sole survivor.—Marine Observation Squadron (VMO-6) Command Chronology*

Captain David F. Underwood's Sikorsky UH-34D, call sign Seaworthy 4-20, was taking on fuel when he heard the direct air support center (DASC) announce over the radio that a reconnaissance team was surrounded by NVA regulars and had to be extracted immediately. One Ch-46 Sea Knight helicopter had already been shot out of the zone while trying to reach the embattled Marines. The airways were filled with reports that the helicopter had taken heavy fire. Underwood contacted the DASC. "I'll give it a try if you want me to do it," he radioed. "Dave Underwood felt like we could accomplish the mission," his wingman Capt. Carl E. Bergman reported. "He knew the gravity of the situation and the seriousness of getting it done, rather than waiting for another '46. The team just couldn't wait that long, so Dave decided to go in."

As helicopter gunships and fixed wing aircraft bombed and strafed the area around the team, Underwood and his copilot, Capt. Tom Burns flew their aircraft through a hail of North Vietnamese automatic weapons fire. They set the helicopter down on a little peak, fully exposed to enemy soldiers who were blasting them at point blank range. "We were taking just unbelievable fire at this point," Underwood exclaimed. "All the glass was blown out of my instrument panel, the windshield was blown out. You could hear the bullets going through the cockpit like bees!" Underwood and his crew were in mortal danger, taking heavy fire while the heavily burdened reconnaissance team struggled to reach them.

RECONNAISSANCE TEAM 2-1

Second Lieutenant Terrence C. Graves, 3rd Force Reconnaissance, was one of the first of his eight-man reconnaissance team 2-1, call sign Box Score, to jump down from the bed of the M35 2½ ton "deuce and half" cargo truck. He quickly led his men into the brush lining the road where they formed a small perimeter and waited, alert for sounds that indicated their covert insertion had been discovered. The truck gathered speed and continued on its way, trying to give the impression that nothing unusual had occurred. The team believed that the enemy was closely watching the roads for this type of insertion. After several minutes Graves gave a signal and the team silently moved out, well aware that this was "Indian Country" and alive with NVA. The veteran Marine reconnaissance teams had made regular contact with heavily armed enemy soldiers in the area. Graves himself had been on a patrol that had made contact and captured a prisoner, who confirmed the presence of a large concentration of his brethren in and around Box Score's patrol area.

The team had been thoroughly briefed on their mission before leaving the confines of the 3rd Force Reconnaissance area at Dong Ha. They were to conduct reconnaissance and surveillance in their assigned zone to determine enemy activity. In accordance with standard procedure, the team was to use supporting arms to engage the enemy ... but was to make every effort to capture a prisoner. Secondarily, the team was to plot helicopter landing zones for future operations. They were cautioned to pay particular attention to the trail network to determine if they were being used by the enemy.

RECONNAISSANCE MISSION
The mission of the lightly armed reconnaissance teams was to find and report enemy activity. The teams operated in small units of 4 to 8 men for short periods of time, normally 5 to 7

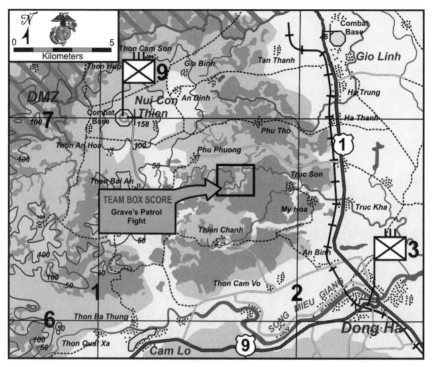

Team Box Score's area of operation in Northern I Corps. *—Lieutenant Colonel R.L. Cody, USMC (Ret.)*

---

days. They were primarily inserted by helicopter or by simply walking into their reconnaissance zone (RZ). The normal RZ, depending on terrain, consisted of six grid squares, 3000 meters long and 2000 meters wide. They avoided becoming directly engaged with the enemy, preferring to use supporting arms . . . artillery and close air support. Often referred to as the "eyes and ears" of the division, the intelligence they gathered was often used by higher headquarters to plan and execute ground combat operations.

The team "broke brush" for the first day, slowly moving further into their patrol area, a location approximately six miles northwest of Dong Ha in Quang Tri Province, just south of the DMZ. According to Pfc. Mike Nation, "the brush was thick and heavy with water from recent downpours. This was to our benefit as wet underbrush does not make much noise as you move through it." They saw "lots of enemy activity, primarily foot prints on the trails," which was not an unusual occurrence for them. The seven enlisted members had worked together on several missions and were comfortable in the enemy's back yard. However, although it was his fourth patrol, this was Lieutenant Graves's first experience as a patrol leader. It was the practice of the company to initially put prospective patrol leaders in subordinate positions to gain experience. The team's two corporals, Robert B. Thomson and Danny Slocum, were considered to be "extremely well qualified reconnaissance Marines." The other five men, LCpl. Steven Emrick, HM3 Steve Thompson, and Privates First Class James Earl Honeycutt, Adrian Lopez, and Mike Nation were typical—all volunteers—physically fit, well trained, and highly motivated Marines.

Team Box Score just after returning from a January 1968 patrol, the first patrol of 2nd Lt. Terry Graves. The patrol members (standing left) are Cpl. Ray Warren; Mr. Giao, a Vietnamese Kit Carson Scout, who was later captured and executed by the NVA in the battle of Hue City; Sgt. William H. "Billy" Andress; Cpl. Danny Slocum; Pfc. Mike Nation and 2nd Lt. Terrance Graves. Kneeling, from left: Cpl. John Kaulu, HM3 Steve Thompson, and Cpl. Robert B. Thomson.—*Colonel Guy Pete, USMC (Ret.)*

AMBUSH

By late afternoon, the team had reached its reconnaissance zone and scouted for a night-time harbor site. "After dark," Nation recalled, "we found a brush covered area that offered good concealment." They established a 360-degree circle and immediately planned close in artillery targets in case of attack. "Every two hours we would rotate the watch," Nation recalled, "which allowed everyone to get some much-deserved rest. The night passed slowly, as it does when you're on patrol . . . but nothing out of the ordinary was observed."

By sunup the next morning the team had moved westerly through thick scrub growth toward a line of hills covered with waist-high elephant grass. About noon, "after crawling through some very low brush," Nation said, "we could see a well used trail just across a stream in front of us." The team paused. "Suddenly we heard Vietnamese voices quite a ways away," he said, "so we all got down, moved to the side of the brush line, and waited to see if they came closer." When they didn't appear, Graves decided to move the team to a better position to observe the enemy and possibly capture one. "We crossed the little stream bed and crawled up the hill to a bomb crater where we formed a 360 circle." Nation explained. "That's when I spotted five NVA carrying packs and rifles coming down the path toward us." The patrol was in something of a bind, caught in the middle of two NVA units. "We didn't have much of a choice but to lay an ambush," Nation said.

Lieutenant Graves passed the word to execute their ambush drill. "We peeled off and set up a hasty ambush alongside the trail as best we could because the brush was only 2 . . . maybe 3 feet high," Nation described. "When it came my turn there was no cover so Honeycutt and I jumped into a 10 feet deep, steep-sided bomb crater. All I could see was sky." Unbeknown to him, the NVA, now numbering seven, continued down the hillside trail. "Four of us [Graves, Lopez, Thomson and Slocum] moved up the hill,"

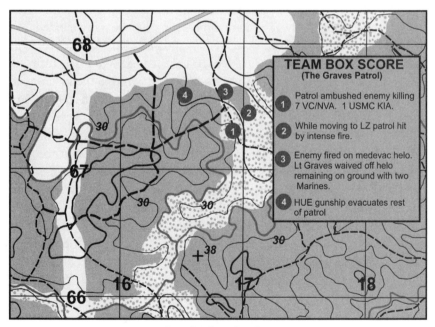

Team Box Score locations.

A reconnaissance team in the bush. Note the radioman in the foreground with a radio concealed in his pack (whip antenna can be seen over his left shoulder).

Slocum recalled, "to ambush them." The NVA approached the kill zone. "One guy got about 15 to 20 feet away from me and kind of looked over my way," he recalled vividly, "and there was another one that just seemed to pop right out of the ground." The slope of the ground prevented Nation from seeing the second enemy soldier. "I think he may have seen me, so I had to open fire. I shot him straight through the head with my M-14 . . . and then everybody opened fire . . . Thomson with an M-79, the others with small arms and a couple of hand grenades."

The team stopped firing and prepared to check out the kill zone. Slocum stood up and started to move to another position when he was wounded. "All of a sudden one or two rounds were fired," Nation recalled. "At first I thought he was hit in the head because he fell back and then he sat up." The team returned fire and then Graves and Thomson crept down into the kill zone to check out the bodies. "They came back a few minutes later with a pack, diary and a few odds and ends," Doc Thompson said. "All the NVA were dead. The trail was just one big mass of blood." In the meantime, he treated Slocum for, "a minor wound in the upper right thigh . . . a 'through and through' wound that basically took out some skin. I put a couple of battle dressings on it and offered Danny morphine but I didn't recommend it because it would slow some of his senses. 'That's fine Doc,' he responded, 'if I need it, I'll let you know.' I believe that decision saved his life." Although relatively minor, the wound was serious enough to prevent Slocum from continuing on the patrol. Graves requested a medevac helicopter and then ordered the team to move to the top of the hill.

HORNET'S NEST

"As we started moving up, we got pinned down by automatic rifle fire," Nation recalled, "kinda like the movies with the rounds bouncing off the ground." The team returned fire, which suppressed the enemy, allowing them to move up the hill where they formed a circle and waited for the medevac helicopter. However, "the NVA seemed to be getting closer, pretty much from all directions," Nation explained. "I could see several. Honeycutt and I started shooting . . . I think he got three and I got one . . . but we started getting rounds in, enough to make us want to stay down low."

While the team held off the enemy with small arms, Graves and Emrick worked the radio directing artillery and air support. "The fire was so heavy," Thompson said, "Lieutenant Graves would sit up and see where the round hit and lay back down and call for adjustment." He also directed Huey gunships that had responded to the call, "troops in contact!" Graves passed the word that the medevac bird was coming in. Nation laid out an air panel to mark their location. "We started towards the hovering helicopter," Thompson recalled, "when all hell broke loose!" The NVA focused their fire on the bird. "It was being riddled with machine gun fire," he said. "It looked to me like the copilot and the gunner were hit." Before the team could reach it, the damaged helicopter lifted out of the zone. "The area was obscured by smoke from rockets that the Hueys and F-8s [Crusaders] were firing," Underwood remembered. "I saw the '46 enter the area and momentarily reappear through the smoke coming back out."

As the damaged helicopter took off, automatic weapons fire raked the team's position. "The lieutenant, Emrick and Thomson all got hit," Nation recalled. "I remember the lieutenant was the first to yell that he got hit." Graves had minor wounds in the upper thigh, which Honeycutt bandaged. The other two were seriously wounded. "Thomson was hit in the lower waist," Doc Thompson remembered. "He said, 'I'm blacking out, Doc, I'm blacking out.' Then he passed out on me, and I think at that moment he died.

I started closed-chest cardiac massage and mouth-to-mouth resuscitation." Nation tried to help the stricken Emrick. "When I flipped him over he said, 'Get the radio off' and that's the last thing he said." Nation administered mouth-to-mouth resuscitation because Lopez said he could still feel a pulse. Graves limped back to work the radio after being bandaged. "He [Graves] directed air strikes," Thompson said, "and kept up a small base of fire to give us some protection."

Back at the reconnaissance company's command post the radio nets were filled with the team's urgent requests for assistance. Their plaintive calls gal-

A reconnaissance team radio operator talking on a PRC-25 radio while his teammate observes.

vanized the entire spectrum of support . . . fixed and rotary wing aircraft . . . artillery tubes . . . an infantry reaction force. Lieutenant Colonel William D. Kent, the battalion commander closely monitored events but, "felt absolutely helpless" because there was nothing he could do that was not already being done for the team.

HOT ZONE

Underwood was orbiting some distance away when he heard about the unsuccessful extraction attempt. "The '46 took heavy fire and couldn't bring the team out," he explained. "So, I left my wingman [in orbit] and went down on the deck to meet the Huey gun to lead me into the zone." Underwood needed a guide because the zone was almost totally obscured by smoke from six gunships and two F-8U fighter bombers that were mercilessly pounding the NVA positions. Captain Bobby F. "Gabby" Galbreath, a friend of Underwood's volunteered to lead him in. "Just follow me and when I break, the zone will be right underneath me," Galbreath radioed. "I followed him in, going flat out," Underwood said. "As he broke left, I button hooked and brought my aircraft into a low hover on top of the ridge." As his helicopter started its descent it came under intense automatic weapons fire. "I could actually see the NVA blasting away with AK-47s . . . unbelievable fire . . . anything except a '34 would have been blown out of the sky," he recalled vividly. "My rotor wash was pushing the elephant grass down . . . and I tried to spot where the guys were because I couldn't see them. I air taxied down the ridge until we finally spotted one of them half-hidden in the grass . . . dragging a guy who'd been wounded."

The team struggled with the casualties . . . Doc Thompson and Honeycutt dragged Thomson, while Nation and Lopez handled Emrick. Graves and Slocum provided covering fire. "We couldn't stand up because the fire was still coming in on us and the grass was so short," Nation recalled. "You had to just kind of kneel down and pull them, while trying to keep them breathing." Underwood remained in the zone over three minutes . . . an eternity when under such heavy fire. "I told my crew chief to lay down suppressive fire and to try and hurry the team up," Underwood said, "but we were going to stay as long as we could to get everyone on board." Thompson recalled that, "the NVA were standing up in the grass shooting at us with AKs [Kalashnikov assault rifles] and machine guns. You could hear the bullets hitting the fuselage." Corporal Mortimer, the crew chief, frantically gestured for the team to hustle. "Two recon members brought up one man [Thomson]," he recalled. "They loaded him on board and then the corpsman came in. He started pounding on the man's heart, trying to keep it going." Nation, Lopez and Honeycutt struggled to load Emrick, "because he was so heavy," according to Nation.

After sliding the mortally wounded man into the cabin, Honeycutt jumped off the '34's step to assist Graves and Slocum in trying to suppress the NVA fire. Lopez also jumped to the ground but a fast thinking Mortimer stopped him. "I grabbed him by the collar and was helping him in when he got shot in the leg." "I'm hit!" he yelled. "At that time we took off and were in the air by the time I pulled him in the plane," Mortimer recalled. Thomson and Emrick lay on the bloody deck of helicopter. The Corpsman was hunched over Thomson massaging his heart, while Nation worked on Emrick. After a few minutes, Nation realized that, "Emrick was gone and I gave up on him." He started working on Lopez who was unconscious from loss of blood. "The Doc [Thompson] gave me his K-bar [knife] and I cut his pant's leg open and pressed a bandage on the wound to get the blood to stop. It was just gushing all over the bottom of the chopper." The bullet severed Lopez' ephemeral artery, ricocheted into his abdominal cavity, and exited through his right hip.

Suddenly the helicopter was riddled by bullets. "The whole side of the chopper seemed to be coming in on us," Nation said, "Some of the stuff hit me in the face." Honeycutt was just climbing in, Corporal Slocum was off to one side and Lieutenant Graves a few feet away. "The lieutenant was screaming at the top of his lungs," Nation exclaimed, "Get out! Get out!' And he just waved at the chopper pilot to get the hell out of there, 'cause he can see that the fuel tanks had been ruptured." Thompson was convinced that, "Terry

[Graves] probably knew that he was not going to live at that point. He knew that the chopper was hit so badly that the extra weight would have kept it from taking off."

Underwood thought he heard the crew chief say that the team was aboard. "I pick this thing up," he said, "and I'm flying on sound alone because my instrumentation is blown out. My carburetor temperature is pegged, I'm streaming gas and oil and I'm losing control because of hits in the motor box and gear servo." Thompson could see that, "the pilot was working as hard as he could to get the chopper in the air, it was severely hit." As the helicopter lifted out of the zone, Underwood saw a man jump out (Honeycutt). "I called my crew chief and asked him how many men we had aboard. I was informed that we only had 5 . . . that 2 had jumped out, obviously in search of a third one who was wounded. At this point there was nothing I could do." Underwood stayed at tree top level and "poured the coal" to his aircraft. "The closest place was Delta Med [Delta Company, 3rd Medical Battalion] at Dong Ha," Underwood said. "I landed there and shut the helicopter down." Nation recalled that, "The crew shouted for us to get out, there was fuel running out all over the place." The aircraft started with 600 pounds of fuel and when it landed, there was only 200 pounds left. The helicopter had taken twenty hits, the majority of them in the cockpit. Underwood said that, "I could not have flown it anymore. In fact it had to be lifted out."

The terror of a helicopter medevac flight under fire shows on the face of wounded Marine Cpl. Larry R. Miklos (center) and an unidentified Navy hospital corpsman as they watch an enemy machine gun shooting toward their helicopter.
—*Department of Defense*

The wounded were rushed into surgery. "They worked as hard as they could on Thomson," a Corpsman said, "but couldn't keep him alive." The doctors were able to stabilize Lopez and evacuate him to a larger hospital at Da Nang but he died the next day. Thompson was devastated. "I remember leaving Delta Med and looked at the helicopter. It was just riddled with bullets and the inside was still covered with blood." Nation was by himself, trying to collect his thoughts. "I sat outside, not knowing what the hell to do. Within 5 minutes someone from my unit arrived and started pumping me . . . 'tell us what happened' . . . and I'm telling them the best I can so we can get a reaction team together to go back and get the others."

NO MAN LEFT BEHIND

Second Lieutenant Graves, Private First Class Honeycutt, and Corporal Slocum scrambled away from the landing zone to the top of the hill, "so we wouldn't catch so much incoming," Slocum said, "And waited for the next helicopter." It was not long in coming. Captain Bergman, Underwood's wingman, followed a gunship toward the new landing zone. "We went in low," his copilot Capt. Ed Egan recalled. "The ground was pretty well obscured by the smoke from WP [white phosphorus], so it was just about IFR down on the deck." They couldn't find the zone and were forced to make three more attempts before they found it. "As soon as we sat down, I could see them at my 1100 o'clock about 10–15 meters away," Egan said, "but they didn't make any move to get in the aircraft. Just about that time, we came under fire. It was so close and so loud that I thought our gunner had opened up." The gunfire was so loud that Bergman did not hear his copilot say that he saw the team . . . and started to lift out of the zone. At that point, "the aircraft gunner got on the ICS [aircraft radio]," Egan related, "and said that the crew chief had been shot in the shoulder and was bleeding badly. I looked down between the seats and I saw blood all over the cabin deck and the crew chief lying there." With a crewman down, the aircraft badly damaged . . . leaking fuel and hydraulic fluid, one of the radios shot up and both windows on the copilot's side shot out . . . Bergman could do no more. He headed for Dong Ha. "I had a decision to make and I made it," Bergman said regretfully. "I didn't accomplish the mission I was trying to do."

With the helicopter gone, the three men on the ground "moved to the "south side of the hill so we wouldn't catch as much incoming," Slocum recalled. "We got all the packs and stuff together that we were going to take. . . . Lieutenant Graves got a radio, I got one and Honeycutt got most of the weapons." With the NVA closing in on the three men on the ground, Captain Galbreath decided to try for a rescue with his Huey gunship. "Don't go in there," Underwood warned, "the fire is too intense, you'll never make it." "Naah," Galbreath responded nonchalantly, "I'm going to go in and try to get them."

Galbreath piloted the vulnerable aircraft through intense machine gun and small arms fire. "They [the NVA] were really putting some rounds in it," Slocum said. "It never quite touched the hill, just kind of hovered about a foot off the ground." The three recon Marines ran for the lives and scrambled aboard. "We all got on and it took off—I'd say not even 5 meters off the ground." Enemy fire riddled the Huey as Galbreath tried to gain airspeed. "I saw the copilot slump over as rounds came through the rear section of the chopper cutting up people," Slocum recalled. "I also think the lieutenant [Graves] got hit again." The damaged Huey lurched out of control. "It was completely spastic," Slocum said, "and crashed on its side across the river, about 50 meters from the bank, right above a bomb crater." The tremendous impact hurled everyone together in a tangled heap. "I was on top of the pile," Slocum described, "so I was able to shimmy out." He jumped to the ground and found "one of the pilots stretched out on ground, semi-conscious."

Seaworthy 4-23 "arrived on site just as Galbreath was hit by enemy fire and crashed," according to the after-action report. "We rolled in and sprayed the tree line where [the] enemy fire came from. On pull off we received two hits entering from the bottom left and striking Corporal Rich, the crew chief. We immediately broke off and flew to Delta Med and left Rich there. We returned to the crash site and continued our gun/rocket runs under control of Fingerprint 25 [the airborne FAC]. With ammo zero we returned . . . reamed and returned to the site and made more gun/rocket attacks until released."

ESCAPE AND EVADE (E & E)

Slocum could see a line of fifteen to twenty enemy soldiers closing in. "One of them was yelling orders, not paying attention to anything. So, I asked the pilot if he had a pistol. He said no, that he had a carbine in the cockpit. I couldn't find it, so I climbed up on the chopper and tried to get the machine gun. Just as I got my hands on it, the gooks opened up, so I jumped off and landed about 5 to 6 meters from the helicopter. I froze near the wreckage of a rocket pod, hoping they wouldn't see me." He heard the NVA soldiers firing one or two rounds at a time. "I think they were killing off what people that were left." Slocum made a break down the stream. "I ran for about 75 yards and took cover in the brush, where I slept part of the night, and then I moved out. I walked right into an NVA harbor site. I knew they were up there because I could hear them talking, clanking canteens and stuff." He backtracked and spent the rest of the night dodging friendly artillery harassing and interdiction (H & I) fire. "The next morning I got up at first light and followed a trail. As I got to the top, I noticed a gook about 15–20 meters away." He quickly backtracked until the trail crossed a stream. "I went up the stream for 100 to 150 meters and crawled up the bank." The NVA were close enough that, "I could hear them talking. They seemed to be coming toward me." Slocum inched his way through the brush to the top of the hill, where he could see helicopters and hear the sounds of a firefight.

Slocum was unaware that late the previous afternoon 2nd Platoon of Bravo Company, 1st Battalion, 4th Marines, was helilifted into the area to aid the recon team. Known as a "Sparrow Hawk" the small reaction force rushed to the scene of the crash. As the platoon approached the downed helicopter, the NVA suddenly opened fire from three sides with small arms and automatic weapons fire. Corporal William A. Lee, the platoon radio operation, was struck in the head and chest and fell mortally wounded. The NVA closed in and threw Chicom grenades [NVA hand grenades] into the ranks of the advancing Marines, slightly wounding four. Under threat of being surrounded and overwhelmed, the platoon commander wisely withdrew his force 150 meters to the southeast and called in mortar and artillery defensive fires throughout the night. An AC-47 gunship nicknamed "Puff the Magic Dragon" circled overhead providing illumination and fire support from its six barreled, rotating, 7.62mm miniguns, which were capable of covering every square foot of a football field with one round, in one minute.

Early the next morning, the platoon was joined by the rest of the company. The combined force reached the Huey and discovered a badly wounded crewman and five bodies. Vietnam veteran Richard A. Guidry in *The War in I Corps* described the scene. "Outside the helicopter lay two dead NVA soldiers, their wounds still dripping blood. 'Five Marines, all dead,' someone from the search party called out from inside the helicopter. From the heap of bloody corpses an angry voice responded, 'I'm not dead, you idiots!' A badly wounded crewman lay beneath the bodies of our dead Marines. He told of how the helicopter was swarmed over by enemy soldiers who stripped it of everything they could carry away, including the watch from his wrist as he played dead. More important, he said that one of the recon team had escaped into the brush." Bravo Company reported the information, evacuated the wounded crewman and started the search for Corporal Slocum, the missing man. Before leaving, the company set fire to the wrecked helicopter.

By continuing to sneak about the battlefield, Slocum unknowingly presented himself as an enemy soldier. "Someone must have seen me and called

men and directed their fire on the approaching enemy. After the fire had ceased, he and 2 patrol members commenced a search of the area, and suddenly came under a heavy volume of hostile small arms and automatic weapons fire from a numerically superior enemy force. When 1 of his men was hit by the enemy fire, 2d Lt. Graves moved through the fire-swept area to his radio and, while directing suppressive fire from his men, requested air support and adjusted a heavy volume of artillery and helicopter gunship fire upon the enemy. After attending the wounded, 2d Lt. Graves, accompanied by another marine, moved from his relatively safe position to confirm the results of the earlier engagement. Observing that several of the enemy were still alive, he launched a determined assault, eliminating the remaining enemy troops. He then began moving the patrol to a landing zone for extraction, when the unit again came under intense fire which wounded 2 more marines and 2d Lt. Graves. Refusing medical attention, he once more adjusted air strikes and artillery fire upon the enemy while directing the fire of his men. He led his men to a new landing site into which he skillfully guided the incoming aircraft and boarded his men while remaining exposed to the hostile fire. Realizing that 1 of the wounded had not embarked; he directed the aircraft to depart and, along with another marine, moved to the side of the casualty. Confronted with a shortage of ammunition, 2d Lt. Graves utilized supporting arms and directed fire until a second helicopter arrived. At this point, the volume of enemy fire intensified, hitting the helicopter and causing it to crash shortly after liftoff. All aboard were killed. 2d Lt. Graves' outstanding courage, superb leadership and indomitable fighting spirit throughout the day were in keeping with the highest traditions of the Marine Corps and the U.S. Naval Service. He gallantly gave his life for his country.

Private First Class James P. Honeycutt, United States Marine Corps, Navy Cross (posthumous) citation:

For extraordinary heroism while serving with the Third Force Reconnaissance Company, Third Reconnaissance Battalion, Third Marine Division (Reinforced), in connection with operations against the enemy in the Republic of Vietnam on 16 February 1968. While on patrol southeast of Con Thien, Private Honeycutt's team established an ambush when seven enemy soldiers were observed moving toward their position. During the initial exchange of fire, one Marine was seriously wounded. Disregarding his own safety, Private Honeycutt moved to an exposed area where he provided covering fire for the corpsman who was treating the injured man. After annihilating the enemy force, the team moved toward a landing zone to evacuate the casualty. As the team moved forward, they were taken under devastating enemy small-arms, automatic-weapons and mortar fire from an estimated two companies of North Vietnamese soldiers. In the initial burst of enemy fire, three Marines were wounded. With complete disregard for his own safety, Private Honeycutt moved across the fire-swept terrain to the side of an injured comrade and administered first aid. He then provided covering fire and assisted in moving the casualties across forty meters of fire-swept terrain to a waiting evacuation helicopter. Displaying exceptional courage, he remained behind to deliver a heavy volume of fire that suppressed hostile fire sufficiently to allow the team to embark. Only after all were aboard did he then embark. Realizing that a wounded man remained in the zone and that the injured team leader had debarked to search the hazardous area, he unhesitatingly jumped from the helicopter to aid his fellow Marines. Upon the arrival of the second extraction aircraft, he then assisted his wounded comrades aboard. By his bold initiative, intrepid fighting spirit and loyal devotion to duty, Private Honeycutt reflected great credit upon himself and the Marine Corps and upheld the highest traditions of the United States Naval Service.

Captain Bobby Frank Galbreath, United States
Marine Corps, Navy Cross (posthumous) citation:
For extraordinary heroism while serving as a Pilot with Marine Observation Squadron SIX, in the Republic of Vietnam on 16 February 1968. Captain Galbreath launched as wingman in a flight of two armed UH-1E helicopters diverted to support the emergency extraction of an eight man reconnaissance team which was heavily engaged with a numerically superior North Vietnamese Army force six miles northwest of Dong Ha. Arriving over the designated area, he immediately initiated his attack and made repeated strafing runs on the enemy positions. Although five Marines had been recovered, subsequent attempts to rescue the remaining men failed due to a heavy volume of ground fire which had seriously damaged three helicopters. Realizing the seriousness of the situation, Captain Gal-

breath volunteered to evacuate the surrounded men. Fully aware of the extreme danger to himself and his crew, he unhesitatingly commenced his approach, but was forced to abandon the landing when his aircraft sustained several hits. Completely disregarding his own safety, he initiated his second approach and skillfully maneuvered his aircraft through the hostile fire into the landing zone. Ignoring the intense fire which was striking his aircraft, he remained in the fire swept area while the men embarked. Lifting from the hazardous zone, his helicopter was struck by a burst of enemy fire and crashed, mortally wounding Captain Galbreath. By his courage, bold initiative and selfless devotion to duty, he inspired all who served with him and upheld the highest traditions of the Marine Corps and the United States Naval Service. He gallantly gave his life for his country.

Captain David F. Underwood III, United States
Marine Corps, Navy Cross citation:

The President of the United States of America takes pleasure in presenting the Navy Cross to Captain David F. Underwood, III, United States Marine Corps, for extraordinary heroism while serving as a Pilot with Marine Medium Helicopter Squadron ONE HUNDRED SIXTY-THREE (HMM-163), Marine Aircraft Group SIXTEEN, First Marine Aircraft Wing, in connection with operations against the enemy in the Republic of Vietnam. On the afternoon of 16 February 1968, Captain Underwood launched as Section Leader of a flight of two UH-34 helicopters in support of the emergency extraction of an eight-man reconnaissance team which was heavily engaged with a numerically superior North Vietnamese Army force six miles northwest of Dong Ha. When the initial extraction attempt by another helicopter was prevented due to intense enemy ground fire, Captain Underwood immediately commenced a low-altitude approach to the besieged unit, which had sustained three serious casualties. Nearing the landing zone, his aircraft suddenly came under a heavy volume of enemy automatic-weapons fire from embark the entire team. Ignoring the intense enemy fire striking his aircraft, he courageously remained in the fire-swept area and calmly directed the fire of his gunners, enabling five of the Marines to embark. Forced to lift from the zone due to the increasing intensity of the hostile fire, which impacted in the helicopter's cockpit and resulted in extensive damage to vital aircraft components, he skillfully maneuvered his damaged aircraft back to Dong Ha. His superior aeronautical ability, resolute determination, and sincere concern for the welfare of his comrades saved the lives of several Marines and inspired all who served with him. By his courage, intrepid fighting spirit, and selfless devotion to duty in the face of extreme personal danger, Captain Underwood upheld the highest traditions of the Marine Corps and the United States Naval Service.

Corporal Robert B. Thomson, Silver Star (posthumous) citation:
For conspicuous gallantry and intrepidity in action while serving as a grenadier with Third Force Reconnaissance Company, Third Reconnaissance Battalion, Third Marine Division (Reinforced), in connection with operations against the enemy in the Republic of Vietnam. On 16 February 1968, Corporal Thomson was a member of a reconnaissance patrol which ambushed seven North Vietnamese Army soldiers southeast of Con Thien. During the ambush, Corporal Thomson's accurate grenade launcher fire quickly silenced the enemy's return fire. When on of the Marines was wounded, as he attempted to search the ambush site, Corporal Thomson volunteered to reconnoiter the area and killed one enemy soldier concealed in the foliage. While waiting for an extraction helicopter, his unit came under small arms and mortar fire and was pinned down. Delivering effective suppressive fire on a suspected enemy mortar emplacement, he quickly silenced the weapon. As a result of the effectiveness of his fire, the North Vietnamese concentrated their fire on his position. With complete disregard for his own safety, he fearlessly stood up and continued to deliver a heavy volume of fire until he was mortally wounded. His steadfast determination and selfless concern for the welfare of his fellow Marines inspired all who observed him and were instrumental in the subsequent safe extraction of his patrol. By his courage, aggressive fighting spirit, and unwavering devotion to duty, Corporal Thomson upheld the highest traditions of the Marine Corps and the United States Naval Service. He gallantly gave his life for his country.

Corporal Danny M. Slocum, United States
Marine Corps Silver Star citation:
For conspicuous gallantry and intrepidity in action while serving as an Assistant Patrol Leader with Third Force Reconnaissance Com-

pany, Third Reconnaissance Battalion, Third Marine Division (Reinforced), in connection with operations against the enemy in the Republic of Vietnam. On 16 February 1968, Corporal Slocum was a member of a reconnaissance patrol moving toward an ambush site southeast of Con Thien when the Marines observed seven North Vietnamese Army soldiers maneuvering toward them. Reacting instantly, Corporal Slocum rapidly deployed his men into advantageous positions and directed their fire upon the enemy force. After the firing had ceased, he advanced toward the hostile position and was wounded in the leg by small arms fire. Ignoring his painful injury, he directed accurate rifle fire on the hostile position and suppressed the enemy fire. While awaiting to be extracted, the patrol suddenly came under a heavy volume of automatic weapons and mortar fire from a numerically superior North Vietnamese Army force and sustained several casualties, including the radio operator. Realizing the seriousness of the situation, Corporal Slocum assumed the duties of radio operator and directed several strafing runs by armed UH-1E helicopters while simultaneously firing his weapon at the hostile soldiers. When the first medical evacuation helicopter landed, Corporal Slocum placed himself behind the aircraft and directed a heavy volume of fire at the approaching enemy force. He then boarded the second helicopter, and as the aircraft lifted from the fire-swept zone, it was hit by hostile ground fire and forced down. After assisting two crew members from the wreckage, he began to climb into the helicopter in order to fire the M-60 machine gun mounted on the aircraft, but was forced to seek cover from the intense enemy fire. Displaying great physical stamina and resourcefulness, Corporal Slocum successfully evaded the hostile forces until rescued by a friendly unit the following day. By his courage, bold initiative and steadfast devotion to duty, Corporal Slocum upheld the highest traditions of the Marine Corps and the United States Naval Service.

Hospital Corpsman Third Class Stephen B. Thompson,
United States Navy, Silver Star citation:
For conspicuous gallantry and intrepidity in action while serving as a Corpsman with Third Force Reconnaissance Company, Third Reconnaissance Battalion, Third Marine Division (Reinforced), in connection with operations against the enemy in the Republic of

Vietnam. On 16 February 1968, Petty Officer Thompson was participating in a reconnaissance patrol deep in enemy controlled territory southeast of con Thien. When the patrol engaged several North Vietnamese soldiers and sustained one casualty, he unhesitatingly exposed himself to enemy small arms fire to render medical aid to the wounded Marine and mover him to covered position. Subsequently, as the patrol was maneuvering toward a landing zone for extraction, it came under intense automatic weapons and small arms fire from a numerically superior enemy force and sustained several additional casualties. Again, Petty Officer Thompson fearlessly exposed himself to hostile fire as he moved to the side of the casualties and, while treating the most seriously wounded Marine, supervised the efforts of several Marines who were rendering first aid to those less seriously wounded. Despite the heavy enemy fire, he directed the movement of the casualties across forty metes of exposed terrain to the fire-swept landing zone where he succeeded in placing them safely aboard the extraction helicopter. When another Marine was wounded by an enemy round which penetrated the helicopter, Petty Officer Thompson efficiently supervised a member of the crew in rendering first aid while he continued his determined efforts to save the life of the critically wounded Marine. Throughout, his professionalism and sincere concern for his companions inspired all who observed him and undoubtedly saved several Marine lives. By his exceptional courage, resolute determination and selfless devotion to duty, Petty Officer Thompson upheld the highest traditions of the Marine Corps and the United States Naval Service.

Corporal Robert B. Thomson, United States
Marine Corps, Silver Star (posthumous) citation:
For conspicuous gallantry and intrepidity in action while serving as a Grenadier with Third Force Reconnaissance Company, Third Reconnaissance Battalion, Third Marine Division (Reinforced), in connection with operations against the enemy in the Republic of Vietnam. On 16 February 1968, Corporal Thomson was a member of a reconnaissance patrol which ambushed seven North Vietnamese Army soldiers southeast of Con Thien. During the ambush, Corporal Thomson's accurate grenade launcher fire quickly silenced the enemy's return fire. When one of the Marines was wounded, as he

attempted to search the ambush site, Corporal Thomson volunteered to reconnoiter the area and killed one enemy soldier concealed in the foliage. While waiting for an extraction helicopter, his unit came under small arms and mortar fire and was pinned down. Delivering effective suppressive fire on a suspected enemy mortar emplacement, he quickly silenced the weapon. As a result of the effectiveness of is fie, the North Vietnamese concentrated their fire on his position. With complete disregard for his own safety, he fearlessly stood up and continued to deliver a heavy volume of fire until he was mortally wounded. His steadfast determination and selfless concern for the welfare of his fellow Marines inspire all who observed him and were instrumental in the subsequent safe extraction of his patrol. By his courage, aggressive fighting spirit, and unwavering devotion to duty, Corporal Thomson upheld the highest traditions of the Marine Corps and the United States Naval Service. He gallantly gave his life for his country.

Private First Class Adrian S. Lopez, United States
Marine Corps, Silver Star (posthumous) citation:
For conspicuous gallantry and intrepidity in action while serving as a Rifleman with Third Force Reconnaissance Company, Third Reconnaissance Battalion, Third Marine Division (Reinforced), in connection with operations against the enemy in the Republic of Vietnam. On 16 February 1968, Private First Class Lopez was a member of a reconnaissance patrol operating southeast of Con Thien when they made contact with several North Vietnamese soldiers, and during the brief fire fight, one Marine was wounded. Exposing himself to the enemy fire, Private First Class Lopez provided covering fire while the corpsman administered first aid t the casualty. Subsequently, while moving to a helicopter landing zone to evacuate the casualty, the Marines suddenly came under intense automatic weapons fire from a numerically superior enemy force and sustained three additional casualties. Realizing the seriousness of the situation, Private First Class Lopez unhesitatingly directed a heavy volume of automatic rifle fire upon the hostile positions attracting the attention and fire of the enemy away from the wounded. Moving to the side of a casualty, he ignored the enemy fire impacting around him and assisted in administering first aid. As a medical evacuation helicopter

approached the landing site, he assisted a companion in moving a wounded man across forty meters of fire-swept terrain to the helicopter. After embarking, he realized that three casualties were not aboard. With complete disregard for his own safety, he jumped from the helicopter in an attempt to rescue the injured men and was mortally wounded by a burst of enemy automatic weapons fire. His bold initiative and sincere concern for the welfare of his comrades were an inspiration to all who observed him and contributed significantly to the accomplishment of his unit's mission. By his courage, exceptional professionalism and steadfast devotion to duty, Private First Class Lopez upheld the highest traditions of the Marine Corp and the United States Naval Service. He gallantly gave his life for his country.

First Lieutenant Paul A. Jensen, United States Marine Corps, Silver Star (posthumous) citation:

For conspicuous gallantry and intrepidity in action while serving with Marine Observation Squadron Six, Marine Aircraft Group Thirty-six, First Marine Aircraft Wing in connection with operations against the enemy in the enemy in the Republic of Vietnam. On the afternoon of 16 February 1968, First Lieutenant Jensen launched as Co-pilot aboard the second aircraft in a flight of two armed UH-1E helicopters diverted to support the emergency extraction of an eight-man reconnaissance team which was heavily engaged with a numerically superior North Vietnamese Army force six miles northwest of Dong Ha. Arriving over the designated area, he pinpointed enemy positions, directed the fire of his gunners and assisted the pilot on repeated strafing runs. Although five Marines had been extracted, subsequent attempts to rescue the remaining men had failed due to a heavy volume of ground fire which had seriously damaged three helicopters. When his pilot volunteered to evacuate the surrounded men, he skillfully assisted the pilot during the approach to the hazardous area, but was forced to abort the landing when the aircraft sustained several hits from the intense enemy fire. Continuing his determined efforts, he ably monitored the aircraft instruments and provided accurate flight data which enabled his pilot to land in the zone. Ignoring the intense fire directed at his aircraft, he calmly directed the fire of his gunners while the men embarked. Lifting from the fire-swept site his helicopter was struck by a burst of enemy fire and crashed, mortally wounding First Lieutenant Jensen. By his courage, intrepid fighting spirit and steadfast devotion to duty, First Lieutenant Jensen upheld the highest traditions of the Marine Corps and the United States Naval Service.

Staff Sergeant Jimmy E. Tolliver, United States Marine Corps, Silver Star (posthumous) citation:

For conspicuous gallantry and intrepidity in action while with Marine Observation Squadron Six, Marine Aircraft Group Thirty-six, First Marine Aircraft Wing in connection with operations against the enemy in the enemy in the Republic of Vietnam. On the afternoon of 16 February 1968, Staff Sergeant Tolliver launched as Aerial Gunner aboard an armed UH-1E helicopter diverted to support the emergency extraction of an eight-man reconnaissance team which was heavily engaged with a numerically superior North Vietnamese Army force six miles northwest of Dong Ha. Arriving over the designated area, he expertly directed a heavy volume of machine gun fire on the enemy positions during repeated strafing runs in support of the extraction aircraft. Although five Marine had been extracted, subsequent attempts to rescue the remaining men had failed due to a heavy volume of ground fire which had seriously damaged three helicopters. When his pilot volunteered to evacuate the surrounded men and made an approach to the hazardous area, the aircraft was damaged by hostile fire and forced to abort the approach. Realizing the seriousness of the situation, he again provided a heavy volume of machine gun fire during his helicopter's second attempt and, after landing, continued to deliver covering fire, enabling the three Marines to embark. Lifting from the fire-swept site, his aircraft was struck by a burst of enemy fire and crashed, mortally wounding Staff Sergeant Tolliver. By his courage, intrepid fighting spirit and steadfast devotion to duty, Staff Sergeant Tolliver upheld the highest traditions of the Marine Corps and the United States Naval Service.

Corporal Harry W. Schneider, United States Marine Corps, Silver Star (posthumous) citation:

For conspicuous gallantry and intrepidity in action while serving with Marine Observation Squadron Six, Marine Aircraft Group

Thirty-six, First Marine Aircraft Wing in connection with operations against the enemy in the enemy in the Republic of Vietnam. On the afternoon of 16 February 1968, Corporal Schneider launched as Crew Chief aboard an armed UH-1E helicopter diverted to support the emergency extraction of an eight-man reconnaissance team which was heavily engaged with a numerically superior North Vietnamese Army force six miles northwest of Dong Ha. Arriving over the designated area, he expertly directed a heavy volume of machine gun fire on the enemy positions during repeated strafing runs in support of the extraction aircraft. Although five Marines had been extracted, subsequent attempts to rescue the remaining men failed due to a heavy volume of ground fire which had seriously damaged three helicopters. When his pilot volunteered to evacuate the surrounded men and made an approach to the hazardous area, the aircraft was damaged by hostile fire and forced to abort the approach. Realizing the seriousness of the situation, he again provided a heavy volume of machine gun fire during his helicopter's second attempt and, after landing, continued to deliver covering fire, enabling the three Marines to embark. Lifting from the fire-swept site, his aircraft was struck by a burst of enemy fire and crashed, mortally wounding Corporal Schneider. By his courage, intrepid fighting spirit and steadfast devotion to duty, Corporal Schneider upheld the highest traditions of the Marine Corps and the United States Naval Service.

Captain Carl E. Bergman, United States Marine Corps, Silver Star citation:

For conspicuous gallantry and intrepidity in action while serving as a Pilot with Marine Medium Helicopter Squadron 163, Marine Aircraft Group Thirty-six, First Marine Aircraft Wing in connection with operations against the enemy in the enemy in the Republic of Vietnam. On the afternoon of 16 February 1968, Captain Bergman launched as Wingman for a flight of two UH-34 helicopters in support of an emergency extraction of an eight-man reconnaissance team which was heavily engaged with a numerically superior North Vietnamese Army force six miles northwest of Dong Ha. After his flight leader had evacuated five of the team members, Captain Bergman skillfully maneuvered his aircraft toward the landing zone and immediately came under intense enemy automatic weapons fire. On three separate occasions, he courageously approached the area, but was unable to locate the landing site due to thick vegetation and the smoke from exploding ordnance. Observing the landing point on the fourth approach, he unhesitatingly landed in the fire-swept zone and attempted to pinpoint the position of the three remaining Marines. Ignoring the heavy volume of hostile fire directed at his aircraft, he steadfastly remained in the hazardous area until forced to lift out when his crew chief and gunner were seriously wounded and his aircraft sustained major damage to vital components. By his courage, bold initiative and selfless devotion to duty in the face of great personal danger, Captain Berman upheld the highest traditions of the Marine Corps and the United States Naval Service.

Lance Corporal Steven E. Emrick,
Bronze Star (posthumous) citation:

For heroic achievement in connection with operations against the enemy in the Republic of Vietnam while serving as a Scout with the Third Force Reconnaissance Company, Third Reconnaissance Battalion, Third Marine Division (Reinforced). On 16 February, Private First Class Nation was a member of an eight man reconnaissance patrol operating southeast of Con Thien. On 16 February 1968, Corporal Emrick's patrol ambushed and killed seven North Vietnamese soldiers southeast of Con Thien. Shortly thereafter, the marines came under heavy small arms, automatic weapons, and mortar fire from an estimated two companies of North Vietnamese troops. With exceptional composure, Corporal Emrick maintained communication with higher headquarters, reporting enemy strength and positions and providing directions for an evacuation helicopter. Fearlessly exposing himself to intense enemy fire, he directed and adjusted artillery fires and air support which enabled the patrol to maneuver to the landing zone and form a defensive perimeter. As he was maintaining communications with the extraction helicopter which was unable to land because of heavy ground fire, Corporal Emrick was critically wounded by a burst of automatic weapons fire. After directing his companions to remove his radial and maintain communication, he succumbed to his wounds. Corporal Emrick's resolute courage, unfaltering determination, and selfless devotion to duty were in keeping with the highest traditions of the Marine Corps and the United States Naval Service. He gallantly gave his life for his country.

Private First Class Michael P. Nation, United States
Marine Corps, Bronze Star citation:

For heroic achievement in connection with operations against the enemy in the Republic of Vietnam while serving as a Scout with the Third Force Reconnaissance Company, Third Reconnaissance Battalion, Third Marine Division (Reinforced). On 16 February, Private First Class Nation was a member of an eight man reconnaissance patrol operating southeast of Con Thien when he observed several North Vietnamese approaching his position. Reacting instantly, he informed his patrol leader of the situation, and the patrol quickly ambushed the hostile soldieries, causing the enemy to flee in panic and confusion. A short while later, the Marine came under intense small arms, automatic weapons and mortar fire from a large North Vietnamese Army force and, during the ensuing fire fight, sustained several casualties. Unhesitatingly, Private First Class Nation ran across the fire-swept terrain to the injured Marines and commenced rendering first aid. Observing that one man had stopped breathing, he administered mouth-to-mouth resuscitation until the casualty commenced breathing. Then, assisted by a companion, he carried the wounded man to an evacuation helicopter, and after boarding the helicopter, Private First Class Nation and another Marine were wounded. Ignoring his own painful injuries, he skillfully treated his comrades during the flight to a medical facility. Private First Class Nation's courage, sincere concern for the welfare of his comrades and unwavering devotion to duty in the face of great personal danger inspired all who observed him and were in keeping with the highest traditions of the Marine Corps and of the United States Naval Service.

––––––––

In an email to the author, George O'Dell, wrote, "There is no question that Underwood should have received the Medal of Honor. I also believe that Bergman should have received the Navy Cross. Likewise in retrospect, Thompson, Slocum and Nation should have received higher awards."

PART III:

THE BITTER END, 1975

CHAPTER THIRTEEN

OPERATION FREQUENT WIND

The country is in a truly perilous situation. We can calculate its continued existence only by the day or week; we cannot calculate it by the month.— Tran Van Don, Defense Minister, Republic of Vietnam

The 1975 North Vietnamese offensive, code named the "Ho Chi Minh Campaign" began on 1 March 1975 and quickly overran the South Vietnamese armed forces, which proved incapable of resisting the onslaught. By the end of April their defense had collapsed on all fronts except in the Mekong Delta. Marine Maj. James H. Kean wrote in *Tears Before the Rain: An Oral History of the Fall of South Vietnam*, "It seemed so sudden to me . . . it was just like a tidal wave . . . and suddenly everything just fell apart." The North Vietnamese troops quickly encircled Saigon, causing panic stricken South Vietnamese officials and civilians to scramble to leave before the city fell. Marine Master Sergeant Juan J. Valdez recalled, "The crowds never appeared dangerous, just desperate—begging [to leave] the country or get their children off to safety." Sergeant Michael Sullivan, an embassy guard, said, "Hell, everyone in the city has been watching those cargo planes lifting out of Tan Son Nhut, most of them carrying the South Vietnam high command. The other day some big-shot general stops a C-141 on the tarmac, pretends like he wants in to search it for draft-age men. Gets inside, buckles himself in, and leaves with the plane." (*Last Men Out: The True Story of America's Heroic Final Hours in Vietnam*)

Operation Frequent Wind was the largest helicopter evacuation in history. A total of 1,373 Americans and 5,595 Vietnamese and third country nationals were evacuated by fifty U.S. Marine Corps and Air Force helicopters. Marine pilots accumulated 1,054 flight hours and flew 682 sorties. Air America and Vietnam Air Force (VNAF) helicopter pilots carried hundreds of additional evacuees out of the threatened city. The operation began in an

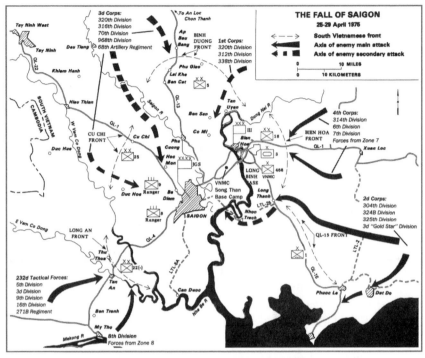

The collapse of the South Vietnamese armed forces allowed the victorious North Vietnamese to encircle the capital.

atmosphere of desperation as hysterical crowds of Vietnamese vied for limited space. It continued around the clock as North Vietnamese tanks breached defenses on the outskirts of Saigon. In the early morning hours of 30 April, the last U.S. Marines evacuated the embassy by helicopter, as Vietnamese civilians swamped the perimeter and poured into the grounds. Many of them had been employed by the Americans, but were left to their fate. North Vietnamese troops overcame all resistance, quickly capturing key buildings and installations. A tank crashed through the gates of the Independence Palace (South Vietnam's presidential residence and offices), and at 1130 hours local time the NLF flag was raised over the building. The event marked the end of 116 years of Vietnamese involvement in conflict either alongside or against various countries, primarily France, China, Japan, Britain, and America

PLANNING THE UNTHINKABLE

On 26 March, the Ninth Marine Amphibious Force (9th MAB) aboard the command and control ship USS *Blue Ridge* (LCC 19) was activated to plan for noncombatant emergency evacuation operations (NEMVAC). Brigadier General Richard E. Carey, Assistant Wing Commander, 1st Marine Aircraft Wing was designated as the commander of the evacuation force. On 11 April the 9th MAB reported to Commander Task Force 76 (CTF-76) for planning Operation Talon Vise, subsequently renamed Operation Frequent Wind and assigned four planning options:

- Option I: Evacuation utilizing all available transportation assets. Controlled by the American embassy to include commercial airlines and steamship lines. Limited military assistance provided in the form of airlift and/or sealift.
- Option II: Primarily fixed-wing aircraft evacuation to include rotary-wing aircraft, a ground security force, and an amphibious force, if required.
- Option III: Primarily sealift evacuation from Vung Tau and/or Saigon to include rotary-wing aircraft, a ground security force, and an amphibious force, if required.
- Option IV: Helicopter evacuation from the vicinity of Saigon that included the same basic provisions as Options II and III.

Brigadier General Carey noted, "The only choice was to plan for all options as best they could be interpreted. Suffice to say that Frequent Wind was a planning nightmare, for with receipt of each new plan a total review of MAB planning to-date was absolutely necessary in order to ensure proper

Brigadier General Richard E. Carey hosts one of the many planning sessions over Saigon contingencies conducted on board the USS *Blue Ridge*. Seated to General Carey's right, from left are Lt. Col. Royce L. Bond, Col. Frank G. McLenon, and Col. Alfred M. Gray.

tasking within the capacity of the force available. Every aspect of the envisioned operation had to be examined minutely." After careful study and review, Carey issued a comprehensive mission statement: "To provide a Ground Security Force (GSF) to Newport Pier, to the Defense Attaché Office (DAO)/Air America Complex, to other LZs as designated by DAO, to Can Tho, to Vung Tau to establish an emergency evacuation/marshalling area, and to provide Marine Security Forces for employment aboard Military Sealift Command (MSC) shipping."

The forces under the 9th MAB's control consisted of a regimental landing team, a provisional Marine air group and a logistic support group.

9TH MARINE AMPHIBIOUS BRIGADE ORGANIZATION

9th Marine Amphibious Brigade Brig. Gen. R. E. Carey
Communications Co (-) (Rein) Maj. R. L. Turley
Regimental Landing Team 4 Col. A. M. Gray
    BLT 1/9 Lt. Col. R. L. Bond
    BLT 2/4 Lt. Col. G. P. Slade
    BLT 3/9 Lt. Col. R. E. Loehe
Provisional Marine Air Group 39 Col. F. G. McLenon
    HMH-462 Lt. Col. J. L. Bolton
    HMH-463 Lt. Col. H. M. Fix
    HMM-165 Lt. Col. J. P. Kizer
    HML-367* Lt. Col. J. R. Gentry
Brigade Logistic Support Group Col. H. G. Edebohls
    LSU 1/9 Maj. D. O. Coughlin
    LSU 2/4 Maj. J. A. Gallagher
    LSU 3/9 Maj. F. W. Jones
Amphibious Evacuation Security Force Maj. D. A. Quinlan

On 12 April an advance party from the 9th MAB flew into Saigon to conduct a reconnaissance of potential evacuation options. They identified six options, two of which eventually became the primary military helicopter

---

* Remained at NAS Cubi Point, Philippines, less detachments aboard USS *Hancock* (CVA-19), USS *Okinawa* (LPH-3), and USS *Blue Ridge* (LCC-19).

landing zones: the DAO/Air America compound and the U.S. Embassy. The DAO tasked Air America with developing other landing zone options. Marine Lieutenant Robert Twigger and veteran Air America pilot Nikki A. Fillipi were involved in the project. "I was attached to a chief pilot in Saigon to work with DAO and I proceeded to look at and survey about 30 plus buildings in downtown Saigon to determine the suitability for landing sites and out of those 37 we chose approximately a dozen rooftops," Fillipi recalled. "With the aid of people from the Pacific Architecture Engineers and local indigenous folks we went out and surveyed and cleared these rooftops of all obstructions so day or night flight operations could be performed." On 9 April they were painted with the letter "H," which designated them as helicopter landing zones. Air America pilot Marcus Burke Jr., a former Marine officer, said, "I was deeply involved in preparations for a final evacuation. The rooftop helipads were to avoid trying to pluck folks out of the crowds. We could buy some time by blocking the entrances to those buildings and pulling people off the roof."

The advance party brought back photographs and sketches of the DAO/Air America compound and the embassy evacuation sites. It was their consensus, as noted in the Operation Frequent Wind after-action report, that "there was a general lack of concern on the part of responsible officials in Saigon as to any sort of evacuation. The first impression of 'Business as Usual' was gained during this visit." During a meeting with U.S. Ambassador Graham Martin he told the advance party that "he would not tolerate any outward signs that the United States intended to abandon South Vietnam. All planning would have to be conducted with the utmost discretion." The next day Brigadier General Carey flew into the city aboard an Air America helicopter for further discussions with Ambassador Martin, the Defense Attaché, Maj. Gen. Homer Smith (U.S. Army), and representatives from CINCPAC and CINPACFLT. Carey's short, formal audience with the ambassador did not go well. Martin tactfully avoided any detailed discussion of the impending evacuation and merely explained that all operations would be coordinated by Major General Smith from the DAO. Martin indicated that he would depart the embassy with a small group of Marines when he was ready. Carey said, "the visit was cold, non-productive and appeared to be an irritant to the Ambassador."

The "business as usual" atmosphere in the embassy was a direct result of Ambassador Martin's refusal to recognize the gravity of the situation. Colonel William E. LeGro, a U.S. Army intelligence specialist said, "Martin dictated

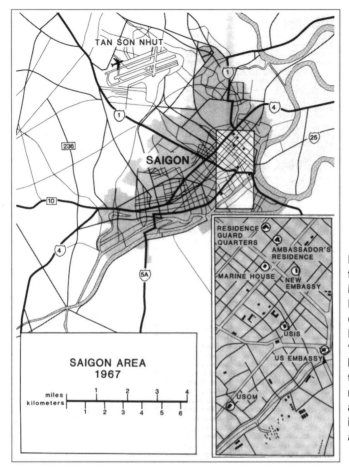

Liaison officers from the 9th Marine Amphibious Brigade visited the embassy and the DAO Compound to "get the lay of the land." They found the visit to be "cold, non-productive and appeared to be an irritant to the ambassador."

a memo on 10 April stating 'the Communists [NVA] would not enter Saigon until a negotiated settlement had been reached with the South." Martin was not prepared to give up the country, or to admit to himself that the military situation was irretrievable. However, by the beginning of April, it was obvious that the South Vietnamese Army was defeated. The entire northern and central sections of the country had fallen to the North Vietnamese juggernaut. The battered remnants of ARVN were fleeing toward the dubious safety of the coastal cities and the capital. On 20 April, the strategically important city of Xuan Loc fell, opening the way for the final assault on Saigon. The next day, President Nguyen Van Thieu bowed to the inevitable and resigned.

PRESIDENT NGUYEN VAN THIEU

By mid-April, Ambassador Martin reached the conclusion that if there was to be any hope of negotiations with the North Vietnamese, President Thieu had to resign. On Sunday morning the 20th of April, Martin met with Thieu and told him that there was, "very little time to avoid an attack on Saigon and if he did not step down, his generals would probably ask him to do so," a declassified CIA report noted, "Thieu listened carefully and dispassionately, and as they departed thanked Marine for his frankness, saying, 'I will of course do what is best for my country.' Martine replied, 'I know that you shall.'" The next day, Thieu delivered a long, bitter, rambling, and tearful speech before the National Assembly blaming the United States for the Republic of Vietnam's plight. "You ran away and left us to do the job that you could not do," he said. The CIA secretly arranged for Thieu to leave the country. After dark on 25 April Thieu and a party of ten gathered at an army compound near Tan Son Nhut, the Saigon airport. Thieu's group was taken by Martin's official limousine and three black station wagons with diplomatic license plates through various checkpoints to the Air America flight line where they boarded a C-118 Liftmaster (military version of the Douglas DC-6) and flew to Taipei. The CIA station radioed that, "Wish to advise that by direction of highest authority, Station has successfully evacuated former President Nguyen Van Thieu and ten others, with wheels up at 2120 hours local, 25 April."

Thieu left the country in the hands of his vice president, Tran Van Huong, who lasted only a week in office. Huong was succeeded by former General Duong Van "Big" Minh, who immediately began implementing plans for negotiations with the North Vietnamese. General Carey noted in his personal log, "[the Ambassador] must be convinced the time to evacuate is at hand and any further delay can only result in increased casualties. I pray for a silver tongue and the wisdom of Solomon, as he is very inflexible." On Tuesday 29 April, Ambassador Martin received an official note from President Minh requesting that the embassy be closed and that all Americans be out of the country within twenty-four hours.

MINH'S NOTE AND MARTIN'S RESPONSE

Dear Mr. Ambassador:
I respectfully request that you give an order for the personnel of the Defense Attaché Office to leave Viet Nam within twenty-four hours beginning April 29, 1975, in order that the question of peace for Viet Nam can be settled early.

Dear Mr. President:
I have just received your note dated 28th of April requesting that I immediately give an order for the personnel of the Defense Attaché's Office (DAO) to leave Vietnam within twenty-four

hours. This is to inform your Excellency that I have issued orders as you have requested.

I trust your Excellency will instruct the armed forces of the Government to cooperate in every way possible in facilitating the safe removal of the personnel of the DAO.

I also express the hope that your Excellency may intervene with the other side to permit the safe and orderly departure of the Defense Attaché and his staff.

With Martin dead set against any evacuation, Major General Smith took it upon himself to alert his people to the danger. "I can tell you that the longer you stay here the more difficult it's going to be in terms of you and your families getting out of here. I'm not suggesting that it [the fall of Saigon] may happen, but, hell, anybody who's got any smarts at all can look at the situation and figure out what kind of risk there is involved." DAO commenced a low-level evacuation of nonessential personnel, which included friends and dependents of Americans. By 21 April, evacuation flights were departing every half-hour. Throughout the month the "thinning out" process continued via fixed-wing aircraft from Tan Son Nhut until the morning of 29 April when Smith recommended ceasing flight operations at the airport. The field had been bombed by rogue VNAF pilots and was then under rocket and artillery fire. Var Green, Vice President, South Vietnam Air America, recalled, "Late Monday afternoon Tan Son Nhut Airport came under 'VC' bombing and

A Vietnamese Air Force C-130 burns after being struck by an NVA rocket on 29 April. The rocket and artillery bombardment forced Ambassador Martin to halt, then cancel, fixed-wing evacuation and commence Operation Frequent Wind.

rocket/artillery attack. The prime target was obviously VNAF assets . . . intermittent rocket/artillery attack continued but frequent secondary explosions of fuel and ammo gave the impression of continuous shelling." It was time for the Americans to leave.

As the situation deteriorated in the vicinity of the DAO compound, General Smith called his boss, Admiral Noel A. M. Gayler, Commander in Chief Pacific Command (CINCPAC), and told him that there was "no way" aircraft could continue to use the runway. Gayler agreed and said that he was going to recommend Option Four to the Joint Chiefs of Staff in Washington. David Butler, a journalist in Saigon at the end of the war, in *The Fall of Saigon* wrote, "Out of deference, Smith called Martin. 'Mr. Ambassador,' he said, 'CINCPAC is at this moment recommending to the Joint Chiefs that we go to Option Four, I thought you should know.' 'It's not their decision,' Martin replied. 'Homer, are you absolutely certain we can't get any more planes in there?' 'Yes, Mr. Ambassador, I am.' 'Okay,' Martin said. At 1048 on 29 April, Martin called Secretary of State Henry Kissinger and told him that it was time to go to Option IV, the helicopter evacuation. Kissinger approved.

TASK FORCE 76

Between 18 and 24 April, Task Force 76 assembled in the waters off the Vung Tau Peninsula, which under Option Three was considered to be absolutely essential for the evacuation of large numbers of Vietnamese. Hundreds of thousands of refugees, as well as remnants of the South Vietnamese Army and Marine Corps units, had fled to the peninsula in hopes of being sealifted from there to safe havens. With the selection of Option Four, at 1108 on 29 April Task Force 76 received the order to execute Opera-

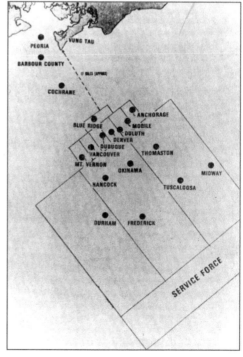

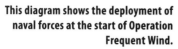

This diagram shows the deployment of naval forces at the start of Operation Frequent Wind.

tion Frequent Wind. At 1244, from a position seventeen nautical miles from the Vung Tau Peninsula, the USS *Hancock* (CVA 41) launched the first wave of helicopters.

TASK FORCE 76 ORGANIZATION

Task Force 76 USS *Blue Ridge* (LCC 19), Command Ship:
Task Group 76.4 Movement Transport Group Alpha:
    USS Okinawa (LPH 3)
    USS *Vancouver* (LPD-2)
    USS *Thomaston* (LSD 28)
    USS *Peoria* (LST 1183)
Task Group 76.5 Movement Transport Group Bravo:
    USS *Dubuque* (LPD 8)
    USS *Durham* (LKA 114)
    USS *Frederick* (LST 1184)
Task Group 76.9 Movement Transport Group Charlie:
    USS *Anchorage* (LSD 36)
    USS *Denver* (LPD 9)
    USS *Duluth* (LPD 6)
    USS *Mobile* (LKA 115)
Aircraft carriers, each carrying Marine and Air Force helicopters (eight 21st Special Operations Squadron CH-53s and two 40th Aerospace Rescue and Recovery Squadron HH-53s):
    USS *Hancock* (CVA 19)
    USS *Midway* (CVA 41)
    USS *Oklahoma City* (CLG 5), Seventh Fleet Flagship.
    Amphibious ships:
    USS *Mount Vernon* (LSD 39)
    USS *Barbour County* (LST 1195)
    USS *Tuscaloosa* (LST 1187)
Destroyers for naval gunfire, escort, and area defense, including:
    USS *Richard B. Anderson* (DD 786)
    USS *Cochrane* (DDG 21)
    USS *Kirk* (FF 1087)
    USS *Gurke* (DD 783)
    USS *Rowan* (DD 782)
    USS *Cook* (FF 1083)
    USS *Bausell* (DD 845)

The USS *Enterprise* (CVN 65) and USS *Coral Sea* (CV 43) carrier attack groups of Task Force 77 in the South China Sea provided air cover while Task Force 73 ensured logistic support.

The Marine evacuation contingent, the 9th Marine Amphibious Brigade (Task Group 79.1), consisted of three battalion landing teams: 2nd Battalion, 4th Marines (2/4), 2nd Battalion 9th Marines (2/9), and 3rd Battalion 9th Marines (3/9), as well as three helicopter squadrons (HMH-462, HMH-463, and HMM-165) along with other support units from Marine Aircraft Group 39 (MAG-39).

Above: Amphibious and MSC ships deploy off Vung Tau awaiting the order to begin Frequent Wind. At the last minute, confusion occurred over the definition of L-Hour and as a consequence the ships did not receive the order to "execute" until 1215 hours 29 April 1975.

Right: HMH-462 (YF) heavy-lift helicopters aboard an aircraft carrier in support of Operation Frequent Wind.

CHAPTER FOURTEEN

SAIGON ROOFTOPS

The military and political opportunity for launching the general
offensive on Saigon is ripe . . . we must launch the attack.
—North Vietnamese Central Political Bureau

A 28 April meeting of senior Air America staff members at Tan Son Nhut had just started when the roar of diving jet planes interrupted their conversation. Almost immediately explosions rocked the building, shattering the windows and sending the men scrambling for cover. Air America pilot Frank Andrews remembered, "Small arms fire erupted throughout the western edge of town. It seemed as though all the soldiers

Tan Son Nhut, adjacent to the Defense Attache Office (DAO), was the most important airport in South Vietnam and the primary site for evacuation. It was also high on the list of NVA targets in the Saigon area.

[ARVN types] who had a rifle immediately started firing in the air—panicked! It seemed to engulf the entire area—people were running, screaming!" The DAO after-action report noted: "Eighteen hundred hours: A flight of five A-37 [captured South Vietnamese] jet aircraft equipped with MK81 ordnance attacked a flight line area of the Tan Son Nhut. A total of six bombs hit the Vietnamese air-force parking area, destroying numerous aircraft (at least three AC-119s and several C-41s). The last two bombs hit between the control tower and the base operations building, which was heavily damaged. No U.S. Air Force aircraft were damaged." Major Stuart A. Harrington, DAO intelligence officer stated, "It [the bombing] signaled the beginning of the end of our fixed-wing evacuation efforts."

TAN SON NHUT BOMBING

Late on the afternoon of 28 April, five captured A-37 Dragonfly fighter bombers of the Vietnam People's Air Force (VPAF) Quyet Thang (Determined to Win) Squadron bombed the airfield at Tan Son Nhut with 250-pound bombs. They were flown by three specially trained VPAF (Vietnamese Peoples Air Force, the North Vietnamese Air Force) pilots and two Republic of Vietnam Air Force (RVNAF) defectors, who had been "volunteered" for the mission after being captured. This was the second mission for flight leader Lt. Nguyen Thanh Trung who had bombed the Presidential Palace in Saigon less than a month earlier. While on a bombing mission against North Vietnamese positions, he suddenly pulled out of formation and dropped four bombs on the palace—one failed to explode—and then strafed the Shell oil storage facility, starting a raging fire. Trung was hailed as a hero by the North Vietnamese who claimed that he had been a Viet Cong agent since 1969 and had infiltrated into the RVNAF where he served with the 540th Fighter Squadron of the 3rd Air Force Division. Trung later revealed that he was originally from Ben Tre Province in the Mekong region, where his father had served as the district secretary of the People's Revolutionary Party. In 1963 Trung's father was killed and his body was mutilated by the South Vietnamese police. Angered by the death of his father, Trung vowed to take revenge on the South Vietnamese government, so in 1969 he secretly joined the Viet Cong after he had been accepted into the RVNAF.

Just prior to the attack, a U.S. Air Force C-130 took off and reported heavy ground fire from 37mm and .50-caliber fire from the vicinity of Tan Son Nhut and Saigon. Captain Ken Rice, 374th Tactical Airlift Wing, reported, "After takeoff we made a right turn-out instead of the normal left turn because the A-37 was off to the left side and we could see that if we had made a left turn, he'd have been right in formation with us. As we flew over the city [Saigon], they [ARVN gunners] just opened up on us. There was ground fire from every direction. It was like the 4th of July!" First Lieutenant Fritz Pingle was in a second C-130. "I made a guard broadcast once we took off—that the airfield was under attack: 'Clark Air Base [Philippines], I don't care who you're talking to—shut up and listen, this is what's happening!' So we finally got the message back to everybody." Air America pilot Thomas Grady watched the bombing from a rooftop. "Shortly after [the bombing] the bad guys started shelling the airfield . . . so we all got ready to do our thing."

Tan Son Nhut air base under attack.

AIR AMERICA: ANYTHING, ANYWHERE, ANYTIME, PROFESSIONALLY (AIR AMERICA SLOGAN)

In early April it was obvious that Air America would have a crucial part to play in the helicopter evacuation of Saigon. The airline's Bell UH-1 Hueys were the only American-controlled helicopters that could land on Saigon's rooftops. On 7 April, veteran helicopter pilot Nikki A. Fillipi reported as Air America's representative to the Special Planning Group of the Evacuation Control Center at the Defense Attach Office (DAO) compound, located at Tan Son Nhut. "We'd been coordinating with the Marines . . . and made the decision that the Marines would handle evacuation from Tan Son Nhut air base and from the U.S. Embassy. Air America would handle evacuation from the downtown sites, bringing the people out to the airport for the Marines to transport out to the fleet. . . ." Fillipi and Marine Lieutenant Robert Twigger worked three eighteen-hour days supervising crews in removing obstructions. They also painted a large letter "H" on each rooftop selected as a helipad to mark the spot for the helicopter skids, indicating that aircraft could land or take off in either direction with guaranteed rotor clearance.

Air America committed twenty-four of its twenty-eight available helicopters, while thirty-one of its pilots volunteered to support the evacuation. This would mean that most aircraft would be flown by a single pilot. According to the U.S. Air Force account of the final evacuation, "This was risky, but Air America was accustomed to such risks and expressed no reservations about that aspect of the Saigon air evacuation." Paul Velte, Air America's managing director and CEO convinced Brig. Gen. Richard M. Baughn (USAF), General Smith's deputy at DAO, to request the temporary assignment of thirty Marine helicopter pilots to provide copilots for the Air America aircraft. When Ambassador Martin learned of the message, he was furious and cancelled the request. On April 9, Secretary of State Henry Kissinger told Ben Bradlee, executive editor of the *Washington Post*, "We've got an ambassador who is maybe losing his cool." The military situation continued to deteriorate. On 18 April Major Harrington noted in his journal, "There are now 11 divisions [NVA] outside of Saigon, with between four and six more on the way down from the overrun northern half of the country. It is evident that they are massing around Saigon, and doing it openly. I think it's a not-too-subtle signal to Washington to get out."

AIR AMERICA

In 1950, the Central Intelligence Agency secretly purchased the assets of the Civil Air Transport (CAT) company to conduct covert operations in Asia in support of U.S. policy objectives. The airline had been started in China in 1946 by Gen. Claire Lee Chennault of Flying Tigers fame and incorporated under the umbrella of The Pacific Corporation, formally Airdale Corporation. The Pacific Corporation became the holding company for several CIA Far Eastern airlines, including Civil Air Transport, Air America, Inc., and Air Asia Co., Ltd. Civil Air Transport continued to fly scheduled passenger flights while simultaneously using other aircraft in its fleet to fly covert missions. During the Korean War, CAT airlifted thousands of tons of war materials to supply U.S. military operations. In 1954 CAT aircrews airdropped supplies to the French at Dien Bien Phu in Indochina. Between 13 March and the fall of Dien Bien Phu on 7 May, CAT pilots flew 682 airdrop missions to the beleaguered French troops. One plane was shot down in early May, and the two pilots were killed; many other Civil Air Transport C-119 Flying Boxcars suffered heavy flak damage, and one pilot was severely wounded. Throughout the 1950s CAT flew this fascinating combination of scheduled commercial flights and clandestine missions.

With the spread of communism throughout Southeast Asia, CAT's mission changed. In 1959 it was renamed Air America and essentially became the CIA's Far Eastern air operator. Under the new corporate name— CAT continued to fly scheduled passenger flights out of

Taiwan—Air America flew all other types of air operations in Laos and South Vietnam. Air America flew civilians, diplomats, spies, refugees, commandos, sabotage teams, doctors, war casualties, drug enforcement officers, drugs, and even visiting VIPs like Richard Nixon all over Southeast Asia. Part of the CIA's support operations in Laos involved logistical support for local tribes fighting the North Vietnamese forces and the Pathet Lao. In addition to food drops (known as 'rice drops) came the logistical demands of the war itself, and Air America pilots flew thousands of flights transporting and air-dropping ammunition and weapons (referred to as hard rice) to friendly forces.

Air America's headquarters was located in Washington, D.C., while its principal North American maintenance base was located at Marana, Arizona.

By 20 April, most of the city's residents sensed that there was little or no hope for their country. Air America pilot Wayne Lannin noted, "The hardest part of living in Saigon in the last days was that we knew it was coming apart. You wanted to leave and get the hell out of there . . . but your personal pride prevented you from leaving." On 21 April, President Thieu resigned in an angry and tearful television address, blaming the country's problems on the United States. Four days later, Major General Smith requested additional security personnel to augment the thirteen embassy Marines at the DAO compound. Air America helicopters airlifted the 3rd Platoon of Company C, 1/9 Marines, dressed in civilian clothes, from the USS *Hancock* to the DAO compound. Despite the fact that the North Vietnamese were funneling thousands of men south on a monthly basis, by the terms of the 1973 Paris Peace Accords the United States was prohibited from exceeding fifty uniformed men in the country at any one time, so the Marines were "snuck" into the country. Air America pilot Burke noted, "It was imperative that we be able to get all our air crews and support personnel together in the minimum amount of time." The same day the Marines flew into the DAO compound, President Thieu left for exile in Taiwan.

On 26 April, Fred Walker wrote, "In addition to not knowing whether or not we are going to get out, there's the constant threat of SA-7 Strela missiles [Soviet shoulder-fired surface-to-air, heat-seeking missiles similar to the American Redeye, the predecessor to today's Stinger]when flying and new anti-aircraft positions. Reds now have a 57mm Firecan radar position 290 degrees, eight miles from the airport." The missile threat was taken very seriously as described by Major Harrington, "We approached Ton San Nhut at 12,000 feet and then executed a dizzying corkscrew descent to the runway.

During the stomach-churning approach, an airman sat in the open door of the C-130 with a flare pistol and scanned the sky for the telltale track of heat-seeking anti-aircraft missiles." Early in the morning on 27 April, the NVA unleashed a rocket barrage that impacted in downtown Saigon and the suburb of Cholon, the first since the ceasefire in 1973. The blasts killed ten people and started huge fires that destroyed five hundred homes and left five thousand people homeless. Simultaneously, heavy fighting erupted all around the capital and the airbase at Bien Hoa came under heavy attack.

With the noose tightening around the city, Air America struggled to evacuate their Filipino employees. Marius Burke tried without success to secure passage for them aboard a Philippine Navy ship. "I called Jacobsen, who was Ambassador Martin's secretary and right hand man, outlining the situation. His response was, 'I wouldn't touch that with a ten foot pole!' No employees got on the ship. I then asked Jacobsen if he would be so kind as to send me a photo of himself so that copies could be made for all flight crews. When the time came to evacuate, we would know who not to pick up!" Burke had a number of meetings with Martin and various staff members. "It became quite apparent to me that they really didn't believe an evacuation would ever take place. In fact, the Ambassador, in one conversation told me that he had good information that Saigon was off-limits to the North Vietnamese and they would never push that far. I countered with the statement that I felt we had no more than two weeks before it was over."

Monday, 28 April was a memorable experience for many of the Air America pilots. Frank Andrews was returning from the downtown area. "As I drove along Cach Mang Street, enroute to the airfield, I noticed several of the shops were shuttered, and I witnessed a woman drawing down the shutters on a small delicatessen. Based on past experience, these actions meant 'trouble' to me." Terry Olson was involved in shuttling evacuees when "a radio operator broadcast on the company VHF radio that Tan Son Nhut was under attack by A-37s." Fred Walker was driving back to the airfield and was "about 100 yards short of the gate when he heard six explosions. Three Americans in the car ahead literally fell out onto the ground with panicky looks and crawled around to the rear door and pulled out flak jackets." He turned his car around and headed for town. Halfway there he "heard multiple explosions and saw hundreds of anti-aircraft [37mm and 40mm] bursts around A-37s." Walker finally decided to hole up with several other Air America pilots in the USAID [U.S. Agency for International Development] billet, a seven-story building located about a kilometer from the airport. Some of the other

A former U.S. Air Force Cessna A-37B Dragonfly used in Vietnam.
In 1975 it was captured by the North Vietnamese.

pilots flew their aircraft to wherever there was a safe location, including U.S. Navy ships offshore.

About 0400 Fred Walker was jarred awake by multiple heavy explosions. "I went to the roof and saw Tan Son Nhut under artillery attack by 130mm cannon, 122mm rocket and mortar fire . . . many aircraft burning . . . at this point we all figured that maybe we'd have to walk and swim to the fleet." Var Green recalled, "Intermittent shelling continued throughout the night, with one rocket landing on our northeast parking ramp . . . near our parked helicopters. Four were unflyable. Incoming fire was intense and by daybreak it was evident an all out attack was in progress." By 0830, the incoming fire had slackened and the airport standby helicopter crew was launched to pick up the flight crews. "[Tony M.] Coalson made the first trip of the day, heading over to the USAID building at 0900 to pick up a load of Air America pilots," Velte recalled. "As soon as he landed, at least nine people climbed aboard . . . and with a full load of fuel on his Bell 204B, he felt that he would not be able to take off." Coalson pointed out that "this was the worst scenario: a full load of pilots [where] everyone is an expert." Velte continued, "The Bell could barely hover—6 to 10 inches—at maximum power. Against his better judgment, Coalson backed up as far as he could and attempted a takeoff. As he went over the side of the seven-story building, his rotor decayed into the red and basically quit flying. The only option was to nose the aircraft over to gain airspeed and reduce collective try and regain engine RPM. Coalson barely managed to avoid the rooftops below. We almost lost the rotary-wing pilots on the first pickup."

Frank Andrews reached the airport on the second flight, grabbed a jeep to check out the helicopters. "As we swung out of the company area . . . a shell exploded right across from us on the ramp . . . a second shell exploded closer this time." He returned to the hanger area where he found, "the mechanics were in the bunkers and in the hallways, trying to stay under cover." Suddenly Andrews heard a helicopter cranking up. "It was obvious that the VNAF were stealing our helicopters." Several pilots and ground crew armed themselves in an effort to provide security for the ICCS flight ramp. This kept other aircraft from being stolen, but not before six were taken, (although one crashed shortly after takeoff). Lyle Genz was preflighting a helicopter when "Six armed VNAF forced their way onto the aircraft demanding they be flown to a ship. I told them it wasn't possible, but that I would take them to a place of safety. I then took off and landed them on the AAM [airline abbreviation code for Air America] ramp where they were disarmed." Ed Adams was more direct, according to Walker. "Ed was about to board his CH-46, and an ARVN soldier tried to forcibly embark. Ed stopped him and the guy started to swing an M-16 [rifle] around to point at him. The soldier got the gun about half way around when Ed knocked him on his ass (busting his hand in the process) and disarmed him. That ended that!"

The Tan Son Nhut airfield by this time was a mass of wrecked aircraft. "We could see the taxiways and military and civilian ramps; a scene of desolation confronted us," Fred Walker recalled. "Burning and bombed out airplanes and helicopters—debris everywhere. Christ, what a sight!" He had to taxi past the "gutted terminal, picking my way around baggage, wrecked automobiles, bicycles, shell holes, shrapnel, you name it." Major General Smith recalled, "The first evacuees departed the DAO compound by Air America helicopters about 1000. We were unable to move personnel earlier because of a lack of air crews. At the time of the rocketing, Air America had only one pilot available at their compound. As others became available during the morning, additional helicopters were activated and in fact Air America finally moved their operational element to the DAO building, since their compound had become untenable as a result of continued rocketing and VNAF interference."

Throughout the morning, Air America helicopters continued to fly evacuees—Americans, Vietnamese and third party nationals—from the rooftop LZs around Saigon to the DAO compound as well as to the fleet.

By early afternoon, however, Air America was down to seventeen flyable helicopters. "We made approximately six trips . . . each time dropping the people
off at the DAO," R. C. Goodwin recalled. "By this time our fuel was running
low, it was getting dark and we had to return to the *Hancock*." Terry Olson
"spent the entire time in Saigon shuttling people from rooftops to the DAO
compound." Fuel became an issue because the Air America compound was
no longer usable. "The only refueling vehicle in their compound required
manual pumping and the internal situation there precluded being on the
ground long enough to refuel . . . accordingly, most refueling operations were
carried out aboard ship," General Smith said. Air America pilot Lyle Genz
recalled, "When fuel became low I flew to an LPD, call sign 'Snow Chief,'
and refueled, then returned to Saigon. I continued to shuttle for the rest of
the day, returning to the Navy LPDs when necessary for fuel." Frank Snepp
noted, "By 1830 Air America ended its rooftop extractions in downtown
Saigon."(At the time of the evacuation, Snepp was in Saigon as the CIA's
chief analyst of North Vietnamese strategy.)

David B. Kendall known as "Farmer John" was flying a "sick" helicopter.
After picking up a load of evacuees, he flew it to one of the Navy ships and
off-loaded his passengers. Before launching he asked for help with fixing a
hydraulic leak. He was told there was no maintenance available and to ditch
the aircraft alongside the ship. After arguing without success, he lifted off,
flew along the port side and jumped, all of which was caught on film and
widely distributed. Fortunately, he was rescued shortly after hitting the water
and taken aboard the ship, none the worse for wear. Thomas P. Grady made
several trips to the fleet but his last flight from the DAO to the USS *Blue
Ridge* was the most memorable. While refueling, several jagged pieces of
metal flew through the air, one of which struck his aircraft. He was amazed
to see a helicopter tail rotor sticking out of the side of the engine. A VNAF
pilot, in a stolen Air America helicopter, tried to ditch in front of the ship.
Instead it crashed into the bow and disintegrated, sending shrapnel skittering
along the deck.

Perhaps the most famous photograph of an Air America evacuation was
mislabeled. Pilot Robert Caron was assigned to pick up several evacuees from
the Pittman Apartments (22 Gia Long Street), the residence of the CIA's
assistant chief of station. As a line of people climbed an outside ladder to the
rooftop, UPI photographer Hugh Van Es took a dramatic shot of an American reaching down to help them up the ladder. The photo received world-
wide distribution with a caption mislabeling it as a military helicopter atop

the roof of the U.S. Embassy. As darkness fell, the Air America pilots were told to shut down for the night aboard the ships of the fleet and to standby to resume operations in the morning. Marius Burke made one of the last flights. "At the USAID building, there were literally thousands mobbing the helipad with Vietnamese calling on the radio for pickups . . . on the same frequency the North Vietnamese were stating that they had the helicopter in sight and would shoot it down if we attempted to land . . . under the circumstances we bypassed it and landed at the DAO where we picked up a load of Americans and took them to the USS *Blue Ridge*."

Operation Frequent Wind was terminated the next day. Air America is credited with evacuating over a thousand people. Frank Snepp said, "That was no small accomplishment, to be sure, particularly in view of the fact that the maximum capacity of each Huey was barely twelve people." Frank Coalson summed up the effort when he said, "We flew our aircraft to their limits and beyond—and we flew ourselves to our limit!"

CHAPTER FIFTEEN

DEFENSE ATTACHÉ COMPOUND

We must seize the opportunity, do it quickly, and do it with certainty.— Le Duc Tho, Democratic Republic of Vietnam Politburo member

The rout of the South Vietnamese forces caused Maj. Gen. Homer D. Smith, the senior defense attaché, to ramp up planning for Option II, primarily a fixed-wing aircraft evacuation to include rotary-wing aircraft, the insertion of a ground security force, and an amphibious force, if required. "We had to devise a plan to fortify and reinforce the compound to hold 10,000 people for 10 days should the situation dictate that in order to accomplish evacuation," Marine Captain Anthony A. Wood, a member of the Special Planning Group recalled, "Immediately I called it 'Alamo' because it seemed obvious that was what we were doing and the name stuck." On 1 April, Smith opened a command and control center named the Evacuation Control Center (ECC) and the Evacuation Processing Center (EPC)

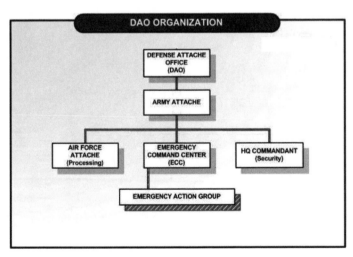

The Defense Attaché Office was the coordination office for the evacuation of personnel during Operation Frequent Wind. The Emergency Command Center (ECC) was organized to process the evacuees.

for processing the anticipated high number of evacuees. Brigadier General Richard M Baughn, USAF was placed in charge of the evacuation. On 4 April, during Operation Baby Lift a U.S. Air Force C5A transport carrying 277 Vietnamese orphans and 37 DAO women staff members experienced an explosive decompression, which blew the rear doors off the aircraft, severing the flight controls, and causing the aircraft to crash. Only one of the DAO volunteers survived.

DEFENSE ATTACHÉ OFFICE

The Defense Attaché Office (DAO) Saigon was activated on 28 January 1973 by Maj. Gen. John E. Murray (U.S. Army) in accordance with requirements established by the Joint Chiefs of Staff, Commander-in-Chief Pacific, and Military Assistance Command, Vietnam. DAO operated from the former MACV compound adjacent to the airfield at Tan Son Nhut, with field offices located in Da Nang, Pleiku, Qui Nhon, Nha Trang, Bien Hoa, Long Binh, Nha Be, Dong Tam, Binh Thuy and Can Tho. It was authorized a staff of fifty military and twelve hundred civilian personnel. DAO Saigon performed the traditional functions of a defense attaché, managed American military affairs in Vietnam after the ceasefire, including the programs for the support of the RVNAF, and furnished housekeeping support to Americans remaining in Vietnam after the ceasefire. Aside from the support of the RVNAF, it reported on operational matters, such as violations of the ceasefire, and produced intelligence information on which subsequent decisions concerning the Military Assistance Program and American interests in Southeast Asia could be based.

Within days of the Baby Lift crash, hundreds of South Vietnamese surrounded the compound, clamoring to enter because they realized the hopelessness of the military situation. In *U.S. Marines in Vietnam, The Bitter End 1973-1975*, it is noted that, "In the next two weeks, these symptoms of decay accelerated to action as mothers started tossing their babies over the fence to other South Vietnamese standing in the processing lines, and the DAO began what Captain Wood called, 'The mobile catch-a-baby drill.'" (Captain Anthony A. Wood, the Joint Casualty Resolution Center's deputy for operations in South Vietnam, was a member of the Special Planning Group.) General Baughn decided it was time to reinforce the DAO's security force, because he had grave doubts that the local Vietnamese guards could provide adequate security. He sent a message to CINCPAC with a frank statement of the grim realities of the situation and called for the commitment of troops for protection. According to Frank Snepp, when Ambassador Martin saw the message "he was infuriated and, without batting an eye, he picked up a secure line, put in a call to the Pentagon and demanded that Baughn be removed immediately, on grounds of insubordination. The following day (11 April) the Pentagon did as Martin demanded, yanking Baughn out of Saigon." From that moment forward everything to do with the evacuation went black (secret) and the Special Planning Group went into deep cover. Captain Wood was assigned to identify evacuation pickup points and bus routes throughout the city. He named the eight routes after pioneer trails in the American West, such as, Colorado, Oregon, Chisholm, Santa Fe, and Texas, which became part of the evacuation vocabulary. As a result, Wood became known as the "Wagonmaster." Wood was skeptical of this plan: "The surface evacuation plan for Saigon was based on planning and bluff, mostly bluff."

The evacuation plan consisted of three phases. The first was the daily evacuation of selected candidates, especially those South Vietnamese who would be targeted for death because of their sensitive assignments, for example, high level government officials, intelligence operatives, and Air America employees. In fact, the DAO had received a report that the NVA had executed the Vietnamese Air America workers after capturing them at the Ban Me Thuot airfield. The second phase concerned the surface and air movement of other evacuation candidates from Saigon and the American Embassy to the DAO compound. The third and final phase involved the massive air evacuation of all the remaining personnel in the DAO installation. Major Harrington thought the plan was in essence "an aerial movement to supplement

CH-53 helicopters in DAO's Landing Zone 38.

Vietnamese being processed for evacuation at the Defense Attaché Office.

the bussing scheme." He felt, "In the event civil disorder precluded movement by bus from the assembly points to the DAO, the plan called for Air America helicopter shuttles from pre-designated pickup points around Saigon to the DAO Compound. [Marine] heavy lift helicopters from aircraft carriers already on station would ferry people from the DAO to the fleet."

Despite the urgency of the situation, General Smith was finding it hard to fill the available evacuation aircraft. By mid-month fewer than 500 people a day were being moved out of South Vietnam. "On 14 April I met with all the DAO contractors in an effort to convince them to leave," he said. "Subsequent to the meeting, however, I was called by one contractor advising me that his people would not leave until we somehow could move even those not legally married." This issue was the heart of the matter . . . many Americans simply would not leave without their "dependents." Smith met with the embassy chief of mission and later with Admiral Gayler and was able to work out an administrative procedure that speeded up the dependent issue. A sponsor simply had to sign a form stating that the individuals listed were his dependents and that he would be responsible for them after their departure from Vietnam. Smith noted, "From 20 April on our numbers of departees grew daily, reaching over 6,000 for 27 April."

Security remained an issue. "We borrowed 16 USMC personnel from the Embassy to help us control personnel being processed," Smith said. The NCOIC of the Marine security guard (MSG) detachment, MSgt. Juan J. Valdez said, "I didn't like the idea of splitting my forces but we were under the operational control of the State Department, and what they said was it."

The 3rd Platoon of Company C, 1st Battalion, 9th Marines, was flown to the DAO compound from Okinawa in civilian clothes to avoid an overt breach of the Paris Accords, which limited the number of uniformed American military personnel in South Vietnam to fifty.

Two of those picked, Lance Corporal. Darwin Judge and Corporal Charles McMahon Jr., were newly assigned to the embassy straight out of MSG School in Quantico, Virginia. "As the week progressed," Smith recalled, "we began losing control again so I asked for a platoon of USMC personnel from the Ground Support Force." On 25 April, 3rd Platoon, Company C, 1st Battalion, 9th Marines, was flown in by Air America helicopters. "This made all the difference in the world," Smith said. "There is something about a United States Marine that demands respect from the Vietnamese people. From the time of their arrival on we had and maintained complete control."

The North Vietnamese bombing of Tan Son Nhut on 28 April completely disrupted the aircraft evacuation flow. "Subsequent to the bombing the government [South Vietnamese] imposed a 24 hour curfew," Major General Smith said. "Later that evening I learned of the decision to discontinue the flow of C-141 aircraft. . . . I was told that 60 sorties of C-130 aircraft could be expected for 29 April." In anticipation of the arrival of the C-130s, a large number of evacuees were assembled and processed for evacuation. Smith recalled that, "Although we did not realize it at the time, the stage for the execution of Frequent Wind was set on or about 0400, 29 April, when Tan Son Nhut came under a rather heavy rocket attack." One of the first rockets hit the guard post near Gate 4, which was manned by two Marines. Sergeant Kevin M. Maloney was one of the first people to reach the scene. "We [Maloney and Corp Otis Holmes] began to move towards Post Number in a fire mission," he recalled vividly, "about five times . . . only five or six rounds but they didn't bother me because I took cover in one if the gook foxholes that covered the hill." An aerial observer (AO) flew over to investigate the suspected enemy soldier. It spotted the young NCO and identified him as the missing team member. "He waved his wings," Slocum recalled, "and circled over me for about an hour before several Hueys showed up." The gunships strafed the ridge trying to keep the NVA at bay. "The Hueys seemed to want me to move toward the grunts [Bravo Company]. I didn't want to do that because I didn't want to get shot again. I didn't have weapon and the gooks were between me and them." Based on the sighting, Bravo Company moved toward the missing man. "[We] spotted something rustling in the brush across a wide clearing," Guidry explained. "The squad fell into position to fire at whoever came into the clearing. A man stumbled out into the clearing. It was one of the missing members of the Force Recon team, fleeing desperately from the enemy." Slocum remembered, "The grunts started moving my way. First I thought they were NVA, so I started moving the other way. The choppers sort of motioned me back in, and it was grunts after all. I walked over to them and they had a medevac come in and pick me up." He was flown to Dong Ha for treatment and after two and a half months recuperation, returned to 3rd Force Reconnaissance Company.

AFTERMATH

The three survivors were interviewed by Captain George W. T. "Digger" O'Dell, the 3rd Force intelligence officer. Based on the interviews, O'Dell was able to piece together the team's desperate fight and make recommendations for individual awards.

Team Box Score Award Citations
The President of the United States in the name of The Congress
takes pride in presenting the **Medal of Honor** posthumously to
Second Lieutenant Terrance C. Graves
United States Marine Corps
for service as set forth in the following
Citation:
For conspicuous gallantry and intrepidity at the risk of his life above and beyond the call of duty as a platoon commander with the 3d Force Reconnaissance Company. While on a long-range reconnaissance mission, 2d Lt. Graves' 8-man patrol observed 7 enemy soldiers approaching their position. Reacting instantly, he deployed his

1 in search of Judge and McMahon," Maloney recalled. "I was searching along the ditch in the darkness and came across McMahon's body ... Judge's body was lying near some burning Honda motorcycles." The two Marines were the first casualties of Operation Frequent Wind and the last two Marines to die on the ground in South Vietnam.

———

Classified Task Force 76 Special Frequent Wind Execution Sitrep:
Reliable source indicates that [NVA] 232 Corps has been ordered to move artillery into new position today and once in position to open fire on Tan Son Nhut runway.

———

Three U.S. Air Force C-130s were on the ground during the attack. Captain Arthur Mallano (USAF) was a pilot of one of the aircraft. "I'll never forget the time—0358—when we thought at first was lighting in the background ... the whole sky lit up and I said to the co-pilot, 'Gee, that thunderstorm is getting a little closer.' The next thing I know, not only was it white, it was red, blue, green. The rockets were hitting the field with accuracy. They were not trying to scare us. They immediately hit a fuel truck, the control tower and an airplane that had turned off the runway." Captain Mallano quickly

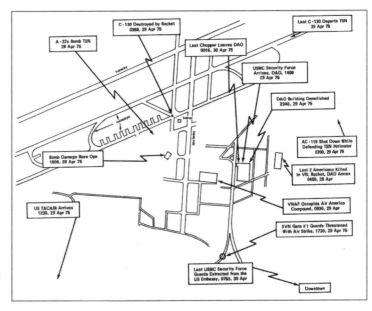

Sketch showing key events at the DAO compound.

taxied out to the runway. He had over 260 passengers in the aircraft, way over the rated capacity. "The rockets were hitting to the left, the right, behind, and in front of us," he recalled. "We went to military power and took off, with the rockets hitting right behind us, right in front of us, right on the sides." A second C-130 was not so fortunate; a rocket hit under a wing and started a fire. "I thought we had lost a crew," he said. "They recognized the situation immediately and got out." The downed crew was rescued and flown out by the third C-130.

The mixed artillery and rocket fire continued to bombard the airfield. Between 0430 and 0800, it was estimated that over 40 rounds per hour was concentrated on the flight line and fuel and ammunition storage areas. One reason for the accuracy of the shelling may have been North Vietnamese infiltrating the city. Major Harrington related an incident that occurred a few days previously. "In a small coffee shop near Tan Son Nhut, several alert ARVN airborne troops noticed an unfamiliar officer wearing their unit insignia. The stranger had a northern accent . . . and an odd unfamiliarity with local prices and customs. The suspicious troopers summoned the military police, who quickly determined that the 'lieutenant's' papers were bogus. Under interrogation, the imposter confessed that he was an NVA artillery forward observer." Author Tiziano Terzani wrote in *Giai Phong, The Fall and Liberation of Saigon*, "Infiltrators were everywhere. Some had arrived separately, one by one, by trucks and buses in the first wave of refugees . . . fifteen hundred Communist commandos had infiltrated themselves around Tan Son Nhut Airport as early as April 25th . . . with the help of local cells of the Front that had survived the Tet offensive . . . Saigon was like a sponge." NVA commander General Van Dung bragged that, "with the help of local people [Viet Cong] we sent our observers to slip in next to the enemy to direct our artillery . . . so that it hit the mark."

Shortly after daybreak on 29 April, despite the shelling, the VNAF began scrambling their aircraft to safety in Thailand. Many jettisoned their external fuel tanks and ordnance on the active runway. Major General Smith said, "It became clear that we were not going to be able to use the field for further fixed wing operations. I relayed this information to Ambassador Martin who chose to come out to the DAO compound for a personal look into the matter." Upon his arrival the ambassador was briefed on the cluttered condition of the runway but still resisted calling off the fixed-wing evacuation. "He discussed the [situation] with me in great detail and, in fact, called LtGen [Brent] Snowcroft in the White House [deputy assistant to the president for national security affairs]," Smith noted. "Subsequent to his departure, he read a message from the White House stating that the C-130 lift would continue as long as feasible." General Smith was flabbergasted. "Within an hour I had discussed the problems of the runways with CINCPAC, who agreed that there was no way we could continue." Smith called Martin and advised him of the phone call. "Mr. Ambassador, CINCPAC is at this moment recommending to the Joint Chiefs that we go to Option IV. I thought you should know." Martin mulled it over and asked Smith again whether he thought the airlift could continue. "After ascertaining that I was absolutely sure that there was no way to continue the airlift, Ambassador Martin agreed that he would call for the rotary wing evacuation. Within the hour the execute message had come through and Frequent Wind was in process." Martin placed the phone call at 1048. Secretary of State Kissinger immediately gave the approval and the American radio station began repeat playing of "White Christmas," which was the signal for American personnel to move to their evacuation points.

EXECUTE OPTION IV

"As the first wave approached the city of Saigon and the Landing Zones, heavy AAA fire was reported."—Command Chronology, PROVMAG-39 DEEP PURPLE . . . DEEP PURPLE . . . DEEP PURPLE . . . THIS IS NO DRILL . . . The 1-MC (a U.S. Navy ship's public-address system) blared the announcement throughout the USS *Hancock* sending the Marine heli-

Pilots from HMH-463 aboard the USS *Hancock* reviewing flight plans prior to launching for Operation Frequent Wind.

copter crewmen scrambling to man their aircraft. Many of the men had been sitting in their helicopters for hours on a one-hour alert and had just been released to go for lunch. Admiral Gayler gave the order to execute Frequent Wind at 1051 but for some unexplained reason it did not reach the *Hancock* until 1215. Captain Kurt A. Schrader recalled, "We had just stood down when the ship's captain came over the 1-MC and announced that the mission was a go but the message directing it had been lost by the *Blue Ridge's* communications center." The *Hancock* went to general quarters at the same time after receiving a report that North Vietnamese torpedo boats might attack.

————————

Provisional Marine Air Group 39 (PROVMAG-39) helicopter mission plan:

- 1st Wave: 12 CH-53s from USS *Okinawa* (HMH-462) with GSF [ground security force] land in LZ at 1500—bring out evacuees if possible.
- 2nd Wave: 12 CH-53s from USS *Hancock* (HMM-463) with GSF land in LZ at 1515—bring out evacuees if possible.
- 3rd Wave: 12 CH-53s from USS *Midway* composed of 3 HMH-463 aircraft and 9 Air Force aircraft, land in LZ at 1520—bring out evacuees if possible.
- All waves will break up into 3 aircraft flights and continue evacuation.
- 2 CH-46s from the USS *Hancock* will be airborne search and rescue (SAR)—holding at Point Wishbone.
- 2 CH-46s from the USS *Okinawa* to provide airborne "Sparrow Hawk" (GSF reaction force), just south of Point Wishbone.
- 2 Cobras from the USS *Hancock* provide protective for aircraft between Point Wishbone and Point Keyhole.
- 2 Cobras from USS *Okinawa* to provide fire for aircraft between Point Wishbone to "feet wet (over the ocean).

Each wave was assigned prescribed routes, altitudes and checkpoints, which were chosen to avoid midair collisions and to avoid the enemy's SAM and SA-7 missile threat: inbound flights 6,500 feet, outboard flights 5,500. The altitudes were also high enough to avoid artillery and small-arms fire. As further protection, both squadrons painted their aircraft with low reflective infrared paint to help prevent enemy missiles from locking on to the helicopters. The flight was approximately eighty miles from the ships to

Saigon. With L-Hour established as 1500, the first wave of helicopters were launched at 1215 to begin cross-decking operations (the ground security force and the helicopters were often positioned on different ships), which required a two-hour lead time to properly position the GSF, get the required numbers of helicopters airborne, and assemble them into their proper waves.

This phase of the operation was extremely complex, requiring meticulous planning and precise timing. Loaded and fueled helicopters had to be repositioned on eight ships: *Okinawa, Hancock, Dubuque, Denver, Duluth, Mobile, Peoria* and *Vancouver*. In addition, large numbers of men and amounts equipment had to be redistributed in order to make the flight schedule work. Fully-loaded helicopters could launch from the various ships at the same time and rendezvous overhead to fly together to Saigon, or unloaded helicopters could be held at an air-orbit point until they could land on the appropriate ship and take on their designated loads at which point the now-loaded aircraft would return to the orbit-point and wait for the flight to depart. In order to accomplish the complicated cross-decking maneuver with the limited space available, all the task force ships had to be used.

COMMAND AND CONTROL

Task Force 76 was responsible for air control operations during the time the helicopters were over the water: feet wet. The helicopter direction control (HDC) aboard the USS *Okinawa*, as an agency of TF-76, had the responsibility for air control during feet wet and for directing outbound helicopters to empty decks for offload of evacuees and for refueling. Once over land, operational control passed to United States Support Activities Group and Commander Seventh Air Force (USSAG/7thAF) located in Thailand. Local control of the air space was carried out by an EC-130E Hercules officially known as the airborne battlefield command control center (ABCCC), call sign Cricket. The commanding officer PROVMAG-39 exercised control of all his assets through the tactical air coordination center (TACC) aboard the USS *Blue Ridge*. Initially, terminal guidance into the DAO landing zone was by strobe light, but this proved unsatisfactory. Subsequently, terminal guidance was by VHF/FM radio utilizing flight-leader identification by a series of landing-light flashes after which the controller at the LZ would provide direction vectors to the landing zone in the DAO to the incoming aircraft. Landing zone departure was at the pilot's option unless specifically directed to hold due to air-traffic conflicts. All departing helicopters were provided advisories on adjacent air traffic, obstacles in the flight path, and hostile fire. Upon clearance from the DAO LZ controller, pilots switched over to the ABCCC.

Fixed-wing fighter bombers were the first aircraft launched. "About 1230, I saw the first American fighters overhead," Lt. Col. John Hilgenberg (USAF), a member of the EPC, noted, "The initial flights looked to be about 10,000 feet and took a lot of ground fire. I could see many airbursts, mostly behind the aircraft. I assumed it was ARVN gunners firing at unknowns, thinking back to the previous night [rogue A-37 bombing]." U.S. Air Force and Navy fighters and fighter-bombers covered the evacuation during daylight hours and were replaced by AC-130 Spectre gunships from Thailand at night. Twelve CH-53s from HMH-462 loaded with Battalion Landing Team (BLT) 2/4 (command groups A and B and rifle companies F and H) comprised the first wave and was scheduled to land in the DAO Compound at 1500: L-Hour.

L-HOUR CONTROVERSY

There was some confusion over the definition and timing of L-Hour. The Navy and Marine Corps defined it as the time a helicopter touched down in the landing zone. The Air Force thought it was the time that a helicopter was launched. The two commands finally agreed to accept the Air Force definition and incorporated the agreement into the planning documents. However, during the later stages of planning, the definition was changed back, which caused the planners to have to modify the entire helicopter flow schedule. Vice Admiral George P. Steel, Commander Seventh Fleet, offered his assessment of the confusion, "This deplorable mix-up over L-Hour never would have occurred, except for the subordination of the Seventh Fleet and the Marines to CG, USSAG." The timing of L-Hour also impacted the unit's alert posture. For example, the plan called for a one-hour alert to allow the forces to get into position before the start of the operation. That one hour, combined with ninety minutes that was needed for cross-decking and the thirty minute flight time from the ships to the DAO, meant that three hours would elapse before the first helicopter would touch down at the landing zone. In addition, the Air Force added another hour for its fixed-wing aircraft to be on station ... which translated into a four-hour window.

Secretary of State Kissinger was upset by the apparent lengthy delay. "Why did it take so long to get the helilift started? Kissinger asked.

Henry Kissinger: I must have told the President three times that the helicopters were ten minutes out [from the carriers]. [Deputy Secretary of Defense] William Clements: I don't know about you, Henry, but I'm just madder than hell about it. I know George [Gen. George S. Brown (USAF), Chairman Joint Chiefs of Staff] is too. Gen. Brown: I don't know, but I suspect we'll need to have an investigation. I suspect that what happened was that some of the local commanders changed their plans at the last minute. Also, I suspect that they miscalculated when they converted the time from Zulu to Saigon time. They miscalculated by about two hours. The result was that we wasted two hours doing nothing. I was sitting over there in the command center doing nothing for two hours.

Classified Task Force 76 Special Frequent Wind Execution Sitrep:
Heavy Anti Aircraft fire northeast of Saigon (estimated .50 caliber or 23mm). Anti-Aircraft fire vicinity of embassy building and light AAA along entire helo route to Saigon.

There was great concern about the NVA antiaircraft capability. A secret Defense Intelligence Agency (DIA) report stated, "Early on 28 April a VNAF helicopter and an A1 Skyraider aircraft were downed by an SA-7/GRAIL in the Cholon section of Saigon. In addition a C-119 was hit by an SA-7 while attempting to take off from Tan Son Nhut and crashed on the airfield. The presence of the highly mobile SA-7/GRAIL missiles seriously threatens U.S. evacuation flights." Major Charlie Brame, a USAF A-7 pilot flying combat air patrol observed, "[My] onboard detection and warning equipment indicated the aircraft was being painted by enemy surface-to-air missile radars . . . several times indications of impending missile launches caused me to take countermeasures." Lieutenant Colonel William A. "Art" Bloomer's detachment, Marine Composite Reconnaissance Squadron One (VMCJ-1), provided electronic countermeasures for the operation. Bloomer said, "this small group of Marines kept jamming radar signals identified with the Firecan radar that controlled the 37mm air defense weapons of the NVA."

MISSILE LAUNCH DEBRIEF
Captain J. J. Porter, Jr. reported, "A missile launch at the helicopter's 4 o'clock to 7 o'clock position, with an angle of approach approximately 60 degrees. I saw red-orange balls of fire

and the white missiles corkscrewing toward the aircraft. Two missiles exploded while the others fizzled out. One of the missiles exploded about 200 feet away after a crewman fired a MK-50 flare, which the missile tracked. I was surprised to see one missile fired from a sampan."

Sergeant T. G. Hamilton reported, "A missile launch three miles southeast of Saigon. I saw the missile and launched a MK-50 and An/ALE-29 flare. The missile exploded in a red ball and then an orange flash. The blast shook the helicopter and caused the tail to dip."

Sergeant Lee Foster reported, "A missile launch five miles southeast of the embassy. I saw the missile and launched four MK-50 flares and 12 AN/ALE flares. The missile detonated prior to hitting the aircraft but the explosion's shock wave moved us 15 to 20 feet to the left.

Corporal Donald Fay reported a sighting. "I saw the missile being shot-off, followed by a secondary flash and then a bright red dot coming towards the aircraft with a trail of smoke behind the missile. When the missile was fired, I immediately fired my MK-50 flare gun and approximately two seconds later the missile started to follow the flare into the river. The missile was about one mile from the aircraft when it started down.

Missiles were not the only threat. The PROVMAG-39 after-action report noted, "As the first wave approached the city of Saigon and the landing zones, heavy AAA fire was reported." Pilot Maj. John F. Guilmartin said, "I and my crew saw a fair amount of fire and returned it." Major Brame was on-station in his A-7. "One of the [helicopter] pilots radioed that he was taking fire and was being hit in the vicinity of the tail rotor. I armed all weapon systems and descended to approximately 800–1000 feet at 500 knots in order to locate this specific threat." Brame was unable to pinpoint the target and aborted the search. An Air Force AC-130 was on station during nighttime hours. "After darkness, the clouds began to clear and we were able to observe the activity below both visually and with our specialized viewing, the infrared and television devices. Many ground fires, fire-fights between ground forces and anti-aircraft firings were present. We took particular interest in one 57mm gun position and smaller caliber AAA which were in close proximity to the [helicopter] flight path . . . we were prepared to fire, but were unable to obtain clearance."

LAUNCH THE HELICOPTERS
Here we go!—Brigadier General Richard Carey
(USMC) upon launching aircraft

At 1315, Brig. Gen. Carey, Col. Al Gray, commander of the 4th Marines, and a small advance staff of communicators and aviation personnel boarded

Brigadier General Richard E. Carey on the bridge of the attack aircraft carrier USS *Hancock* while visiting with BLT 1/9 and HMH-463. General Carey, the 9th MAB commander, served on the *Hancock* many years earlier as a corporal in its Marine detachment.— *Department of Defense*

two UH-1Es and departed the USS *Blue Ridge* for the DAO compound. The flight was uneventful until the aircraft reached the vicinity of Tan Son Nhut where NVA artillery and rocket fire was plastering the airfield. Plumes of thick black smoke marked burning buildings and aircraft. The burned out hulk of a VNAF C-130 littered the runway, while other damaged and destroyed aircraft cluttered the taxiways. The pilots carefully gauged the strike of the shells and determined that they could land near the DAO headquarters. The passengers quickly disembarked and made their way to the emergency command center and established communications. DAO staff operations officer Lt. Col. Arthur E. Laehr (USAF) remembered, "General Carey landed at 1406 and reported some ground fire on his ingress. As he entered the ECC, it was apparent that he was upset from learning that some kind of delay message had been passed to the troop carrier helicopters." L-Hour had been postponed an hour, from 1400 to 1500.

———

Classified Task Force 76 Special Frequent Wind Execution Sitrep:
Entire first wave of 34/7 USMC and USAF CH-53 and H-53 helos from Okinawa, Hancock and Midway have departed launch area enroute Saigon.

———

Lieutenant Colonel Herbert M. Fix, HMH-463's (Pegasus) commanding officer, led the squadron's first three CH-53s (Pineapple 5-1, 5-2, 5-3) off the deck of the USS *Hancock* at 1240. "We proceeded to the USS *Vancouver* for the pickup of the GSF [117 Marines] and proceeded to *Hancock* for refueling." The squadron operations officer, Maj. J. R. Howell and a flight of three(Pineapple 6-1, 6-2, 6-3) "took off from USS *Hancock* twenty minutes later and proceeded to USS *Vancouver*. Pineapple 6-1 was the first to land and pick up his load of 40 GSF . . . then proceeded to USS *Mt Vernon* to await L-Hour. During this time Pineapple 6-2 and 6-3 landed on USS *Vancouver*, loaded up 22 GSF, 2 mules [small, flatbed, self-propelled vehicles] carrying 106s [recoilless antitank weapons], and awaited L-Hour. At approximately 1430 Pineapple 6-1 departed *Mt Vernon*, flew over *Vancouver* collecting the rest of his flight and started inbound to Point Hope." Flight after flight executed the evacuation flight schedule in a complicated aerial ballet.

SIKORSKY CH-53 SEA STALLION

The Sikorsky CH-53 Sea Stallion is the Marine Corps's heavy-lift transport helicopter. Delivery began in 1966, with the first aircraft arriving in Vietnam in 1967. The CH-53A featured a six-bladed main rotor and four-bladed tail rotor. To save space on board naval vessels, the tail boom and the rotors folded. The rotor system was initially driven by twin General Electric T64-6 turbo shaft engines providing 2,850 shaft horsepower (2,130 kW) each, with an engine on each side of the forward fuselage. Experience in Vietnam's tropical climates proved that heavy lifting demanded more power, so an improved variant was acquired, the CH-53D, with upgraded engines. Both the CH-53A and the CH-53D served alongside each other through the rest of the Vietnam War.

The Sea Stallion has a fuselage design similar to the Sikorsky S-61R/Jolly Green Giant series, with a passenger door on the right side of the fuselage behind the cockpit and a power-operated rear loading ramp. The fuselage is watertight, though not intended for amphibious use, and only lands on water in emergencies. The Stallion has mechanical flight controls which are backed by three independent hydraulic systems. Armor protects crew and vital systems. The CH-53 carries a crew of four (pilot, copilot, crew chief, and an aerial observer), a load of thirty-eight troops or twenty-four litters with medical attendants, an internal cargo load of 8,000 pounds (3,600 kg) or an external load of 13,000 pounds (5,900 kg) on the single-point sling hook. The CH-53D is equipped with twin .50 BMG (12.7mm) M2/XM218 machine guns that point out to each side of the fuselage.

Upon reaching Point Hope, a control feature located at a point of a land just west of Vung Tau, the flights were released by the helicopter direction center aboard the *Okinawa* to proceed to their landing zones. "We reached Point Hope and . . . directed to hold for approximately 13 minutes due to the complete saturation of the inbound route," Major Howell, Pineapple 6-1, recalled. After being cleared to continue, Howell's flight "came under small arms fire, which was arching under the aircraft so no retaliatory fire was returned." Pineapple 6-1 flight was cleared to the next checkpoint, Wishbone, and then authorized to proceed to Check Point Keyhole, the entry point to the DAO compound's landing zones. The pilots in the first wave reported the weather as 2,000 feet scattered clouds, 20,000 feet overcast with 15 miles visibility. A haze over Saigon further decreased line of sight visibility to 1 mile, while a solid layer of clouds more than 2 miles high obscured the sun. CH-46 pilot Capt. Edward J. "Jim" Ritchie recalled, "The sky was completely overcast, meeting the ground in the distance with the lights of the city and the burning buildings reflecting off it, giving one the impression that you were seeing a strange movie about the Apocalypse." HMH-463's command chronology stated, "The pilots had to fly 100 miles over enemy terrain with broken cloud cover and no NAVAIDS or radar control." Weather conditions continued to deteriorate as the operation continued.

Classified Task Force 76 Special Frequent Wind Execution Sitrep:
First flight on deck at USDAO LZ. GSF inserted. Second flight (2 helos) above USDAO LZ.... [Twelve minutes later the Task Force reported,] First flight departed USDAO LZ with 149 evacuees.

CH-53Ds from HMH-462 carrying elements of 2nd Battalion, 4th Marines, approach the DAO landing zones. The first helicopter landed in the DAO compound at 1506 on 29 April 1975.

Vietnamese board CH-53s in LZ 39, a parking lot in the DAO Compound.—*Department of Defense*

As the aircraft began the descent into the DAO compound, their radar-homing and warning devices lit up, indicating the present of three SA-2 batteries [the SA-2 Guideline was a missile system similar to the U.S. Army's Nike Ajax] to the north and northeast of Tan Son Nhut, all of which were within range. Pineapple 6-1 landed in LZ-37 (tennis courts), 6-2 and 6-3 in LZ-35 (exchange parking lot) where they dropped off the ground security force and picked up a total of 203 evacuees. Lieutenant Colonel Hilgenberg recalled, "At 1512 three Marine CH-53s roared overhead at about 50 feet. To me the sight was almost too good to be true . . . the crowd broke into a huge cheer with hand clapping and the first smiles I had seen in days." As the helicopters landed, the GSF disembarked. "The Marines spilled out in full battle gear and ran, crouching, to perfect positions to guard against the threats that faced them," David Butler wrote in *The Fall of Saigon.* Hilgenberger said, "It went off with the precision of a maneuver, [just] like a movie" and that the helicopters "loaded rapidly with three 65-evacuee groups through the rear cargo doors of each aircraft, and they were airborne within two to three minutes."

DAO/AIR AMERICA LANDING ZONES
The DAO/Air America complex was situated adjacent to the Tan Son Nhut airfield. With some preparation numerous landing zones were available in the DAO compound, the Annex, and across the road on the Air America apron. The DAO complex was divided roughly into two separate areas, one called the Alamo and the other the Annex, with the Alamo housing the main headquarters building and the emergency command center (ECC). The Annex consisted primarily of the exchange and the gymnasium.

Landing Zones:
- Exchange parking lot—LZ-35, capacity three CH-53s
- Softball field—LZ-36, capacity three CH-53s
- Tennis court area—LZ-37, capacity three CH-53s
- Parking lot—LZ-38, capacity two CH-53s
- North parking lot and motor pool—LZ-39, capacity one CH-53
- Air America ramp area—LZ-40, capacity one CH-53

A preliminary inspection by the 9th MAB of these landing zones found that they were not suitable as-is for helicopter operations. The MAB requested permission to commence engineering efforts, a request that was denied by the embassy. Despite this decision improvements to the LZs were initiated with obstacles were removed and windsocks and markings installed under the cover of darkness, so prying eyes could not observe the preparations.

Marines of BLT 2/4 guard the perimeter of the DAO Annex landing zone. LZs 34 and 35 were located here. All operations from the Annex were completed before sunset on 29 April.—*Department of Defense*

The helicopters flew outbound via Newport Pier toward the ships of Task Force 76. Upon reaching Point Mercy they reported feet wet and were then vectored to the ships that had enough deck space to accommodate them. On one flight Major Howell reported receiving, "AAA fire which seemed to explode about 500–1000 feet below the aircraft." Several aircraft reported taking automatic weapons fire as they approached the various landing zones. Many pilots thought it was South Vietnamese troops embittered at being abandoned by America. Fortunately none of the helicopters were hit. The evacuation continued like clockwork, with flights in and out on a ninety-minute cycle. By late afternoon, darkness threatened the evacuation, especially during the approach to the landing zone. Pineapple 7-1 recalled, "The weather was getting pretty bad with squall lines developing along with the darkness. The flight inbound was intermittently IFR with visibility low." The compound was still well lit by several floodlights, as well as automobile headlights, but the ballpark was black. "These zones required near vertical approaches over buildings and trees, Lieutenant Colonel Hilgenberg noted. "During a landing, two aircraft, one flying level across the field, another climbing after a missed approach, had an extremely near miss, less than 50 feet before the lower pilot saw the higher aircraft and broke violently to the right in the darkness." Lieutenant Colonel Bolton told his pilots to "turn on their lights to help avoid a mid-air collision."

By1730 hours, Lieutenant Colonel Hilgenberg reported, "all evacuees were gone. Huge piles of luggage left by the crowds stood about the area . . . and were being pilfered by ARVN paratroopers and civilians from the surrounding area." With the Vietnamese evacuees and most of the Americans gone, it was time for the remaining DAO personnel and the GSF to pull out. At 1930, the security force tightened its defensive perimeter until it encompassed just LZ-36 and the Alamo. A half hour later, Major General Smith and his remaining staff boarded two helicopters and departed the compound. Finally, at 2250, Brigadier General Carey ordered the withdrawal of the GSF. Just after midnight at 0030, the last elements of the GSF prepared to lift off. Major James Livingston recalled, "Two guys came out of nowhere, saying 'Don't leave the two of us." Captain Raymond McManus and MSgt. William East, an explosive ordnance disposal (EOD) team, had been assigned to destroy sensitive documents, communications gear, and over $3 million in U.S. currency to keep it from falling into NVA hands. "They had about 10,000 pounds of thermite packed all around the gear," Livingston said. "We managed to get them on, and somehow this helicopter . . . struggled to get off the ground. The North Vietnamese were right outside the fence when we pulled out."

DESTRUCTION OF CLASSIFIED MATERIAL AND U.S. CURRENCY

On 19 April, a two-man explosive ordnance disposal team was sent to the DAO compound to prepare all the classified or sensitive material, telecommunications equipment, crypto machines, and other designated control areas for destruction. There was simply too much equipment to be evacuated in the short time frame remaining before the North Vietnamese captured the compound. Nothing of value was to fall into their hands. The EOD team used eighteen 44-pound drums of thermite powder, over 120 thermite grenades and 220 thermite slabs. The telecommunications center alone required 15 drums of thermite, 30 thermite grenades, and 200 thermite slabs. In addition the team prepared to destroy the $13.5 million satellite tracking station. "High powered explosives [were used] around the base of the antenna dish," according to CIA analyst Frank Snepp, "and the ARVN computer complex and the quarters once occupied by General Westmoreland." The team was also directed to prepare the destruction of over 3.5 million U.S. dollars and 85 million RVN piastres (at the time worth U.S. $113,787). Art Laehr recalled, "On the afternoon of the 29th we took all the money into the open courtyard and deposited it [in] barrels by layers with thermite between layers." Lieutenant Colonel Laehr observed the EOD team "wire the barrels for automatic burn when they destroyed the rest of the DAO building." By the evening of 29 April, all the preparations had been completed. As the last helicopter arrived, the EOD team pulled the fuses Lieutenant Colonel Laehr said, "Sheets of flame swept through the complex as the bombs went to work. The heat from the explosions was so intense that . . . this fabled bastion of American power in Vietnam crumpled and collapsed like a ribbon of cheap tin."

A CH-53 departs LZ 39 after depositing its security force. After the withdrawal of the last ground forces at 0030 hours 20 April, flight operations ceased for nearly two hours.

Time Magazine correspondent William Stuart described the flight out, "For the next three minutes as we gained altitude, we held our breaths. We knew the Communists had been using heat-seeking missiles, and we were prepared to be shot out of the sky. Forty minutes later we were aboard the USS *Denver* . . . and safety." Frank Snepp wrote, "As the big CH-53 lunged up over the edge of the compound . . . as far as [I] could see, the airfield was littered with fireballs, each going from blue to green to brilliant white as it rolled its way through rows of parked aircraft."

Classified Task Force 76 Special Frequent Wind Execution Sitrep:
Last GSF out of USDAO at 291610Z Apr [date/time group]. No casualties at DAO since execute.

The DAO evacuation lasted a total of nine hours and involved over fifty U.S. Marine Corps and Air Force helicopters. A total of 395 U.S. citizens and an estimated 4,475 refugees were evacuated. Colonel Edward Pelosky, USA, a member of the DAO staff praised the evacuation. "My hat is off to those individual planners and participants who got us out of Saigon. It was a deliberate exercise pulled off with precision, confidence, and the great skill of the aviators—a textbook version."

CHAPTER SIXTEEN

THE EMBASSY

Note evacuational signal. Do not disclose to other personnel. When the evacuation is ordered, the code will be read out on American Forces Radio. The code is: THE TEMPERATURE IN SAIGON IS 112 DEGREES* AND RISING. THIS WILL BE FOLLOWED BY THE PLAYING OF I'M DREAMING OF A WHITE CHRIST-MAS—from SAFE (Standard Instruction and Advice to Civilians in an Emergency), a fifteen-page booklet distributed by the U.S. Embassy in Saigon

The American embassy, known as the Norodom Compound, was located in downtown Saigon along Embassy Row, several blocks from the Presidential Palace, and across the street from the British Embassy. The French Embassy's property abutted it on the south side. A gate in the wall allowed access into the French garden. Authors Bob Drury and Tom Clavin in *Last Men Out, The True Story of America's Heroic Last Hours in Vietnam*, noted that the embassy "was actually two separate compounds, a consulate and the embassy Chancery proper, which were divided by an eight-foot wall bisected by a steel gate. The three-story consulate was located in the southern third of the grounds and took up about an acre of land. . . . The larger area to the north housed the six-story Chancery building." A parking lot, motor pool and a combined recreation area (CRA), with a swimming pool, canteen, bar, and small theater, was located on the northwest side of the Chancery. "Both the consulate and embassy grounds were pocked with multiple warehouses and utility sheds built into an eight-foot wall, embedded with glass shards and topped with concertina wire, which sealed the entire complex," according to Drury and Clavin. Most of the American staff worked

---

* Some accounts report it as the temperature is 105 degrees and rising.

in the Chancery, a distinctive white concrete building, with a lattice facade that served to both cool the building and deflect rockets and other projectiles. At the time of its construction it was one of the tallest buildings in the city.

Aerial view of the American embassy in Saigon. The embassy was never considered a primary helicopter evacuation site because its rooftop helipad couldn't accommodate anything bigger than a CH-46. However, the large tree in the parking lot was cut down allowing CH-53s to land.

The embassy had a long-standing evacuation plan, but it was hopelessly out of date. It did not include using the grounds as a major evacuation site. The embassy's ground-level landing zone could only accommodate a single CH-53 and its rooftop landing pad, which was meant to be used to evacuate the ambassador, a small staff, and the embassy's Marine guard, could take one CH-46. Deputy Chief of Mission Wolfgang Lehmann noted, "the heavy CH-53 had to land in the courtyard where the famous, beautiful Banyan tree was located. It was always obvious that, when push came to shove, the tree would have to come down. One of the problems was that the tree was not only large but it was always visible from the street. The streets were getting increasingly crowded as panic was beginning to slowly develop in the city . . . [and] the removal of the tree would be visible act that would undoubtedly spread like wild fire throughout the city."

THE BANYAN TREE

When Wolfgang Lehmann, the deputy chief of mission, learned that the helicopter evacuation had been approved, he told Administrative Counselor Hank Boudreau, "Okay, Hank, now you can tell 'em to take down the dammed tree!" Lehmann was talking about a large Tamarind tree that had been planted by the French. It dominated the lawns and gardens outside the main foyer . . . and more importantly it obstructed the only space within the embassy grounds that could handle a CH-53 helicopter. Major James H. Kean, commanding officer Company C, Marine Security Guard (MSG) Battalion, and Ground Support Force Commander United States Embassy Compound, had come to the conclusion that, "we had to get rid of the [tree] that blocked access to helicopters landing. Ambassador Martin had spoken to me personally and told me that if I laid one finger on that tree that I would be in very big trouble." To Martin the tree had become a symbol . . . once the tree fell, America's prestige would fall with it. Major Kean recalled, "Someone actually strung a rope around the tree and tied a fire axe to it with a little sign that read, 'Feeling frustrated? Take a whack!'" With Option Four approved, the tree came down. Australian journalist John Pilger was an eyewitness to the great logging effort. "The tree-cutters assembled, like Marlboro men run to fat. These were the men who would fell the great tamarind; a remarkable group of CIA officers, former Special Forces men (the Green Berets) and an assortment of former GIs supplied by two California-based companies to protect the embassy. They were issued with axes and a power saw, and secretaries from the embassy brought them beer and sandwiches." The crew made short work of the tree and cleared the landing zone within minutes.

Company E, Marine Security Guard Battalion, forms in the American embassy parking lot which was designated an evacuation site. The tree in the center of the photo was felled on 29 April to permit CH-53 helicopters to land.

Soon after Brigadier General Carey set up shop at the DAO, he learned that over two thousand people were waiting to be evacuated from the embassy. This came as a big surprise, for there had been no indication at all that the embassy would be used as an evacuation center. Major Kean, reported, "I called from the Deputy Chief of Mission's office to alert the Fleet of our needs and to request the diversion of helicopters to our LZ. Until my call the Fleet thought that all Embassy personnel had been taken by bus to the DAO Compound and they had accordingly scheduled only two planned lifts for Marines and the Ambassador's party." Carey immediately ordered "Cricket" and the airborne command control center (ABCCC) began directing helicopters to either the DAO Compound or the embassy, depending on the availability of space and the type of helicopter. Major Kean recalled, "From ten in the morning until noon we moved vehicles, cut trees and shrubbery, and began to organize the 2500 evacuees within the compound. I ordered the Seabees to mark the Embassy rooftop LZ and parking lot with luminous paint and directed the Mission Warden Fire Chief to soak the parking lot area with water to keep down the debris when the helos began to fly."

By midday, security in the embassy was rapidly deteriorating, threatening to overwhelm the security force and the Marines guarding the embassy. Major Kean, said, "The American Embassy had shifted from controlled façade to controlled pandemonium . . . it was obvious that the critical period had arrived. . . . Marines held the walls against an estimated ten thousand people!" The Marines were given orders to prevent the embassy from being overrun, which meant keeping the Vietnamese from breaching the walls. Master Sergeant John Valdez, NCO in charge of the embassy guard explained, "For a while we were opening the gates, but every time we did that masses of people kept pushing the gates and then we had to push them back out. At the end we just kept the gates closed and if somebody pointed out a Vietnamese that had to be evacuated, we would just jump on each other's

Marines from BLT 2/4 arrive in Saigon to assist with embassy security.

shoulders, reach the top of the gate, and yank them inside the compound." Major Stuart Harrington recalled, "In their efforts to comply with these orders, our young Marines resorted to the use of force, which was regrettable but their determined performance of duty prevented the embassy landing zone from being overrun . . . had this happened, no one would have escaped." Late in the afternoon it was obvious that the Marine security guard needed help. Brigadier General Carey ordered three platoons (130 men) from BLT 2/4 and a landing-zone-control team from BLT 1/9 to be helilifted into the embassy. Harrington explained, "After the arrival of the Marine reinforcements, the walls were secure." CIA station chief Thomas Polgar exclaimed, "Thank God! I think we now have a chance."

However, the situation inside the Chancery was anything but secure. Ken Moorefield, the Ambassador's personal aide recalled that the air strike on Tan Son Nhut had "thrown the embassy into a panic. Secretaries spent half the night throwing typewriters down the stairwells . . . and were shredding secret documents like crazy because Martin had been unwilling to evacuate a number of our secret files. The generators or I should say the incinerators on the roof of the Embassy were going full blast and reverberations could be felt throughout the building. And we could hardly hear ourselves talk on the top floor of the Embassy." Major Harrington noted, "Inside the embassy building, tight-lipped American civilians were preparing to depart. Many walked around in a daze, their faces registering disbelief at what was happening." As Harrington made his way around the compound, he became convinced that, "we faced a complex and dangerous situation." The embassy and the combined recreation area were jammed with people—Americans, Vietnamese, Korean diplomats and a sprinkling of third country nationals—who were taking advantage of the situation. "Looting was in progress in the CRA restaurant . . . [however], more disturbing was the problem of the club's abundant stock of unsecured liquor. The drinks were on the house, and the crowd was taking full advantage of the situation," according to Harrington.

Classified Task Force 76 Special Frequent Wind Execution Sitrep:
Two CH-46 and two CH-53 helos started flow to evacuate embassy. Intend to maintain flow with 53 and 46 landing every 10 minutes.

The first CH-46 touched down on the roof of the embassy at about 1700 and the larger CH-53s started landing shortly thereafter. Captain Gerry Berry was piloting one of the first CH-46s. "[It] was absolute chaos," he said, "there were hundreds inside the compound and literally thousands in the streets surrounding the embassy. The crowd was not getting any smaller. If anything, it was getting larger . . . like a bottomless pit. Every time you land, there's more people than there were before!" Pilot Charles "Chic" Schoener recalled, "the ambassador's people were intermixed with people swarming inside. People he [Ambassador Martin] wanted to get out were locked outside the gates and people who weren't important were inside. It was all messed up." Captain Glynn Hodges brought his CH-53 down into the compound. "My troops couldn't believe the scene. People were trying to climb fences along the embassy wall. It was bedlam. We were afraid of the crowd. We wore flak vests [that] were hot and heavy. We were really uncomfortable and scared too." Major Kean acted as the evacuation ground control in the parking lot. "We loaded as many as 85 Vietnamese on many birds. If the helicopter could lift off, the pilot would yell, 'Put some more on!'"

The Embassy's landing zones posed serious challenges for the pilots. Wolf Lehmann said, "The helicopter lift operation out of the embassy was a difficult one because there were high walls around the compound. It was a tough job for the pilots to get over them." The embassy's 300-foot radio tower's four heavy steel anchor cables stretched across the parking lot until Major Kean had them cut. The embassy rooftop landing zone proved to be a difficult evacuation site. At one point, the task force received a report that the embassy was on fire. The embassy incinerator was located close to the landing pad. Frank Snepp recalled, "We were still shredding our secret documents, and as the helicopters came in they had to fight their way through billows of smoke from the incinerators and bags of shredded material were blown open and you had classified material flying about the embassy grounds like confetti." Ken Mooreland, Ambassador Martin's aide, assisted evacuees up from the embassy stairwell into the helicopters. "We were dealing with a ninety-mile-an-hour rotor blast and there was no guardrail. For people who were tired, fatigued, or disoriented, it was somewhat dangerous. One of our Marines had fallen off the helicopter pad onto the roof below and cracked his skull."

The courtyard was also tricky. Bob Drury and Tom Clavin described a typical landing:. "The Sea Stallion [CH-53] leader descended first. As he dropped below the roof line, the steady drone of rotor blades, augmented by the shriek of turbine engines, increased tenfold . . . halfway to the ground, the pilot nipped the branches of another smaller Tamarind tree. . . . They found the top of the vertical tunnel, slowed their forward progress, hovered for an instant, and one at a time made the dizzying seventy-foot drop as if hurtling down an elevator chute. If they strayed ten feet or so in any direction on the descent, the rotors would whirl into either the side of the embassy building or the wall separating it from the CRA compound."(*Last Man Out, The True Story of America's Heroic Final Hours in Vietnam*) The onset of darkness dramatically increased the flying hazards. Captain Hughes said, "Air traffic was very crowded at night, [and] we didn't have night-vision goggles. The worst fear I had was running into another airplane."

Captain Berry explained that, "Nighttime was definitely more difficult. There's no radar separating all those helicopters flying around Saigon. You have at any one time probably forty or fifty during parts of the day and the early parts of the evening going in and out of one place. That's stressful when you're moving in and out of the clouds, and it's dark." Shortly after 2300 hours, a CH-46 search and rescue (SAR) bird, call sign Swift 14, crashed into the sea on its approach to the *Hancock*. The pilot, Captain William C. Nystul and copilot 1st Lt. Michael J. Shea were killed, while the two enlisted crewmembers, Corporals Stephen R. Wills and Richard L. Scott were rescued.

Classified Task Force 76 Special Frequent Wind Execution Sitrep:
Helo crash at sea, two personnel still missing. SAR in progress, search continuing. Incident occurred during Frequent Wind execution.

SWIFT 14 CRASH

Shortly after 2330, the Search And Rescue helicopter from the USS *Hancock* crashed into the sea and two of its crew members were killed. Corporal Stephen R. Wills, the crew chief, was one of two survivors. " . . . there was no conversation in our aircraft, except for a comment made by Captain Nystul that, 'Someone is going to die up here tonight.' On returning to the ship I was asked if we were clear for a left turn. I gave the OK and no sooner than that I heard, 'Pick it up,' "Pick it up,' Pick it up.' I braced myself . . . then everything went black. I came to under water. I was able to inflate one side of my LPA [life preserver assembly]. The right side was torn. When I hit the surface . . . I found my pen flares and fired two of them. Corporal Scott was yelling that he couldn't swim. We both tried to get to each other, but the current was pulling him further from me. I couldn't move because my right hip was dislocated and my left leg had a compound fracture eight inches above the knee. After firing my pen flares, I was able to light my strobe light. The first two Navy SH-3s tried to get us out with their hoist, but we couldn't hookup. The rotor wash from the CH-53 that came over us just kept pushing us under water . . . the three [aircraft] backed off. I was blacking out from loss of blood and shock."

Another CH-46, call sign Swift 07, launched from the *Hancock* and picked up Corporal Scott with a hoist. Wills was more difficult. The pilot, Capt. Steve Haley, and copilot 1st Lt. Dean Koontz brought their aircraft down in pitch-black conditions until it was in the ocean, then water-taxied to the seriously injured Wills. An eyewitness, Cpl. Chris Woods recalled, "Then all of a sudden I watched as the bottom of the anti-collision light on the Phrog (CH-46) went underwater. I thought God, not another crash." Corporal Wills remembered, "There was seawater in the cabin section when they pulled me through the cabin door. I heard the emergency throttles come up and remember the whine of the engines and the slapping of the blades . . . I can still remember seeing the rotor blades and thinking that the helo was crashing on top of me." Corporal Wills exclaimed, "The aircrew of that ship will always live in my heart and mind as my guardian angel."

Flight conditions continued to deteriorate. Navigation to the city had become even more difficult as a line of thunderstorms stood astride the flight path, and upon arrival, the pilots would often have to use their instruments

Captain John W. Bowman and 1st Lt. David L. Androskaut shortly after being pulled from the sea after their Cobra crashed.

to land. Pineapple 7-1 reported, "The weather was getting pretty bad. Squall lines were developing. The flight inbound was intermittently IFR and visibility low." Pineapple Flight 6-0 departed the USS *Hancock* after dropping off over a hundred DAO evacuees and, as the three CH-53s headed for the embassy, "they encountered heavy cloud buildup which required the flight to climb to 9,000 feet. Once on the other side of the cloud bank, Saigon could be seen through a scattered and broken layer," according to the HMH-463 after-action report. Lieutenant Colonel Hilgenberg reported, "Almost on cue, it started to rain and low black clouds began to roll in from the south. I personally thought that the evacuation might be curtailed because of the weather . . . ceilings looked to be no more than 1500 feet." Captain Berry recalled, "Up above a certain level you don't have to worry about that as much. But as the weather comes in you're forced down because there's no real navigation aids to allow you to land on the embassy roof."

The approaching darkness and enemy anti-aircraft fire added to the difficulties. As Pineapple 6-0 approached the embassy, Pineapple 6-3 broadcast a heart pounding, "Mayday, hit and going down!" At the same time, Pineapple 6-2 reported, "multiple SA-7 launches, am releasing flares and taking evasive action!" The flight leader, Pineapple 6-1 swung around to provide support but it was not needed, 6-3 radioed that his aircraft was OK and landed in the embassy parking lot. After checking his aircraft for damage, 6-3 lifted out of the embassy with forty-eight evacuees. The flight leader quickly landed and picked up another sixty-four before heading back to the fleet.

Additional antiaircraft reports:

- Pineapple flight 5-0: Began receiving light to medium AAA fire from the vicinity of Vung Tau but no hits were received. After descent into the city, at 500 feet, 5-3 was fired upon by an SA-7. The crew chief immediately fired a MK-50 flare and the aircraft applied power, turned, and successfully evaded the missile.
- Pineapple flight 7-0: The flight took automatic weapons fire going in to the DAO Compound and upon lifting out. While in the LZ, a mortar round dropped approximately 25 feet behind 7-3. Upon entering the city, 7-1 encountered heavy automatic weapons fire and two SA-7s which were diverted by the use of flares.
- Pineapple flight 8-0: On the return flight we took heavy AAA and automatic weapons fire north-northwest of Vung Tau at 6500–7000 feet altitude. Many tracers in heavy bursts were reported by all three crews, once

completely enveloping 8-2. . . . 8-3 also reported isolated grey puffs of flak. . . . 8-1 fired 3 ALE-29 flares on an unconfirmed missile launch and 8-2 fired 1 ALE-29 flare by mistake.

- The USS *Midway* reported in a message dated 291562Z: Ground fire from .50 cal. Or small arms received from within city grid square XS 8395. Silenced by Jolly Green 12-2. 37mm AAA fired from north of NE end of TSN [Tan Son Nhut]. Large convoy entering city across from Newport Bridge.* SA-7 launches at helo from vicinity of XS 9085. Two AN/ALE 20 flares dispensed and helo commenced evasive turns, no detonation observed. No damage to aircraft . . . munitions expended 2 CBU-58, 2 CBU-71, 1 AGM-45, 250 7.62mm, 4 ALE-20 flares.
- A USAF fighter escort reported: I caught a flash out of the corner of my eye as a burst of AAA passed between Larry and I. The AAA burst was gorgeous. I could see a series of four or five streaks that through the flight, went on up to about 1,000 feet, and exploded. The next burst of AAA fire came from the heart of the city.

As flight hours increased, mechanical problems cropped up. Pineapple 6-2 reported mechanical problems and headed to the *Hancock* for repairs. Enroute to the *Duluth*, 7-1 lost a generator and smelled fumes of a possible electrical fire which was extinguished upon turning off the vent blower. After being directed to the *Hancock*, the aircraft shut down and was not launched again. Pineapple 8-1 experienced problems and turned back; 9-3 also experienced mechanical problems and was grounded. Admiral Whitmire was so concerned about mechanical problems and crew rest that he halted flight operations. A postoperational Joint Chiefs of Staff investigation noted, "Following the extraction of the GSF from the DAO compound all H-53 helicopters were directed by CTF-76 to return to base for aircraft servicing and crew rest." The Navy/Marine flight crews exceeded the number of flight hours allowed in a twenty-four-hour period, but kept flying, except for the Air Force helicopters. "The Air Force, also over their crew day (i.e. having

---

* General Van Tien Dung, NVA commander, said that a deep-strike unit advanced into Saigon, "Our fighters were sitting in trucks, wearing neat new uniforms, and all had red armbands so they could recognize each other easily when they entered the city. With leafy branches camouflaging people and vehicles, the whole unit roared off at 1500 . . . truck after truck stretching out in a long line, bravely advancing toward the center of Saigon.

flown in excess of the 12 hours allowed in one day) did not resume the airlift. Their eight CH-53s and two HH-53s shut down after the final sortie from the DAO Compound and did not launch again."(*U.S. Marines in Vietnam: the Bitter End 1973–1975*)

In a conversation with Ambassador Martin, Carey learned that the flow of helicopters had slowed down to a trickle. Upon reaching the *Blue Ridge*, he discovered that RAdm. Donald E. Whitmire, commander of TF-76, had ordered a stand-down without informing the 9th MAB commander. "I was damned angry at this stopping my helos," Brigadier General Carey said hotly, "and I made this point in no uncertain terms." The issue was also taken up by Fleet Marine Force Pacific commander Lt. Gen, Louis H. Wilson Jr. He went so far as to say that he would prefer charges against any officer who ordered his Marine pilots to stop flying so long as there were Marines still on the ground in Saigon. "If General Carey was damn angry, I was out of my mind. I told Admiral Gayler [CINCPAC] and Admiral Weisner [CINC-PACFLT] on the phone, that there was no such thing as Marines not evacuating Marines." Rear Admiral Whitmire conceded the point and promptly ordered the launch of the Marine helicopters.

As darkness settled over the city, Major Kean was told by a pilot that the CH-53 evacuation from the parking lot would stop at dark because it was too dangerous. "I explained our predicament [hundreds of evacuees remained] and assured them that the zones could be well lit. I directed the lower zone to be boxed with vehicles with the engines running and the headlights and Embassy security lights on." Major Harrington recalled, "An alert embassy staffer produced a 35mm slide projector, which we mounted on the roof overlooking the landing zone. As the big birds began their harrowing vertical descents, a Marine turned on the projector and bathed the LZ in a rectangle of white light." By 0215 hours, one CH-46 and one CH-53 were landing every ten minutes. By this time the pilots had been flying ten to twelve hours and they were exhausted. As an AH-1J Cobra approached the LPH USS *Okinawa* it ran out of fuel and crashed into the sea. The pilot, Capt. John W. Bowman and copilot 1st Lt. David L. Androskaut were rescued without injury.

Classified Task Force 76 Special Frequent Wind Execution Sitrep:
Report of major aircraft accident (combat zone): A/C was assigned as escort

for evacuation helos into and from a highly contested area. During the final phase of evacuation, A/C became Airborne Zone control providing zone briefs and sequencing in addition to gun cover. Due to the urgency of the evacuation, the crew elected to remain overhead until minimum fuel to ensure that maximum number of evacuees would be assisted. In bound to the LPH the A/C reached fuel exhaustion. No. one engine flamed out followed with seconds by no. two engine flame out. Jettison attempts were made unsuccessfully from both cockpits. When entering water used rotor brake as A/C rolled right. Floated for 20-30 seconds on right side. Front co-pilot escaped by opening canopy and stayed with the A/C while it floated. Pilot in command in rear had trouble releasing seat belt due to bullet vest overlapping buckle . . . belt finally released. Two red star cluster (pen gun) flare were fired. One strobe light was turned on and worked properly. Rescue effected by whale boat from USS Kirk within 15 minutes of ditching. [The two airmen were flown to the Okinawa by pilots from the *Kirk*, who were given five gallons of strawberry ice cream for the favor.]

———————

Major Harrington recalled, "by 0300 the chopper flow had become a near traffic jam. We worked frantically to hustle the evacuees onto the CH-53s, which had begun landing and departing almost on top of one another." Pineapple 7-1 picked up sixty-eight evacuees but encountered heavy automatic weapons fire and two SA-7s on the inbound flight and outbound flights. Italian journalist Tiziano Terzani wrote in *Giai Phong, The Fall and Liberation of Saigon*, "In these brief flashes of light one could discern on the roof of the American embassy the black shapes of people scurrying under the rotating blades to board the helicopters. All night the sky's black void was punctuated by the intermittent red lights of these strange birds of prey that lowered themselves slowly onto the roofs, oriented themselves by throwing a long white ray of light at intervals from their single eye, alighted for four or five minutes, then slipped away loaded with people, taking pains each time to avoid the tall radio antenna above the post office building and the two pointed bell-towers of the cathedral."

Secretary Kissinger, who was closely monitoring the evacuation in the White House, was furious that a large number of Vietnamese were being evacuated. "Can someone explain to me what the hell is going on!" he exploded. "The orders are that only Americans are to be evacuated. Now, what the hell is going on?" Ambassador Martin had directed that as many Vietnamese were to be evacuated as possible and was stonewalling the decision to stop the evacuation. Seventh Fleet commander Admiral Steel noted, "One thing not generally known is that Ambassador Martin was attempting to get large numbers of Vietnamese evacuated from the embassy. It appeared to be a bottomless pit, and as our men and machines began to tire I began pressuring the embassy to get all Americans and the Ambassador out. I did not want him captured . . . in my opinion he was going to keep that evacuation going by not coming out himself." At 0327 hours, President Ford directed that no more than nineteen additional lifts would be flown and that the ambassador would be on the last one. "At four o'clock this morning I find out that nobody is off the ground yet," Kissinger grumbled. "Now what the hell is going on. . . . I'll instruct the Ambassador to get those people out . . . those are his bloody orders, goddamnit!" Thirty minutes later Ambassador Martin sent a final message: "Plan to close mission Saigon approximately 0430 Saigon time, dependent on performance of military evacuation channels. Due to necessity to destroy commo gear, this is the last Saigon message to sec-state."

Deputy Chief of Mission Lehmann said, "a very peremptory message did come through direct from the White House directing the ambassador and the remaining staff to leave by the next helicopter." Brigadier General Carey notified Captain Berry, flying a CH-46 call sign Lady Ace 09, that he was to bring out the ambassador on the next lift. "We land on the roof and actually loaded up a group of Vietnamese and I had to say, 'We're not leaving the rooftop until the ambassador's on board," Berry said. The Vietnamese were hustled off his aircraft. "[It] couldn't have been more than a minute and the ambassador and his whole entourage are on top of the roof getting ready to get on. The ambassador looked as haggard as I've ever seen anybody. I think all he wanted was for someone to tell him he had to go." At 0458 Berry lifted off. "I made the call, 'Tiger, Tiger, Tiger,'" the code word to let the fleet know we had the ambassador on board and we were enroute to the *Blue Ridge*," he said. Berry's message was relayed to the command ship: "Pilot Lady Ace 09 reported the U.S. Ambassador and 23 staff aboard—lift off at 0458 from the rooftop, American Embassy." As he flew over the city, Berry recalled, "I could see fires. The [South Vietnamese troops] were retreating into the city and some of them were still putting up a good fight, especially in the north end of the city. It was the end of a culture as we knew it. After 20 years of fighting, it was a tough thing to watch."

Frank Snepp described the evacuation flight. "The roof of the embassy was a vision out of a nightmare. In the center of the dimly lit helo-pad a CH-46 was already waiting for us, its engines setting up a roar like a primeval scream. The crew and controllers all wear what looked like oversized football helmets, and in the blinking under-light of the landing signals they reminded me of grotesque insects rearing on their hind quarters. Out beyond the edge of the building a Phantom jet streaked across the horizon as tracers darted up . . . into the night sky. . . . Almost imperceptibly the chopper began rising straight up. Through the open exterior door, where the tail gunner was now crouching over his weapon, I watched numbly as the edge of the pad sank slowly out of sight. . . . Then the cabin lights dimmed, and the chopper banked and arched up over the center of the city." Lehmann noted, "As we were leaving the Saigon area, I could look out of the helicopter and I could see the approaching North Vietnamese columns with their headlights out and beginning to enter the outskirts of the city."

The departure of the ambassador and his staff left only the Marines of the GSF and Marines of the embassy guard remaining in the embassy compound. The Marines had pulled back to form a semicircle at the main entrance to the Chancery. "I passed the word that we were buttoning up," Major Kean recalled. "Suddenly, the crowd outside realized it was being abandoned and came at us. A big Seabee chief grabbed the huge timber that was used to bar the doors, put it across the small of his back, wrapped his arms around it and started spinning. The rushing crowd, afraid of getting hurt, faltered and we bolted the door." The men retreated floor-by-floor, locking grill gates behind them, and dropping tear gas canisters down the stairs. The crowd drove a truck through the embassy doors and surged up the stairs. By this time there were about sixty Marines left. Major Kean recalled, "On the top floor, there was a passageway to the roof, with heavy fireproof doors at each end. We filled that hallway with wall lockers, fire extinguishers, and other junk. Corporal Stephen Bauer stayed there to hold the frantic people off with [tear] gas grenades. When the crowd would try to break through, he would toss one through a broken window in a door and the people would back up to avoid the stinging gas."

Helicopters continued to take the Marines off the roof until only eleven embassy guards remained. "All of us were zombies," Major Kean recalled, "[after] working feverishly for more than 70 hours!" There was a lull toward dawn—not a helicopter in sight. "We were scared to death," Major Kean said, "but the older Marines had an obligation to look stoic for the sake of the younger men, who asked, 'They're coming aren't they?'" From their rooftop vantage point the Marines could see looters carrying off their prizes, drunken revelers deliberately crashing vehicles in the street . . . and most poignant of all, "Vietnamese were still sitting on their luggage in the embassy parking lot, waiting to be called for a flight out of the city." Finally, off in the distance, one of the men spotted sunlight glinting off a helicopter. Captain John E. Rhodes, piloting Swift 22, swept in for landing. "We all bolted for the tailgate of the helicopter," Kean recalled. "It was 0758 Saigon time."

––––––––

Classified Task Force 76 Special Frequent Wind Execution Sitrep:
Last members of GSF lifted off embassy roof outbound to USN shipping. No firing in the embassy area. Last American out of Saigon, all GSF accounted for. This is final special sitrep for the execution phase of Frequent Wind.

MARINE CORPS HELICOPTER DEVELOPMENT 1948-1969

The Marine Corps' foray into rotary-wing aviation began on 9 February 1948 when the newly formed Marine Helicopter Squadron 1 (HMX-1) took delivery of the first two helicopters at the Marine Corps Air Station Quantico. The two aircraft, Sikorsky HO3S-1s, were to be used by HMX-1 to develop techniques and tactics for the ship-to-shore movement of assault troops in amphibious operations. The concept called "vertical envelopment" was an answer to critics who said the days of landing troops on a hostile shore in the atomic age were long past. The helicopter offered an opportunity to place an assault force well inland, instead of attacking shoreline defenses. The May–June 1997 issue of *Naval Aviation News* noted, "The establishment of HMX-1 at Marine Corps Air Station Quantico, Virginia, on 1 December 1947 started a revolution in Marine Corps aviation and tactical doctrine."

MARINE HELICOPTER SQUADRON 1 (HMX-1) NIGHTHAWKS

Marine Helicopter Squadron 1 (HMX-1), the first Marine rotary-wing squadron, was activated on February 1948 to test helicopter doctrine in accordance with recommendations of a special board headed by Maj. Gen. Lemuel C. Shepherd, a future Commandant of the Marine Corps. The new doctrine, published by the Marine Corps Schools was titled *Amphibious Operations— Employment of Helicopters (Tentative)* or Phib-31, was the first manual for airmobile operations. Phib-31 termed helicopter tactics as "vertical assault," and viewed rotary-wing aircraft as an alternative to ship-to-shore movement by surface craft. HMX-1 was initially manned by seven commissioned-officer pilots and three enlisted men but quickly grew to eighteen pilots and eighty-one enlisted men by the time the first Sikorsky HO3S arrived. Within three months, the squadron was operating off the escort carrier USS *Palau* (CVE-122) developing ship-board flight operations and ship-to-shore procedures.

Interestingly, the "X" in its squadron designator originally stood for experimental, emblematic of its original mission of testing new helicopters and flight systems. However, as its operational role in VIP transportation overshadowed its operational test and evaluation role, the experimental moniker was dropped, although the squadron designator was left unchanged. Currently mustering more than seven hundred personnel, HMX-1 is the largest Marine Corps helicopter squadron. It is divided into two sections. The White side (White House) flies two unique helicopters—both specially configured Sikorsky executive transports—the VH-3D Sea King and the VH-60N Seahawk. From HMX-1's Quantico, Virginia, headquarters the Green side provides basic helicopter indoctrination training for ground troops, tests new concepts and equipment, and assists the Marine air weapons and tactics squadron. HMX-1 is responsible for flying the President and members of his staff.

HMX-1 continued in the forefront of vertical assault development under combat conditions. In 1950, at the start of the Korean War, four HMX-1 HO3S-1 helicopters, seven officers and thirty enlisted men, under the command of Maj. Vincent J. Gottschalk, were attached to VMO-6 and assigned to the 1st Provisional Marine Brigade during the Battle of the Pusan Perimeter. The brigade commander, Brig. Gen. Edward A. Craig said, "They have been used for every conceivable type of mission . . . liaison, reconnaissance, evacuation of wounded, rescue of Marine flyers downed in enemy territory, observation, messenger service, guard mail at sea, posting and supplying of outguards on dominating terrain features and the re-supplying of small units by air." Colonel Gottschalk declared, "Perhaps the most important use of the helicopter in the early months of the Korean War concerned command and

The Sikorsky HO3S-1 was first used in combat during the Korean War when four aircraft were assigned to the 1st Provisional Marine Brigade during the Battle of the Pusan Perimeter.

control. The flexibility provided the Brigade Commander to control his forces, change direction of movement, give personal instructions to subordinate commanders, and observe the resultant battlefield movement in a dynamic fast moving situation provided a new dimension to tactical control of the battlefield in a difficult terrain setting."

In the decade following the Korean War, the Corps continued to expand its rotary-wing fleet. By 1962, there were 341 aircraft in its inventory, the most common of which was the Sikorsky-built UH-34D Sea Horse (HUS until September 1962) with 225 helicopters assigned to eleven Squadrons in four Marine Air Groups (MAG): MAG-16, Futema, Okinawa; MAG-36, Santa Ana, California; MAG-26, New River, North Carolina; and MAG-13, a fixed-wing group located at Kaneohe, Hawaii. Another 11 helicopters were assigned to VMO-6 at Camp Pendleton, California. Finally, several helicopters were assigned to HMX-1 to continue the development of tactics, techniques and equipment for landing-force operation. From the late 1950s until the CH-46 entered service in 1965, the UH-34D operated as the mainstay of Marine Corps helicopter units. During the Vietnam War, over 150 UH-34Ds were lost due to battle damage and accidents.

The Marine Corps's interest in a heavy-lift helicopter resulted in another Sikorsky development: the HR2S designated the CH-37 and nicknamed the Duce. Originally there were to be nine squadrons equipped with twenty HR2S helicopters each, but only two squadrons were commissioned: HMR(M)-461 (later redesignated HMH-461) and HMH-462. The Duce was described as a monster of a helicopter—it was the largest helicopter in the Western world—with a five-bladed main rotor 68 feet in diameter and a four-bladed tail rotor 15 feet across. Its round nose was split by two hydraulically operated doors opening on a cabin 30 feet 4 inches long, 7 feet 8 inches wide, and 6 feet 8 inches high. Ramps in the nose doors and reinforced tracks in the floor allowed jeeps and other vehicles to drive in and out. The pilot and copilot sat

A Sikorsky CH-37 twin-engine helicopter is seen recovering a damaged UH-34. The CH-37 was used primarily to airlift supplies and equipment.

on a flight deck reached from the cabin by a folding ladder. The cabin had space for twenty-six Marines, two combat assault squads. It could be configured for twenty-four casualty litters. In 1963, four CH-37s were deployed to Vietnam to provide heavy lift support. They remained in-country until 14 May 1987 when they were replaced by the CH-53. Only one of the big machines was lost in Vietnam due to combat action.

In the spring of 1962, the Marine Corps selected the Bell Helicopter Company's UH-1E Huey as its assault-support helicopter. The U.S. Army was already using them in Vietnam and with a few modifications the aircraft was quickly added to the Corps's inventory. The first aircraft were delivered to VMO-1 in February 1964 and within four years almost two hundred had been delivered. Tactical doctrine at the time required the Huey to perform observation, reconnaissance, rescue missions, and "armed helicopter support for transport helicopters," which brought into the open a raging debate about arming helicopters. Many Marine aviators were adamantly opposed to helicopter gunships, arguing that it was the role of fixed-wing aircraft to provide air support. The issue was settled when Commandant of the Marine Corps General Wallace M. Greene came down on the side of arming the Huey. He directed "a high priority project to develop, evaluate and service test a readily installable weapons kit for the UH-1E helicopter."

In 1966 the armed Hueys were assigned to three observation squadrons in Vietnam: VMO-2, VMO-3 and VMO-6. The gunships were armed with four fuselage-mounted M60 machine guns, two to four 2.75-inch rocket pods, and two door M60 machine guns. In 1967, a pod containing two M60 machine guns that could be aimed and controlled (traversed and elevated)

An unarmed Bell UH-1E helicopter approaches a landing zone in Operation Prairie. The unarmed Hueys were commonly called Slicks, and used for a variety of missions, not the least of which was medical evacuation. Armed Hueys carried four fuselage-mounted M60 machine guns and two to four 2.75 inch rocket pods to be used in landing-zone preparation and in a ground-support role.

The CH-53A Sea Stallion heavy-lift helicopter was developed for the Marine Corps by Sikorsky and placed in service in 1964. The heavy assault transport has a four-man crew and can carry thirty-eight troops at a cruising speed of 170 miles per hour.

by the pilot was mounted below the nose of the aircraft. Clean, unarmed Hueys, referred to as slicks, could carry seven to nine fully equipped troops and were often used for the insertion and extraction of small reconnaissance teams. Marine pilot David Ballentine flew the UH-1E in 1966–1967. "The Huey was simply a great helo, versatile, strong, simple and fun. [It] was a re-markable combination of engine, airframe, and rotor system." Over 140 Hueys were lost to combat and operational accidents during the war.

By the end of 1961 the CH-37 was approaching the end of its service life and a replacement was becoming imperative. Sikorsky eventually won the contact based on its successful Duce and the company's willingness to cut research and development costs. The first of two prototypes rolled off the assembly line on 28 May 1964 but the aircraft did not reach the fleet until September 1966 when HMH-463 accepted the first four. Designated the CH-53A and named the "Sea Stallion," a total of 141 were built. Its primary mission was to move cargo and equipment, with a secondary role of trans-ferring troops ashore in an amphibious assault. The first CH-53As arrived in Vietnam in January 1967. Seventeen of the Sea Stallions were lost due to accidents or combat.

The Marine Corps closely watched the U.S. Army's development of an attack helicopter, the UH-1H, called the Huey Cobra or simply the Cobra. After its success in Vietnam, the Marine Corps requested sufficient Cobras (designation changed to AH-1G, AH for attack helicopter) to provide a squadron of twenty-four in each of the active wings. The first Cobras arrived in Vietnam on 10 April 1969 and were assigned to VMO-2. On one of its first missions it was reported, "With [Cobras] covering, a Marine rifle company was moving out cautiously. Shots came from around the bend and the [Cobras] covered the area with fire. When the Marines got there, five Viet Cong were horizontal; four dead and one wounded. The wounded VC was shouting and banging his fists into the dust. One company commander asked the interpreter what all the shouting was about. 'He's apparently the squad leader,' the interpreter replied. 'He's yelling, "If I told them once, I told them a thousand times—don't shoot at that kind of helicopter!"' In 1971, the AH-1G was upgraded with twin engines and designated the AH-1J. Ten Cobras were lost during their Vietnam deployment, four through combat and six in operational accidents.

The Marine Corps's Vietnam-era rotary-wing fleet has undergone many upgrades over the years, but many of those birds are still being flown. The CH-46, CH-53, UH-1J, and the UH-1E are currently (2013) in the inventory, but replacement aircraft types are on the way. The most well known is the Bell Boeing tiltrotor MV-22 Osprey, which has completed combat deployments to Iraq and Afghanistan.

The Bell AH-1 Super Cobra is a twin-engined attack helicopter. It was initially developed in the mid-1960s for the U.S. Army and later modified to meet Marine Corps requirements. Marine AH-1J Sea Cobra arrived in Vietnam for evaluation in February 1971. It carried a three-barrel 20mm cannon in its nose turret, capable of firing 750 round per minute.

CAPTAIN STEPHEN PLESS (USMC) RECOMMENDATION FOR MEDAL OF HONOR

Colonel Joseph A. Nelson, commanding officer VMO-6, congratulates Maj. Stephen Pless, who received the Medal of Honor for saving the lives of several U.S. Army soldiers from a Viet Cong attack.

MARINE OBSERVATION SQUADRON 6
Marine Aircraft Group 36
lst Marine Aircraft Wing
Fleet Marine Force Pacific
FPO, San Francisco 96602

10:JAN:krp
1650
AUG 2 6 1967

From: Commanding Officer

To: Secretary of the Navy (Navy Department Board of Decorations and Awards)

Via: (1) Commanding Officer, Marine Aircraft group 36
        (2) Commanding General, lst Marine Aircraft Wing
        (3) Commanding General, III Marine Amphibious Force
        (4) Commander, United States Military Assistance Command, Vietnam
        (5) Commanding General, Fleet Marine Force, Pacific
        (6) Commander in Chief, United States Pacific Fleet
        (7) Commander in Chief, Pacific
        (8) Commandant of the Marine Corps (Code DL)
        (9) Chief of Naval Operations (OP-09B2E)

Subj: Medal of Honor; recommendation for

Ref: (a) SecNavInst P1650.1C (revised)
        (b) ForO 1650.1C
        (c) FMFPacO P1650.1A

Encl: (1) Proposed Citation [see paragraph 2 below...Editor]
        (2) Statement of Captain Rupert E. Fairfield, USMC
        (3) Statement of Gunnery Sergeant Leroy N. POULSON, USMC
        (4) Statement of Lance Corporal John G. PHELPS, USMC
        (5) Statement of Warrant Officer James F. VAN DUZEE, USA
        (6) Statement of Warrant Officer Ronald L. REDEKER, USA
        (7) Statement of Staff Sergeant Lawrence H. ALLEN, USA
        (8) Pictorial Representation of Scene of Action

1. In accordance with the provisions set forth in references (a), (b), and (c), it is recommended that Captain Stephen Wesley PLESS, United States Marine Corps attached to and serving with Marine Observation Squadron Six be awarded the Medal of Honor for conspicuous gallantry and intrepidity at the risk of his life above and beyond the call of duty.

2. On 19 August 1967, while serving as pilot-in-command of an armed UH-1E helicopter attached to Marine Observation Squadron Six in the Republic of Vietnam. Captain PLESS was assigned to fly an armed escort for an H-34 Medical Evacuation helicopter. In the course of a regularly assigned mission, Captain PLESS monitored a call on an emergency frequency which stated that four Americans from an aircraft forced down by enemy fire were being attacked by a large force of Viet Cong. Heavily armed with automatic weapons and grenades, the Viet Cong were assaulting the small group, which was trapped on a small strip of beach.

When Captain PLESS determined that the H-34 he was assigned to escort could proceed with the mission unassisted, he flew directly to the area given in the distress call. On arrival at the site, a small section of beach one mile north of the mouth of the Song Tra Khuc River, he found that the tiny America force by now out of ammunition, had been overwhelmed by an estimated thirty to forty armed Viet Cong. As the Americans lay helpless on the sand, the Viet Cong, in a frenzy, were bayoneting and beating them with rifle butts. Several other aircraft were orbiting the area futilely, unable to assist due to heavy enemy fire and an apparent lack of coordination.

Despite the obvious danger and apparent hopelessness of the situation, Captain PLESS, threw his aircraft at the enemy. As he made his first low pass directly over the heads of the enemy troops, the Viet Cong, completely surprised, began to move away from their victims toward the shelter of a tree line running parallel to the beach. They were immediately subjected to a vicious series of rocket and machine gun attacks delivered by Captain PLESS. Pressing his attacks to below tree top level, Captain PLESS, despite the heavy fire of the now resisting enemy troops, rained a hail of fire on the Viet Cong, often flying through the debris of his own ordnance explosions.

During one of these low level attacks Captain PLESS saw one of the severely injured Americans raise his arm and gesture for help. Completely disregarding the enemy troops located only scant yards from the wounded, Captain PLESS maneuvered his aircraft into a violent turn and landed between the wounded men and the enraged enemy. Using his aircraft as a shield, Captain PLESS directed his crew to load the Americans aboard.

Captain PLESS's aircraft remained stationary on the beach for nearly ten minutes, subjected to attacks by individual and groups of Viet Cong who often closed to within ten feet of the helicopter in an attempt to destroy it.

With the Americans safely aboard, Captain PLESS, encircled on three sides by the frantic Viet Cong, had but one route of departure open to him. Forcing his aircraft, which was now nearly five hundred pounds over safe take-off weight, into the air, Captain PLESS turned out to sea. Jettisoning his empty rocket pods and ordering his crew to throw all excess gear over-board, Captain PLESS skipped over the water. On four separate occasions Captain PLESS's aircraft settled onto the waves, and four times, in an unbelievable display of airmanship, Captain PLESS brought it back into the air. Finally becoming safely airborne, Captain PLESS set a course direct to the nearest medical facility, while his crewmen applied first aid enroute.

Captain PLESS, by his willingness to expose himself to almost certain death in order to help his comrades-in-arms, was able to thwart a determined enemy effort to kill three of four American soldiers. In so doing, he also inflicted heavy casualties on the heavily armed enemy force. His actions were those of a man of uncommon bravery and ability, and were in keeping with the highest traditions of the United States Naval Service.

3.   The facts contained in the proposed citation are completely substantiated by the statements of eye-witnesses and contained herein as enclosures (2) through (7).

4.   Captain PLESS has received the following personal decorations: The Bronze Star Medal; The Air Medal, 1st through 18th awards; The Navy Commendation Medal; The Purple Heart Medal; The Korean Military Merit IN HUN.

5.   Captain PLESS has been recommended for but has not yet received the following personal awards: The Air Medal, 19th through 36th awards.

6.   Captain PLESS is due for detachment from this organization during September 1967.

7.   There are no foreign awards being recommended for this same action.

8.   Roster of VMO-6 personnel involved in this same action

Pilot   Captain Stephen W. PLESS
Copilot   Captain R. E. FAIRFIELD
CrewChief   Lance Corporal J. G. PHELPS
Gunner   Gunnery Sergeant L. N. POULSON

9. The following additional award recommendations are being submitted in connection with this same action:

AWARD	NAME	RANK	SERNO	LETTER
Navy Cross	R. E. FAIRFIELD	Capt.	*[Redacted]*	CO, VMO-6 ltr 10:JAN:kpr over 1650 of AUG 26 1967
Navy Cross	L. N. POULSON	GySgt.	*[Redacted]*	CO, VMO-6 ltr 10:JAN:kpr over 1650 of AUG 26 1967
Navy Cross	J. G. PHELPS	LCpl.	*[Redacted]*	CO, VMO-6 ltr 10:JAN:kpr over 1650 of AUG 26 1967

(SIGNED)
J. A. NELSON

NAVY UNIT COMMENDATION TASK FORCE 76

The Secretary of the Navy takes pleasure in presenting the
NAVY UNIT COMMENDATION
to
COMMANDER TASK FORCE 76
for service as set forth in the following
CITATION:
For exceptionally meritorious service on 29 and 30 April 1975 during Operation FREQUENT WIND, the emergency evacuation of Saigon, Republic of Vietnam. During this period, the units of Commander Task Force 76 displayed exceptional teamwork and professional competence in supporting and accomplishing the helicopter evacuation of nearly 7,000 United States citizens, Vietnamese refugees, and third country nationals. Although under constant threat of enemy reaction and attack from both land and sea, they selflessly devoted themselves to the task of saving evacuees lives. In addition, the operation was severely complicated when scores of South Vietnamese helicopters loaded with armed and often panic stricken Republic of Vietnam Army troops and their dependents descended upon every unit of Commander Task Force 76 with a helicopter landing deck. By their courage, resolute determination, and mutual cooperation, the officers and men of Commander Task Force 76 contributed significantly to the success of Operation FREQUENT WIND', thereby reflecting 'great credit upon themselves and upholding the highest traditions of the United States Navy Service.

/s/ J. William Middendorf
Secretary of the Navy

BIBLIOGRAPHY

Ballentine, David A. *Gunbird Driver, A Marine Huey Pilot's War In Vietnam.* (Annapolis: Naval Institute Press, 2008).

Butler, David. *The Fall of Saigon.* (New York: Simon and Schuster, 1985).

Dorr, Robert F. *Marine Air, The History of the Flying Leathernecks in Words and Photos.* (New York: Berkley Caliber, 2005).

Drury, Bob and Tom Clavin. *The Last Men out: The True Story of America's Heroic Final Hours in Vietnam.* (New York: Free Press, 2011).

Englemann, Larry. *Tears Before the Rain: An Oral History of the Fall of South Vietnam.* (New York: Oxford University Press, 1990).

Hammel, Eric. *Khe Sanh, Siege in the Clouds, an Oral History.* (New York: Crown Publishers, 1989).

Livingston, James, E., Colin D. Heaton, Anne-Marie Lewis. *Noble Warrior: The Story of Maj. Gen. James E. Livingston, USMC (Ret).* (Minnesota: Zenith Press, 2011).

McCoy, James W. *Secrets of the Viet Cong.* (New York: Hippocrene Books, 1992).

Mersky, Peter B. *U.S. Marine Corps Aviation, 1912 to the Present.* (Annapolis: The Nautical & Aviation Publishing Company of America, 1983).

Munter, Weldon. *My Downside Up Life.* (Victoria: Trafford Publishing, 2005).

Petri, Thomas. *Lightening from the Sky, Thunder from the Sea, the First Anglico Story.* (Bloomington: Anchor House, 2009).

Prados, John and Ray W. Stubbe. *Valley of Decision, The Siege of Khe Sanh.* (New York: Houghton Mifflin Company, 1991).

Snepp, Frank. *Decent Interval, An Insider's Account of Saigon's Indecent End.* (New York: Random House, 1977).

Steinman, Ron. *The Soldiers' Story, Vietnam in their own Words.* (New York: Barnes and Noble, 1999).

Stoffey, Bob. *Cleared Hot, A Marine Combat Pilot's Vietnam Diary.* (New York: St. Martin's Press, 1992).

Terzani, Tiziano. *Giai Phong! The Fall and Liberation of Saigon.* (New York: St. Martin's Press, 1976).

UNPUBLISHED SOURCES

Marine Corps University Archives and Marine Corps History Division

Located at Quantico, Virginia, the Marine Corps University archives and the Marine

Corps History Division are rich sources of material for researchers of Marine Corps history. Their resources include nearly four thousand collections of papers donated by active-duty and former officers and enlisted personnel, documenting every conflict involving Marines. Of particular importance to this book were the oral histories that have been collected by the Marine Corps History Division over the years. The following Marines' oral histories were used in this book:

Thompson, Sgt. Stephen, 23 June 2004
Bergman, Capt. Carl E., 16 August – 19 July 2004
Nation, Pfc. Michael, 29 November 2002
Underwood, Col. Dave 24 July 2002

3rd Reconnaissance Battalion Interviews:
Slocum, Cpl. Danny, 17 February 1968
Nation, Pfc. Michael P., 17 February 1968

U.S. GOVERNMENT PUBLICATIONS

1st Marine Aircraft Wing Command Chronology for the period 1–13 January 1968.

3rd Battalion, 26th Marines Command Chronology for the period 1–31 January 1968.

2nd Battalion, 3rd Marines Command Chronology for the period 13–31 May 1967.

1st Battalion, 3rd Marines Command Chronology for the period 1–31 May 1967.

History and Museums Division. *U.S. Marines in Vietnam, an Expanding War 1966.* (Washington, D.C.: GPO, 1982).

History and Museums Division. *U.S. Marines in Vietnam, The Landing and the Buildup 1965.* (Washington, D.C.: GPO 1978).

History and Museums Division. *U.S. Marines in Vietnam, The Advisory & Combat Assistance Era.* (Washington, D.C.: GOP 1977).

History and Museums Division. *U.S. Marines in Vietnam, Fighting the North Vietnamese 1967.* (Washington, D.C.: GPO 1984).

History and Museums Division. *U.S. Marines in Vietnam, 1954–1973, An Anthology and Annotated Bibliography.* (Washington, D.C.: GPO 1985).

History and Museums Division. *Marines and Helicopters 1962–1973.* (Washington, D.C.: GPO 1978).

History and Museums Division. *A History of Marine Medium Helicopter Squadron 161.* (Washington, D.C.: GPO 1978).

History and Museums Division. *Whirlybirds, U.S. Marine Helicopters in Korea.* (Washington, D.C.: GPO 2003).

History and Museums Division. *U.S. Marines in Vietnam, The Defining Year 1968.* (Washington, D.C.: GPO 1997).

History and Museums Division. *U.S. Marines in Vietnam, Vietnamization and Redeployment 1970–1971.* (Washington, D.C.: GPO 1986).

History and Museums Division. *U.S. Marines in Vietnam, The Bitter End 1973–1975.* (Washington, D.C.: GPO 1990).

History and Museums Division. *Marines and Helicopters 1946–1962*. (Washington, D.C.: GPO 1976).

History and Museums Division. *Marines and Helicopters 1962–1973*. (Washington, D.C.: GPO 1978).

Marine Air Group 16 Command Chronology for the period 1–30 October 1965.

Marine Observation Squadron 6 Command Chronology for the period 1–29 February 1968.

Marine Observation Squadron 6 Command Chronology for the period 1–31 August 1967

Marine Medium Helicopter Squadron 262 Command Chronology for the period 1–29 February 1968.

Marine Medium Helicopter Squadron 262 Command Chronology for the period 1–31 March 1968.

Marine Medium Helicopter Squadron 262 Command Chronology for the period 1–31 April 1968.

Marine Medium Helicopter Squadron 262 Command Chronology for the period 1–31 May 1968.

Marine Medium Helicopter Squadron 164 Command Chronology for the period 1–31 July 1966

Marine Medium Helicopter Squadron 164 Command Chronology for the period 13–31 May 1967.

Marine Medium Helicopter Squadron 165 Command Chronology for the period 1–31 May 1967.

Marine Heavy Helicopter Squadron 463 Command Chronology for the period 28 March–14 May 1975.

9th Marine Amphibious Brigade Command Chronology for the period 26 March–30 April 1975.

Marine Air Group 36 Command Chronology for the period 1–31 January 1968.

United States Mission in Vietnam. *The Impact of the Sapper on the Vietnam War, a Background Paper*. (Saigon: U.S. Army, 1969).

Commanding General III MAF. *Viet Cong Attack of Marble Mountain Air Facility and Chu Lai Airfield of 28 October 1965*. (Honolulu: U.S. Marine Corps, 1965).

PERSONAL INTERVIEWS

Kufeldt, Col. Edward, 2011

Fiorillo, Col. Mike 2012

Nation, Michael P.

O'Dell, Lt. Col. George "Digger," 2009

Rosental, Lt. Col. George 2011

Crookall, Charlie

Crutcher, Robert

ARTICLES

Burrows, Larry. "War with a Brave Crew in a Deadly Fight." *Life Magazine* (April 16, 1965)

Camp, Richard D. "The Lang Vei Rescue Attempt." *Leatherneck* (March 2012): pp 18–21.

Camp, Richard D. "Last Full Measure of Devotion: Extraction of Team "Box Score." *Leatherneck* (November 2009): pp 18–23.

Davis, Steven A. "They played White Christmas as Marine Choppers Flew and Saigon Fell." *Leatherneck* (May 2000): pg. 18–23.

Kelly, Michael L., "Operation Frequent Wind, the Evacuation of the DAO Compound and the Saigon Embassy." *Leatherneck* (April 2011): pgs 22–27.

LeGro, William E. "Intelligence in Vietnam after the Cease-Fire. *INSCOM JOURNAL 20, no. 2* (March–April 1997).

Vietnam War: Saigon Evacuation After Action Report: Operations Analysis Group, report no. 2–75, 16 May 1975, BACM Research.

INDEX

1st Cavalry Division, 7
1st Marine Air Wing, 17, 74, 107–108, 140, 187
3rd Marine Division, 7
4th Air Commando Squadron, 67
9th Cavalry, 8
20th Field Artillery Regiment, 8
52nd Aviation Battalion, 28
68th Aviation Company, 56
117th Aviation Company, 28
119th Aviation Company, 28
278th Sapper (Special Operations) Company, 46
324th B Division, 82, 91
374th Tactical Airlift Wing, 197
III Corps, 19
III Marine Amphibious Force (III MAF), 37–38

A-1 Skyraider, 217
A-1E Skyraider, 69
A-1H Skyraider, 28, 29, 30–32, 34, 70
A-4 Skyhawk, 42, 69, 76, 83, 112, 140, 141, 143
A-4E Skyhawk, 143
A-7, 217, 218
A-37, 197
A-37B Dragonfly, 202
AC-47, 67, 169
AC-130, 216, 218
Adams, Ed, 203
AH-1 Super Cobra, 247

AH-1G, 246–247
AH-1J Cobra, 237, 247
Air America, 198–205
Allen, Albert N., 32–33
Allen, Lawrence H., 115, 116–118
American Embassy, 227–241
Amphibious Ready Group Alpha (ARG-A), 95
Anderson, D. N., 109–110
Anderson, Richard E., 48–49
Andress, William H. "Billy," 160
Andrews, Frank, 196–197, 201, 203
Androskaut, David L., 234, 237
Arrotta, Robert J., 139–140
ARVN 1st Division, 83
ARVN 5th Airborne Battalion, 56
ARVN 5th Division, 24
ARVN 7th Division, 24
ARVN 21st Division, 19, 21
Ashau Valley, 64–79
Assum, David P., 139

Bailey, Gary L., 89
Ballentine, David, 246
banyan tree, 228–229, 233
Barden (Colonel), 84
Bauer, Stephen, 240
Baughn, Richard M., 199, 207–208
Bench, Arnold E., 83
Bergman, Carl E., 157, 167, 180–181, 182
Berry, Gerry, 232, 233, 235, 239
Blair, John D., IV, 67, 68, 69, 73–74, 78

Blakeman, Wyman, 74–75, 76, 77
Bloomer, William A. "Art," 217
Bolton, J. L., 188, 224
Bond, Royce L., 187, 188
Boudreau, Hank, 228–229
Bowman, John W., 234, 237
Braddon, John Rendall, 29, 31, 33–36
Bradford, John, 67
Bradlee, Ben, 199
Bradley, James, 14
Brame, Charlie, 217, 218
Breeding, Earle G., 134, 135
Brown, George S., 217
Brown, Leslie E., 42, 43, 44–45
Brule, Lawrence, 47
Burke, Marcus, Jr., 189, 200, 201, 205
Burns, Tom, 158
Burrows, Larry, 56–57, 58, 59, 63
Bush, Tyler, 13, 15, 16, 18–19, 25
Butler, David, 193, 222
Byrd, R. W., 105

C5A, 207
C-119, 217
C-123, 68
C-130, 41, 192, 197–198, 211, 213, 219
Camp Adenir, 48, 50
Carey, John, 17
Carey, Richard E., 140, 187–188, 189,
    191, 218–219, 224, 229–230, 231,
    237, 239
Carl, Marion, 73, 79
Caron, Robert, 204–205
Carter, Tennis "Sam," 67, 69, 74
Cassada, William E., 49
CH-3, 68
CH-37, 52, 84, 244–245
CH-46, 103, 105, 110, 111, 114, 128,
    130, 134, 136–137, 140, 141, 143,
    157, 203, 214, 220–221, 228, 231–
    232, 233, 234, 237, 239–240, 244,
    247

CH-46 Sea Knight, 84, 152
CH-46A, 8, 110
CH-46-A, 84, 85, 88, 89
CH-47 Chinook, 115, 116
CH-53, 131, 145, 155, 208–209, 214,
    216, 219, 220, 222, 225, 226, 228–
    229, 231–233, 234, 235, 237, 238,
    245, 247
CH-53A Sea Stallion, 246
CH-53D, 221
CH-54 "Flying Crane," 7
Chancey, John A., 132–134, 142
Chennault, Claire Lee, 199
Chu Lai Airfield, 37–38, 40–46, 48
Civil Air Transport (CAT) company,
    199
Civilian Irregular Defense Group
    (CIDG), 66, 77, 79, 148
Clapp, Archie J., 13, 14, 15, 17, 19,
    20–23, 24–25
Clavin, Tom, 227, 232–233
Clements, William, 217
Coalson, Frank, 205
Coalson, Tony M., 202–203
Cobras, 214
Colby, Dwain A., 81
Collins, Willard, M., 67
Condon, John, 17
Connelly, Joseph C., 98, 101
Conti, Edward P., 85–87
Corfield, S. L., 114
Corps Tactical Zone, 108
Coughlin, D. O., 188
Craig, Edward A., 243
Crookall, Charlie, 152, 153–154
Crutcher, Robert, 152–153, 154–155
Culver, R., 105
Cunningham, William, 32–33

Dabney, William H. "Bill," 125,
    127–128, 139, 141
Dalbey, R. M., 111

Darger, Rocky, 112
Davis, Raymond G., 7–8
Deadlock, 99–100
Defense Attaché Compound (DAO), 196, 206–213, 220–221, 222–223, 226, 229–230, 237
DeLancy, Michael, 134
Demilitarized Zone (DMZ), 81, 95, 107–108, 148
Dickey, Steve, 130
Drury, Bob, 227, 232–233
Duong Van "Big" Minh, 191–192
Duphiney, Randall Wallace, 49–50

"Eagle Flight," 23–24
East, William, 224
Ebersbach, William M., 91
Edebohls, H. G., 188
Egan, Ed, 167
Eliason, Wendell T., 57
Emergency Control Center (ECC), 206, 222
Emrick, Steven E., 160, 163, 165, 181–182
English, Lowell, 83, 92
Ensign, Jerry A., 88–89, 90
Esslinger, John Thomas, 138–139, 141
Evacuation Processing Center (EPC), 206
Ewers, Norman, 57, 62
explosive ordnance disposal (EOD) team, 224–225

F-4 Phantom, 111
F-4B Phantom, 76, 83, 143
F-8U, 164
Fairfield, Rupert E., 115–118, 119, 121–122
Farley, James C., Jr., 56, 58, 59–60, 63
Fay, Donald, 218
Fay, Robert J., 55
Faylor, Dwight G., 100, 102

Fillipi, Nikki A., 189, 198
Fiorillo, Michael, 84n
Fisher, Bernard F., 69–71
Fix, Herbert M., 188, 219
Ford, Gerald, 239
Foster, Lee, 218

Galbreath, Bobby F. "Gabby," 157, 164, 167–168, 172–173
Gallagher, J. A., 188
Gallo, James A., 101
Garner, Cecil Aubrey, 60–61, 62
Gayler, Noel A. M., 193, 209, 214, 237
Gelien, Walter J., 51
Gentry, J. R., 188
Genz, Lyle, 203, 204
Giao (scout), 160
Goddard, Bernard G., 129
Gomez, Ernesto "Gooie," 136–138
Goodwin, R. C., 204
Gottschalk, Vincent J., 243–244
Graboskey, Edward E., 52
Grady, Thomas P., 198, 204
Graves, Terrence C., 158, 159, 160, 161, 163, 165–166, 167, 168, 170–171
Gray, Alfred M., 187, 188, 218–219
Gray, Roy C., Jr., 65, 73, 75, 77–78, 79
Green, Var, 192–193, 202
Greene, Wallace M., 245
Gregoire, Paul, 58
Gregory, William J., 76
Guidry, Richard A., 169, 170
Guilmartin, John F., 218

H-21 Shawnee, 13
H-34, 74, 78, 136
H-53, 219, 236
Haley, Steve, 234
Hamilton, T. G., 218
Harper, Richard C., 83, 88, 90
Harrington, Stuart A., 197, 199, 200–201, 208–209, 212, 231, 237, 238

Harris, John, 85–86, 89–90
Harrison, Robert, 130–131
Heim, D. C., 112
Heintges, John A., 73
HH-53, 237
Higgins, Marty, 111
Hilgenberg, John, 216, 222, 224, 235
Hill, Mike, 135–136
HMAS *Hobart*, 95, 97
HMH-461, 244
HMH-462, 214, 216, 221, 244
HMH-463, 131, 213–214, 219, 221, 235, 246
HMM-162, 26, 56, 105
HMM-163, 25, 26, 56–63, 64–65, 76, 78
HMM-164, 84, 88, 101, 103, 105
HMM-165, 103, 105, 106–114, 132
HMM-261, 26
HMM-262, 112, 114, 128, 130–131, 136, 140, 152, 153
HMM-263, 53, 95, 99, 102
HMM-265, 84, 88, 90, 112
HMM-361, 26, 49, 53, 113
HMM-362, 13, 14, 16, 17, 20, 24, 26, 113, 130
HMM-363, 68
HMM-364, 26, 27–36, 132, 143
HMM-365, 26
HMM-462, 195
HMR(M)-461, 244
HMX-1 (Marine Helicopter Squadron 1), 242–243, 244
Ho Chi Minh Campaign, 185
HO3S-1s, 242, 243
Hodges, Glynn, 232
Hoilien, Wayne L., 56, 63
Honeycutt, James Earl, 160, 161, 163, 164–165, 166, 167, 171–172
House, Charles A. "Chuck," 64, 65, 74–76, 77–79
Howell, J. R., 220–221, 223
HR2S, 244

Hugel, David, 14
Hughes (Captain), 233
HUS-1 "Sea Horse," 15

Jacobsen, 201
Jasper, Norman, 129
Jenson, Paul A., 157, 178–179
Johnson, David "Doc," 135, 145
Joint United States Public Affairs Office (JUSPAO), 72
Jones, F. W., 188
Judge, Darwin, 210

Kalas, W. D., 109
Karch, Frederick J., 44
Kaulu, John, 160
KC-130, 140
Kean, James H., 185, 229–230, 232, 237, 240–241
Kendall, David B., 204
Kent, William D., 164
Khe Sanh Combat Base (KSCB), 125–146, 148, 150, 152, 153–154, 155
King, Huberg, 69
Kirby, Edward K., 98, 99–100, 101
Kirby, William, 80–81
Kissinger, Henry, 193, 199, 213, 216–217, 238–239
Kizer, J. P., 188
Koontz, Dean, 234
Kufeldt, Edward, 147, 152–153, 154–156
Kyle, Wood B., 83
Kyllo, Kellan, 131–132

L-19 Bird Dogs, 67
La Voy, John "Big John," 27, 28, 29, 32, 34, 36
Laehr, Arthur E., 219, 225
Lang Vei Special Forces Camp, 147–156
Lannin, Wayne, 200
Lathrop, R. G., 143–144
Laurence, John, 72–73, 78–79

Lee, Michael, 139
Lee, William A., 169
Leftwich, William G., Jr., 111
LeGro, William E., 189–190
Lehmann, Wolfgang, 228, 232, 239, 240
Leohe, R. E., 188
L-Hour, 215, 216
Life Magazine, 56
Livingston, James, 224
Lofton, Kreig, 129, 130
Lopez, Adam, 160, 161, 163, 165, 166
Lopez, Adrian S., 177–178
Lownds, David, 126, 127, 152

MACV briefing, 72–73
MAG-11, 83
MAG-12, 42–43, 44, 83
MAG-16, 47, 49, 53, 244
MAG-26, 244
MAG-36, 49, 136, 244
MAG-311, 69
Magel, James E., 58, 63
Mallano, Arthur, 211
Maloney, Kevin M., 210–211
Mann, Bennie, 61
Marble Mountain Air Facility, 37–38,
    46–55
Marine Air Base Squadron-16 (MABS-
    16), 18, 26
Martin, Graham, 189–192, 199, 201,
    208, 212, 229, 232, 237, 238–239
Maves, William, 135
McAllister, T. C., 89–90, 91
McCormick, John W., 100–101
McCosar, Bunnie, 91
McCoy, James W., 109, 113
McCutcheon, Keith, 48
McGrath, Fred, 151
Mckee, Dennis T., 29
McLenon, Frank G., 187, 188
McMahon, Charles, Jr., 210–211
McManus, Raymond, 224

McRaney, Curt, 153, 154
Medal of Honor criteria, 120
Medlin, L. R., 112–113
Merchant, Robert A., 27, 28, 32
Middendorf, J. William, 252
Miklos, Larry R., 166
Military Region 5 (MR-5), 27
Miller, Keith, 91
Miller, Thomas J. "TJ," 143
Mobile Construction Battalion 9
    (MCB-9, Seabees), 46, 48
Mobile Construction Battalion 11
    (MCB-11), 148
Moorefield, Ken, 231
Mooreland, Ken, 232
Mortimer, Eugene, 47, 165
Munter, Weldon, 15
Murgallis, Patrick, 131
Murray, John E., 207
MV-22 Osprey, 247
Myers, Dafford W. "Jump," 69–71

Nation, Michael P. "Mike," 159,
    160–163, 165, 166–167, 182
Naval Advisory Detachment, 55
Nelson, Joseph A., 119, 248
Nesmith (Captain), 111–112
Nguyen Don, 27
Nguyen Thanh Trung, 197
Nguyen Van Thieu, 190–191, 200
Ninth Amphibious Force (9th MAB),
    186–187, 188
Nixon, Richard, 200
Norodom Compound (American
    embassy), 227–241
Novotny, Stanley J., 62–63
Nung mercenaries, 66, 69, 70, 73–74, 76
NVA 95th Regiment, 64, 66–67
NVA 324B Division, 81, 82
Nystul, William C., 233–234

O-1 Bird Dog, 68

O'Connor, Thomas J., 47–48, 54n, 79
O'Dell, George W. T. "Digger," 170, 182
OE-1 "Bird Dog," 15, 17–18, 25
Olson, Terry, 201, 204
Operation Baby Lift, 207
Operation Beau Charger, 95–103, 104, 108
Operation Belt Tight, 103–105
Operation Delaware, 7
Operation Frequent Wind, 185–195, 205, 206, 210–211, 213–214, 217, 219, 221, 226, 231, 233, 237–238, 241, 252
Operation Hastings, 82–92
Operation Hickory, 103–105, 108
Operation Homecoming, 155
Operation Lockjaw, 20
Operation Nightingale, 21
Operation Shawnee, 108
Operation Shufly, 13, 17, 19, 25, 26
Operation Talon Vise, 187
Operation Union I, 108
Operation Union II, 108, 113
O'Shannon, Leonard, 47–48
Owens, Billie, 58, 63

Pacific Corporation, 199
Paris Peace Accords, 200, 210
Pelosky, Edward, 226
Perryman, James, 18
Peterson, Delbert R., 67
Pham Van Hoa, 31
Phelps, John G., 116–119, 123–124
Phib-31, 242
Phillips, William R., 152
Pilger, John, 229
Pingle, Fritz, 198
Pless, Stephen W., 115–119, 120–121, 248–251
Pleva, J. F., 110
Polger, Thomas, 231
Porter, J. J., Jr., 217–218

Poulson, Leroy N., 116, 117–119, 122–123
Powell, David, 141–142, 145–146
Prados, John, 126, 129, 148
Project Delta, 112–113
PT-76, 147–148
Puckett (Sergeant), 76

Quantico, 242–243
Quinlan, D. A., 188

Reap, T. S., 88
reconnaissance missions, 158–159
Redeker, Ronald L., 119
Reinders, Ray, 50–51, 53
Rhodes, John E., 241
Rice, Ken, 197–198
Rich (Corporal), 168
Richards, Robert J., 153
Richey (First Lieutenant), 91
Riley, J. T., 131
Ritchie, Edward J. "Jim," 221
Romine, Richard E., 111, 132
Ropelewski, Robert, 128
Rosental, George, 147, 154–155
Rowland, Thomas P., 53

S-61R, 220
Saal, Harve, 151
Sapper Team Four, 48
Sapper Team One, 50
sappers
    at Chu Lai, 43
    description of, 38–40
    at Marble Mtn., 46, 48, 49, 50–51
Schneider, Harry W., 157, 179–180
Schoener, Charles "Chic," 232
Schrader, Kurt A., 214
Schreiner, Andrew M., Jr., 45–46
Scott, Richard L., 233, 234
Sellers, W. J., 88–89, 90
SFODA-102, 66

SFODA-503, 66
SH-3s, 234
Shamrell, Richard, 47, 48, 51, 55
Shauer, Walter H,., 130
Shea, Michael J., 233
Shelton, Jim, 15, 16–17
Shepherd, Lemuel C., 242
Sherrer, O. M., 56
Shirley, Larry D., 14, 18–19
Slade, G. P., 188
Slocum, Danny M., 160, 161–162, 165, 167–170, 174–175, 182
Smith, C. E., 131
Smith, Homer D., 189, 192–193, 200, 203, 204, 209, 210, 212–213, 224
Smith, Terry L., 139, 140
Snepp, Frank, 204, 205, 208, 225, 226, 232, 239–240
Snowcroft, Brent, 212–213
Special Forces Camp (Ashau), 65–69
Special Landing Force Alpha (SLF-A), 95
special landing force (SLF), composition of, 95–96
Spink, Shepard, 64, 65, 74
Spooky 70, 67
Stahl, Mike, 129
Stanton, Jim, 152
Steel, George P., 216, 239
Steinberg, Melvin J., 132, 136–137
Stoffey, Bob, 47, 48, 49, 51–52, 53–55
Stuart, William, 225–226
Stubbe, Ray, 126, 148
Sullivan, Michael, 185
Super Gaggle, 140–142
Sure Wind 202 (Quyet Thang 202), 27–36
Swift 07, 234
Swift 14, 233–234
Swift 22, 241

TA-4F, 140, 143

Tan Son Nhut, 196–198, 200–202, 203, 207, 210, 211, 217, 219, 222, 231, 236
Task Force 76, 187, 193, 194–195, 215, 223, 237, 252
Team Box Score, 157–182
Terzani, Tiziano, 212, 238
Therriault, Anton E., 130
Thompson, Dennis, 153, 155
Thompson, Stephen B., 160, 162, 163, 164–167, 175–176, 182
Thomson, Robert B., 160, 161–162, 165, 174, 176–177
Thomson, Steve, 166
Tiroch, Peter, 147–148
Tolliver, Jimmy E., 157, 179
Tolson, John J., III, 7
Tran Van Don, 185
Tran Van Huong, 191
Tri, Do Cao, 27
Trumfeller (Captain), 144
Turley, R. L., 188
Twardzik, George, 64, 76–77, 78
Twigger, Robert, 189, 198

U-10s, 28
UH-1 Hueys, 198
UH-1 Iroquois, 81–82
UH-1B Huey, 27, 29–30, 32, 56
UH-1E, 52, 53, 55, 74, 80–81, 84, 100, 103–104, 110, 115, 116, 136, 140, 143, 152, 219, 245–246, 247
UH-1E Iroquois, 76
UH-1H, 7
UH-1H Cobra, 246–247
UH-1J, 247
UH-34, 74, 76, 99, 100, 102–103, 130, 136
UH-34D, 8, 25, 27, 29, 30, 32, 33, 34, 52, 53, 56, 57, 58, 68, 125, 157
UH-34D Sea Horse, 15–16, 20, 22, 244
Underwood, David F., III, 157–158, 163, 164–166, 167, 173–174, 182

Underwood, Victor, 68–69, 70, 71, 73, 75, 78
Urban, Norm, 65, 67, 74–75
USS *Bayfield*, 95
USS *Blue Ridge*, 186, 187, 204, 205, 214, 219, 237, 239
USS *Boston*, 95
USS *Denver*, 215, 226
USS *Dubuque*, 215
USS *Duluth*, 215, 236
USS *Edson*, 95
USS *Fechtler*, 95
USS *Hancock*, 194, 200, 204, 213–214, 215, 219–220, 233, 234–235, 236
USS *Joseph Strauss*, 95
USS *Kirk*, 238
USS *Midway*, 214, 236
USS *Mobile*, 215
USS *Mt Vernon*, 220
USS *Okinawa*, 95, 97–98, 99, 101, 214, 215, 220, 237
USS *Palau*, 242
USS *Peoria*, 215
USS *Point Defiance*, 95, 97
USS *Princeton*, 13–15, 17, 103
USS *Saint Paul*, 95, 97
USS *Summer*, 97
USS *Valley Forge*, 99
USS *Vancouver*, 215, 219–220
USS *Whitfield Country*, 95

Valdez, John, 230–231
Valdez, Juan J., 185, 209
Vale, Summer A., 83, 85, 91
Van Dung (General), 212
Van Es, Hugh, 204–205
Van Tien Dung, 236n
Vasdias, Richard A., 68
Vaughn, S., 105
Velte, Paul, 199, 202

Vertol CH-46 "Phrog," 8
VH-3D Sea King, 243
VH-60N Seahawk, 243
Vietnamese 7th Division, 20
VMA-214, 45
VMA-224, 42
VMA-311, 69
VMO-1, 245
VMO-2, 50, 52, 55, 74, 76, 80, 84, 99, 103, 105, 245, 246
VMO-3, 245
VMO-6, 109, 111, 113, 140, 152, 243, 244, 245
Vogel, Peter, J., 56, 58–59

Walker, Fred, 201–202, 203
Walt, Lewis W. "Lew," III, 73, 92
Walters, Francis M., 17
Warren, Ray, 160
Watson, W. C., 84
Weisner (Admiral), 237
Westmoreland (General), 82, 225
Whaley, Bob, 13
White, William J., 140, 153
Whitesides, Walt, 125
Whitmire, Donald E., 236, 237
Wilkinson, James B., 126–127, 152
Willoughby, Frank, 148, 151
Wills, Stephen R., 233, 234
Wilson, Donald R., 57
Wilson, Franklin E., 136
Wilson, Louis H., Jr., 237
Wood, Anthony A., 206, 207, 208
Woodmansee, Jack, 29–32, 33, 34, 35–36
Woods, Chris, 234

Xavier, Augusto M. "Gus," 69

Yankee Papa 13 (YP-13), 56–57, 58, 59, 60, 63